AUTOCOURSE
INDY CAR
1995-96

HAZLETON PUBLISHING

FROM THE PAINT LEADER TO THE POINT LEADER...CONGRATULATIONS.

PPG CONGRATULATES JACQUES VILLENEUVE, WINNER OF THE 1995 PPG CUP.

Jacques Villeneuve has reason to smile. As winner of the PPG Cup Points Championship for the 1995 PPG Indy Car World Series, Jacques and Team Green earned a check from PPG for $1,000,000 and the coveted PPG Cup.

Jacques' outstanding performance was highlighted by four trips to the winner's circle including a win at the Indy 500. He topped all other Indy Car drivers by grabbing the pole position six times.

As the world leader in automotive finishes, PPG is proud to recognize this outstanding achievement in motorsports racing.

The world leader in automotive finishes.

CONTENTS

PUBLISHER
Richard Poulter

EDITOR
Jeremy Shaw

ART EDITOR
Steve Small

PRODUCTION MANAGER
Steven Palmer

MANAGING EDITOR
Peter Lovering

BUSINESS DEVELOPMENT MANAGER
Simon Maurice

SALES PROMOTION
Clare Kristensen

CHIEF PHOTOGRAPHER
Michael C. Brown

US Advertising Representative
Barry Pigot
2421 N. Center Street
Suite 128
Hickory, North Carolina 28601
Telephone and fax: (704) 322 1645

INDY CAR 1995-96
is published by
Hazleton Publishing Ltd.,
3 Richmond Hill,
Richmond, Surrey
TW10 6RE, England.

Color reproduction by
Barrett Berkeley Ltd., London, England.

Printed in England by
Butler and Tanner Ltd.,
Frome.

ISBN: 1-874557-51-9

Michael C. Brown

ACKNOWLEDGMENTS

The Editor and publishers wish to thank the following for their assistance in compiling the *Autocourse Indy Car Yearbook 1995-96*: Andrew Craig, Jeff Kowalczyk, Cathy Lyon, CeCe Pappas, John Procida, Adam Saal, Mark Williams; Marilyn DiTeodoro, Carol Wilkins; Peter Waswo; Susan Bradshaw, Kim Carmine, Francois Cartier, Mark Christian, Allyson Clark, Gayle Coyne, Amy Dangler, Kevin Diamond, Roger Elliot, Anne Fornoro, Robbin Herring, Christine Horne, Steve Horne, Trevor Hoskins, Deke Houlgate, Hank Ives, Dan Luginbuhl, Kevin Kennedy, Gordon Kirby, Michael Knight, Kathi Lauterbach, Mai Lindstrom, Chris Mears, David Phillips, Craig Pollock, Steve Potter, Scott Reisz, A.B. Shuman, Rick Shaffer, Marc Spiegel, Carole Swartz, Scott Tingwald, Tony Troiano and Tamy Valkosky.

DISTRIBUTORS

UNITED KINGDOM
Bookpoint Ltd.
39 Milton Park
Abingdon
Oxfordshire OX14 4TD

NORTH AMERICA
Motorbooks
International
PO Box 1
729 Prospect Ave.
Osceola
Wisconsin 54020, USA

AUSTRALIA
Technical Book and
Magazine Co. Pty.
289-299 Swanston Street
Melbourne
Victoria 3000

NEW ZEALAND
David Bateman Ltd.
P.O. Box 100-242
North Shore Mail Centre
Auckland 1330

"One thing you learn in racing is that they don't wait for you." *Roger Penske*

When he was fourteen years old, Roger Penske's father took him to see his first Indianapolis 500. "The crowd, the excitement—it just got to me," Penske recalls. "I said to myself, 'Someday I'm going to compete here.'"

Eighteen years later he made it to Indy as the leader of Team Penske. To date, they have won ten Indy 500 victories, and are the most successful team ever.

In addition to managing his racing team, Penske runs an international multi-billion-dollar transportation business. "I try to teach my people that it's up to them to innovate, to make things happen."

Roger Penske combines a focus on results with attention to detail. "What I like about Rolex," he explains, "is that they don't compromise either. That's why I've worn a Rolex for over two decades."

ROLEX

Rolex Oyster Perpetual Day-Date Chronometer in 18kt gold with matching concealed-clasp President bracelet.
Write for brochure. Rolex Watch U.S.A., Inc., Dept. RLX, Rolex Building, 665 Fifth Avenue, New York, N.Y. 10022-5383.
Rolex, ♔, Oyster Perpetual, Day-Date and President are trademarks.

FOREWORD

by Jacques Villeneuve • 1995 PPG Cup champion

Having been raised in Europe, I had no idea that my career would bring me to North America and Indy cars – my only aspiration was 'F1.' Actually, it's been a very important stage of my racing.

To have a chance in racing is like most things in life, you need to catch the opportunities and make the most out of them. I'm glad that Player's Ltd. and Team Green gave me a chance to come to North America to try it out. It has been three years of fun, friendships and, most of all, racing in a highly competitive series.

The Indy Car series in 1995 had the competitiveness normally found in smaller series. And to me, the hard fighting (on the track) in a tough series like this year's is almost as rewarding as winning. The '500,' the championship and most of the races in 1995 really had a special flavor. And to get that, a driver needs special people behind him.

Those people for me are Barry Green and all his crew. Not only are they the best, they always give the most they can. It's very important when you're driving on the edge, trying to get that extra 'tenth,' to feel that they are behind you.

I will now move on to new challenges. And I hope, as a spectator in years to come, the Indy Car series will give me the excitement of great racing (even some wheel-banging) which will bring back fond memories.

I am happy to be able to participate in the making of this year's edition of the *Autocourse Indy Car Yearbook*, which very competently summarizes the season.

So long . . .

Michael C. Brown

5

Yes, Son, this is where

Before we designed VTEC engines for our sporty Preludes, Accords and del Sols, we built engines for championship Formula One cars. As a matter of fact, we've put together more than 200 championships in everything from SCCA and IMSA to Grand Prix motorcycle racing.

At Honda, we like to put ourselves through the most grueling tests possible. Which explains our

entry into the PPG Indy Car World Series. From the Slick-50 200 in Phoenix to the Indy 500, our engineers, engine technology and teammates on the LCI Honda Indy Car will be measured on a new learning curve almost every week. Sometimes an oval. Sometimes a Super Speedway. Or sometimes a twisting, turning street course. But no matter what, it'll be a high-speed endurance

Hondas come from.

challenge testing our mettle at every possible level.

So eventually, when our engineers go back to their regular jobs in California or to one of our plants in Ohio, they'll take some meaningful experience along with them. Like the preparation that goes into being ready for race time. And how to work as a team when the green flag drops. Not to mention a few ideas they wouldn't get driving production

cars around a test track in Marysville, Ohio.

The Honda VTEC engine and double wishbone suspension are just some of the engineering innovations we've picked up from racing over the years. Which means the materials, technology and engine management systems we use on this Honda may very well become part of the Honda your kids will drive tomorrow. **HONDA**

GETTING BETTER

ALL THE TIME . . .

The PPG Indy Car World Series just continues to grow in stature, to broaden its appeal. It gets better and better. And 1995 provided the most enthralling season to date. Record crowds poured through the gates at almost every event and the fans were treated to some spectacular action, featuring wide-open competition among a well-matched field of veterans and rookies.

Significantly larger television audiences, with interest booming in all parts of the globe, also served as a measure of Indy Car racing's continued progress and prosperity. Why, for those seeking a legal interlude, the series even boasted a courtroom drama of its own.

By the midpoint in an electrifying 17-race campaign, as many as 10 drivers still held a legitimate hope of lifting the PPG Cup crown. Then sophomore sensation Jacques Villeneuve, who had earlier won at Indianapolis, cracked open the title-chase with a string of impressive performances in Team Green's Player's Ltd. Reynard-Ford/Cosworth. The superbly gifted 24-year-old French-Canadian capped his championship-winning season by confirming he would bid adieu to the Indy cars at the end of the season and instead switch his attention to Formula 1.

Marlboro Team Penske also garnered its share of the headlines. That in itself should come as no surprise, since Roger Penske's battalions dominated the title-chase in 1994. But this time Penske wasn't always in the news for what one might consider the 'right' reasons.

First of all, it came as a major surprise to see Al Unser Jr. and Emerson Fittipaldi struggling among the midfield runners during the season-opening race in Miami. Nevertheless, that story paled into insignificance a couple of months later when, in one of the most shocking developments in Indy Car history, defending champion Unser and Fittipaldi failed to make the field at Indianapolis. They simply weren't fast enough. Even with all their experience, knowledge, expertise and resources, both Penske drivers missed the cut. Amazing.

It didn't end there. Unser and Penske were back in the limelight at Portland in June, after Unser had sped to the most convincing win of the season . . . only to be promptly disqualified when his car failed to pass technical inspection. The team protested its innocence and commenced a long, messy saga which continued until after the final race of the season at Laguna Seca in September. Penske's initial motion for reinstatement was denied. Then the matter went to a Court of Appeals, which finally decided in Penske's favor.

The entire episode did not reflect well on the IndyCar organization. In this instance, the sanctioning body was fortunate, because the championship already had been decided and the overturning of the stewards' original decision had no bearing on the top 20 championship positions. Nevertheless, IndyCar President Andrew Craig took full responsibility for the timing and freely admitted that the affair had taken far too long to be settled. Accordingly, IndyCar will take a hard look at its procedures over the winter. Craig also confirmed that action would be taken to prevent a repetition of the confusion caused by the employment of two distinct methods of measuring Unser's car, one by the IndyCar officials and one by the volunteer technical inspectors who have traditionally provided valuable assistance to the small cadre of IndyCar professionals during race weekends.

The spirit of competition, of course, ensures that rules always will be stretched to the limit by the combatants, but the technical team will be charged with attempting to close some of the loopholes prior to the commencement of the 1996 season.

Craig had plenty more to occupy his mind during the year. Indeed much of his time was spent in attempting to analyze the ramifications of Indianapolis Motor Speedway President Tony George's proposed new Indy Racing League, which is due to begin in January, 1996 with a 200-mile race on a brand-new oval at Walt Disney World in Florida.

The United States Auto Club, which also sanctions the Indianapolis 500, initially issued a rules package for 1996 based upon down-sized 2.2-liter engines and revised chassis and aerodynamic configurations. These were later rescinded when it became apparent the existing engine suppliers were content with the current regulations. Then, after Championship Auto Racing Teams confirmed its intention to introduce new limitations on the cars for '96, aimed at reducing downforce and, consequently, cornering speeds, as well as requiring more protection for the drivers in the cockpit area, the IRL once

The closely matched field prepares for battle at Phoenix. The race produced a typically tight finish, Robby Gordon holding off a charging Michael Andretti to win by 0.788 seconds.

The runaway success of the PPG Indy Car World Series has attracted a host of new drivers, teams, sponsors and suppliers to the championship over the last couple of seasons. Brazilian rookie Andre Ribeiro's magnificent victory in the New England 200 at the wheel of the Tasman team's Firestone-shod LCI International Reynard-Honda confirmed that the new boys can take on Indy Car racing's established players on equal terms.

Michael C. Brown

more flew in the face of convention by announcing that its rules for next season, including the Indianapolis 500, would be exactly the same as those governing the cornerstone event in 1995.

Suddenly, therefore, the IndyCar teams were faced with the prospect of not only developing their own new cars for the 1996 PPG Cup season, but also retaining their 1995-specification equipment solely for use at Indianapolis. And worse was to come. In July, apparently in response to the prospect of meager support for the IRL series, Tony George dropped another bombshell by stating that 25 of the 33 starting positions in the 1996 Indianapolis 500, irrespective of qualifying speed, will be reserved for entrants who are prepared to commit to the IRL.

The IndyCar teams responded by crying 'foul!' Said one particularly irate owner: 'For the first time, the race won't be open to the 33 fastest cars. All the tradition, the heritage of Indianapolis has gone out of the window.'

Many of the issues raised by George's formation of the IRL remain unresolved as this is written. But one point is clear: the battle lines have been drawn. George, effectively, has issued an ultimatum: 'If you want to be sure of a place in the field at Indianapolis, you'd better run the IRL races at Walt Disney World (January 27) and at Phoenix (March 24).' The IndyCar teams, meanwhile, countered by saying, 'We already have our own, thriving series. We don't have the capacity, either financially or physically, to contest additional races – especially to a different set of regulations.' Impasse.

Both sides, however, remain adamant that they would prefer to reach a compromise of some sort.

'I want to make it clear,' said highly respected three-time PPG Cup champion and car owner Bobby Rahal, 'and I think I speak on behalf of all the team owners, we want to race at the Indianapolis 500. That's the best-case scenario and that's what we're working on. But if we go there it has to be on the basis of open competition, as it's always been. The problem is that the rules have been changed. It's no longer an open competition.'

Sadly, but inevitably, all the rhetoric tended to detract somewhat from a truly magnificent season. The competition was more closely matched than ever. The racing was

intense. In all, nine different winners emerged from the 17 races, equaling a record set in 1985. There were four first-time winners – a new single-season high – and nine different pole winners, also a record. A staggering total of 21 drivers led at least one lap of PPG Cup competition, while no fewer than 17 claimed the honor of a podium finish. Again, both are records. Incredibly, 11 races were decided by a margin of less than 2.5 seconds.

The bare statistics bear witness to the astonishing quality of the racing in 1995. They confirm, too, how high the standard had been boosted in comparison, even, to 1994, when the Marlboro Penske team dominated with its PC24 chassis.

The general consensus prior to the season suggested that the customer chassis suppliers, Lola and Reynard, would raise the level of their game substantially in order to combat the Penske steamroller. And so it proved. Just ask Stefan Johansson, who this year struggled to match the customer cars with one of the previously all-conquering Penskes: 'Heck, in Toronto, I was nine-tenths [of a second] off the pole and 18th on the grid,' noted Johansson. 'Last year I was one second off the pole and seventh on the grid. And it's the same every race.'

The level of competitiveness ensured a measure of unpredictability unrivaled in any other major category of auto racing. All three engine manufacturers experienced the spoils of victory, including Honda, which made a quantum leap forward in its sophomore season; and for 1996 the prospects are even more exciting, with Toyota well-advanced on plans to enter the fray and challenge the established might of Ford/Cosworth, Mercedes-Benz and Honda.

The overall caliber of the drivers also reached an all-time high, as evidenced by the likes of Gil de Ferran, Andre Ribeiro and Christian Fittipaldi eschewing promising careers in Europe in favor of a chance to drive in the PPG Cup series with a competitive, top-line team. Home-grown talent also rose to the surface. Robby Gordon and Scott Pruett both joined the ranks of proven winners during 1995, while Bryan Herta and Jimmy Vasser came close. Perhaps their chance will come in '96. It promises to be one heck of a show.

Jeremy Shaw
Columbus, Ohio
September 1995

In Memoriam

Henry Banks, a ceaseless campaigner for safety during his many years with USAC, died December 18, 1994, at the age of 81. Banks, whose family emigrated from England when he was a child, began racing in 1932 and went on to win the 1950 AAA National Championship title. He retired from driving in 1954 but returned to the sport in 1959 to succeed Duane Carter as USAC's second Director of Competition. He was inducted into the Auto Racing Hall of Fame at Indianapolis in 1985, one year after finally retiring from the USAC organization.

Bobby Grim, who passed away June 14 in Indianapolis following a lengthy illness, will be remembered as one of dirt track racing's most popular stars. After winning four consecutive IMCA sprint car championships between 1955 and 1958, Grim moved into the USAC ranks and won rookie of the year honors at Indianapolis in 1959. Grim won one National Championship race, on the Syracuse Mile in 1960, and raced nine times at Indianapolis. He retired in 1971 with 199 career wins to his name. Grim was 70.

Rouem 'Haff' Haffenden, a vastly experienced chief mechanic on the Formula 1 and Indy Car circuits, died February 26. Haffenden, born in Sussex, England, worked with Dan Gurney in Europe before moving to California in the late 1960s. He became chief mechanic on Gurney's Indy Car team and prepared the Eagle with which Jerry Grant recorded the first-ever 200 mph lap at Ontario Motor Speedway in 1972. Haffenden, who was 55, also worked with the Vel's-Parnelli Jones, Interscope, Psachie/Garza and Kraco Racing Indy Car teams.

Nick Kranz, general manager of Dick Simon Racing, died suddenly at his home June 29. Kranz, a close friend of Simon for more than 25 years, raced modified and stock cars in the 1960s, and himself sponsored Simon's efforts at Indianapolis in the early 1970s. More recently he had been responsible for concluding the deal to bring Mexican Carlos Guerrero and sponsor Herdez to Simon's team this season. Kranz was 52.

Bernie Myers, universally liked and admired as an occasional crew member for Payton-Coyne Racing, for whom his three sons, Bernie (Jr.), Doug and Mark, all have worked for several years, died suddenly June 11. The elder Myers, a plumber by trade, had chosen not to attend the race at Detroit and instead was working on the team's new race shop in Plainfield, Illinois, when he died at the age of 59.

Chuck Stevenson, who captured two of his four career wins, at Milwaukee and DuQuoin, en route to the 1952 AAA National Championship, died August 21. He was 75. Stevenson raced nine times at Indianapolis between 1951 and 1965, recording a best finish of sixth in 1961. He took a sabbatical following the tragic death of his chief mechanic, Clay Smith, in 1954, but won the first-ever USAC-sanctioned stock car race at Saugus, California, in 1956, and twice claimed stock car class honors in the Carrera Panamericana.

Charlie Thompson, who had been associated with the Indianapolis Motor Speedway since 1958 and succeeded Clarence Cagle as Superintendent of Grounds in 1977, holding the post until his retirement in 1994, succumbed to cancer August 3. The well-liked and respected Thompson, a life-long resident of Indianapolis, Indiana, was 66.

In motorsports,
all the physical processes
are merely prepatory steps
for the mental challenges.

Face your fears.
Live your dreams.

Marlboro
TEAM PENSKE

Follow us

INDY CAR'S WORLDWIDE WEB

The PPG Indy Car World Series is now truly international – and stronger than ever. The participation of top drivers from around the world has brought the sport to a massive new worldwide audience, which, in turn, has led to the involvement of even more major multinational sponsors and suppliers.

Once upon a time the PPG Indy Car World Series was a backwater of international racing – a place where aging Formula 1 stars went to pasture, failed Formula 1 drivers went to earn a living, and promising American and Canadian talent hit a solid, if sometimes lucrative, dead end. In short, Indy Car racing was largely irrelevant outside of North America.

Not any more. For the second time in the past four years, the PPG Cup champion has signed on with a top Formula 1 team. Indy Car racing now enjoys the largest worldwide television audience of any annual sporting series. And the PPG Indy Car World Series has become a destination – not just a layover – for emerging drivers from every corner of the globe.

One reason for Indy Car's ascendancy in the international arena is a sensible, stable set of rules which ensures that driving talent and teamwork have at least as much influence on the outcome of races as the latest technological breakthrough. Apart from some adjustments to the maximum allowable turbo boost, the rules for Indy Car engines are little changed in the past 10 years. During that same period, chassis regulations have evolved in a logical, step-by-step fashion with safety the paramount concern.

Indy Car rules-makers learned a lesson from Formula 1 in the 1980s when developments like carbon brakes, active suspension and electronics worthy of the Starship Enterprise drove costs through the stratosphere and detracted from the competition. Thus active suspension, traction control, carbon brakes and ultra-sophisticated engine materials have been banned from Indy Car racing.

Yet the modern Indy car is hardly a Stone Age piece of equipment. Today's chassis from Penske, Lola and Reynard boast wind tunnel-honed aerodynamics and advanced composite construction, while Ford/Cosworth, Honda and Ilmor/Mercedes-Benz have developed ultra-sophisticated engine management and data acquisition systems to match.

As a result, Indy Car is high-tech enough to attract manufacturers and sponsors, but common sense enough to keep technology from running amuck. With Ford, Honda, Mercedes-Benz and, beginning in 1996, Toyota up to their collective necks in Indy Car racing, the PPG Cup series enjoys a level of involvement by the world's automotive manufacturers that is without precedent in the 80-year history of the national championship.

'There's a good balance between technology and cost controls,' says Tom Elliott, president of American Honda, Inc. 'There are enough limitations on technology that everybody's got to work hard to find something extra. Simply spending more money is no guarantee of success.

'And you can have an advantage one year and lose it the next. Look at what happened when Penske won everything in 1994: It stimulated everybody to do better. As a result, 1995 was much more competitive.'

The 1995 season also saw Firestone return to Indy Car racing after a 20-year absence, a move that made sense in light of its tradition of success in the Indianapolis 500 but which was also practical thanks to the IndyCar rules.

'First and foremost we wanted to re-energize the Firestone brand name,' says Al Speyer, Firestone motorsports manager. 'We felt the best way to show that Firestone is alive and well was to return to Indy Car racing where we have a legacy of great accomplishments.

'However, the fact that IndyCar has such a reasonable formula for balancing the conflicting goals of high technology and cost control made our decision to come back to Indy Car racing an easy one.'

In recent years, tire wars have wreaked havoc on Formula 1 and NASCAR. Again, IndyCar learned from others' mistakes. Working in concert with Goodyear and Firestone, IndyCar established a workable set of rules that discouraged profligate spending and ensured a level playing field for both manufacturers.

Perhaps as a result of the rules stability and manageable costs, the atmosphere at Indy Car races is remarkably relaxed. The camaraderie among drivers may also be a by-product of racing at 220 mph where there's no place for grudges. Whatever the reasons, the PPG Indy Car World Series has long enjoyed a reputation for having its priorities right: the racing is ferocious, but at the end of the day, it's still a sport.

Formula 1 refugees Teo Fabi, Derek Daly and Raul Boesel raved about Indy Car racing in the early 1980s, but it wasn't until Emerson Fittipaldi won the PPG Cup series and the Indianapolis 500 in 1989 that the world took notice. Here was a man who had won two World Championships but retired unhappily from racing in 1980 after his dreams of a Brazilian Formula 1 team were shattered.

Fittipaldi discovered a fountain of youth in Indy Car racing, and he was not shy about proclaiming its virtues to the rest of the world.

'In America when I am preparing to go to a race I know it won't be just one big aggravation,' said Fittipaldi shortly after winning the Indianapolis 500. 'I have time to race and time to be with my friends. That doesn't exist in Formula 1. The mentality is completely different here.'

Not only did the world start listening, Fittipaldi's presence attracted the attention of Brazil to Indy cars – and with it, much of South America. Fittipaldi's coming to Indy Car racing set in motion the events

by David Phillips

that would ultimately see Indy Car's international television market grow from virtually nothing to the envy of the sports world.

The next big step came in the early 1990s when IndyCar's plans to race in Australia ignited a simmering dispute with FISA regarding Indy Car racing's place in the international racing calendar. A renegade organization in the eyes of the world since splitting from USAC in 1979, IndyCar faced the threat of sanctions before an agreement was hammered out with FISA. IndyCar agreed that the balance of its schedule would be conducted in North America and that any additional foreign events would be held on oval tracks.

These developments set the stage for a remarkable chain of events that saw World Champion-elect Nigel Mansell turn his back on Formula 1 to drive for Newman-Haas Racing in 1993. Mansell enjoyed a season with more ups and downs than a Coney Island roller coaster before winning the PPG Cup championship. More significantly, his presence was a boon to Indy Car racing's international profile. The fact that a reigning World Champion had forsaken the defense of his crown to race Indy cars endowed the PPG Indy Car World Series with instant credibility around the world.

Thanks to Mansell's enormous popularity, racing fans everywhere clamored to see the 1993 Indy Car

series. As a result, Indy Car's international television distribution and print media coverage skyrocketed.

In 1992, the last year of the 'pre-Mansell era,' Indy Car racing was televised to some 90 countries outside North America. That number jumped to more than 130 in 1993 and well in excess of 150 in 1994. What's more, IndyCar estimated that 11 percent of its 1994 season press credentials were issued to publications that likely wouldn't have been covering the sport sans-Mansell.

And the world liked what it saw. Nobody who watched the 1993 New England 200, when Mansell, Fittipaldi and Paul Tracy swapped positions at 180 mph while carving their way through thick knots of traffic, will ever forget it. And though Mansell's honeymoon came to a swift end the following season, the seed had been sown. When Mansell returned to F1 (briefly) in 1995, the world continued to watch Indy Car racing in increasing numbers. This year Indy Car television coverage reached a cumulative worldwide audience of some 1.2 billion people.

Mansell was also a trend-setter in that he became the first of several 'hot' European properties to turn his back on F1 in favor of Indy cars. Although Mansell returned to F1, one of that sport's bright young stars already had confirmed his intention of moving in the opposite direction; none other than Christian Fittipaldi,

nephew of Emerson, arrived on the Indy Car scene in 1995 to drive for Walker Racing fresh off a three-year stint in F1 with the Minardi and Footwork teams.

Like his uncle, Christian quickly embraced Indy Car's blend of competition and sportsmanship.

'We laugh and joke, but when it comes time to go racing we race as hard as anyone, anywhere,' says Fittipaldi. 'But just because the racing is serious is no reason why everyone has to wear a frown all the time. Take it from me, I am fresh from Formula 1 and I am fresh to Indy cars. The atmosphere in Indy cars is what true sport is about.'

Nor was he alone. Fittipaldi was joined by fellow Brazilian Gil de Ferran, third in the 1994 FIA International Formula 3000 Championship, who accepted an offer to drive for Hall Racing. De Ferran made no bones about his decision to come to America.

'For me Indy cars was always an interesting proposition, even when I was racing in Formula 3,' he says. 'Indy Car is one of the top two series in the world; it's single seaters, fast cars and the idea that you can be competitive with a good team is very appealing.

'In Indy cars I had a chance to win, it's as simple as that. The way the rules and the championship are structured, you have 10 or 15 guys out there who can win a race – and the statistics this year prove that.

What I'm most interested in as a sportsman is being able to compete on a level playing field, where my performance is reflected in the results. This is as level a playing field as there can be in racing.'

The tables will be turned in 1996 when Villeneuve joins the Williams Formula 1 team. As the son of one of Formula 1 racing's most beloved heroes, Villeneuve will not only have a daunting legacy to live up to, he will be carrying the reputation of Indy Car racing on his young shoulders as well.

But Villeneuve won't be alone in spreading Indy Car's international profile. In one of the most exciting developments in recent Indy Car history, the PPG Indy Car World Series will make its international oval track racing debut in Brazil in March, at a specially constructed oval at the Jacarepagua circuit near Rio de Janeiro.

Indy Car racing's vast popularity in Brazil, coupled with the fact that upward of a third of the field will be composed of Brazilian drivers, virtually ensures the event will be a success. And with Firestone, Honda and Toyota in the fray, it is only a question of when – not if – Indy Car racing will spread its wings to Japan.

It may have taken the best part of 80 years, but Indy Car racing has become a fixture on the international racing scene. What's more, it's here to stay.

At 200 plus miles per hour...

 Mercedes-Benz

Official Sponsors of IndyCar

... you may not have noticed some of the quality companies supporting IndyCar.

Championship Auto Racing Teams • 755 West Big Beaver Road • Suite 800 • Troy, MI 48084 • (810) 362-8800

1996 PPG INDY CAR WORLD SERIES SCHEDULE

March 3	**Homestead Motorsports Complex, Miami, Florida**
March 17	**Nelson Piquet International Raceway, Rio de Janeiro, Brazil**
March 31	**Surfers Paradise Street Circuit, Queensland, Australia**
April 14	**Long Beach Street Circuit, California**
April 28	**Nazareth Speedway, Nazareth, Pennsylvania**
June 2	**Milwaukee Mile, West Allis, Wisconsin**
June 9	**Belle Isle Park Street Circuit, Detroit, Michigan**
June 23	**Portland International Raceway, Portland, Oregon**
June 30	**Burke Lakefront Airport Circuit, Cleveland, Ohio**
July 14	**Exhibition Place Circuit, Toronto, Ontario, Canada**
July 28	**Michigan International Speedway, Brooklyn, Michigan**
August 11	**Mid-Ohio Sports Car Course, Lexington, Ohio**
August 18	**Road America, Elkhart Lake, Wisconsin**
September 1	**Concord Pacific Place Circuit, Vancouver, British Columbia, Canada**
September 8	**Laguna Seca Raceway, Monterey, California**

Schedule correct at time of going to press

Our fastest moving parts.

The piston in the Ford Zetec-R Formula One engine accelerates from 0-100 miles per hour in just one thousandth of a second.

Moving quickly on, the turbo in the Ford Cosworth engine which won the 1995 Indy 500 and PPG Indy Car Championship spins at 80,000rpm.

And yet, from 1996, Cosworth's fastest moving parts will be castings.

Up to one million castings per year will be produced using the patented Cosworth process at a new, highly automated UK foundry in which £25 million has been invested.

Phase A alone has already produced full order books to supply high quality, precision engine castings to companies such as General Motors, Jaguar, Ford and many other manufacturers around the world.

This is all part of our fast moving success in the field of automotive technology.

COSWORTH

CASTINGS • ENGINEERING • MANUFACTURING • RACING

1992

St James Mill Rd   Northampton NN5 5JJ   United Kingdom   Tel: + 44 1604 732100   Fax: + 44 1604 732113

Cosworth is a registered trade mark belonging to Vickers PLC.

Vickers

A division of
Vickers PLC

TOP TEN DRIVERS

Chosen by the Editor, Jeremy Shaw, taking into account their racing performances and the equipment at their disposal

Photographs by Michael C. Brown

1

Jacques Villeneuve

Date of birth: April 9, 1971
Residence: Indianapolis, Indiana
and Monte Carlo, Monaco
Indy Car starts in 1995: 17
PPG Cup ranking: 1st
Wins: 4; Poles: 6; Points: 172

At the age of 24, Villeneuve became the youngest man ever to capture the PPG Cup title. He did so by virtue of a mature-beyond-his-years blend of speed, confidence, aggression, intelligence and consistency. Also, crucially, during a year which boasted a parity among cars and teams without parallel in the history of PPG Cup racing, he had Lady Luck riding on his side – at least until the final stages of the season, and by then the crown was virtually within his grasp.

Villeneuve owed much of his success to the Team Green organization, which provided him with excellent equipment as well as ample engineering and moral support. His relationship with team owner Barry Green – and with highly respected race engineer Tony Cicale – was based on mutual respect, trust and friendship; it developed into one of those rare sporting marriages which seemed destined to bear fruit.

After winning the opening race in Miami, thanks more to persistence than outright speed, Villeneuve remained locked in a battle for championship honors with several other drivers until mid-season. Then came his maiden pole in Portland. It coincided with a dramatic rise in tempo and gave observers the first glimpse of his rare ability to produce an extraordinarily fast lap right at the end of qualifying. His new-found talent was exemplified by his season-high tally of six poles, achieved within the space of just nine races. Thereafter he was almost always near the front of the grid, save at New Hampshire, where, after starting only 15th, he derived intense satisfaction from a gritty drive to finish fourth, which effectively put his points total beyond reach.

jacques

VILLENEUVE

2

al UNSER *jr.*

Talk about a roller-coaster season! Unser's year began badly, his Penske team desperately off the pace in Miami, although some hastily arranged extra testing ensured a dramatic improvement in form. He won handily in Long Beach. Then came the debacle at Indianapolis, where Unser, the defending champion, failed to make the field. As if that wasn't bad enough, a dominant win in Portland was overturned after his car failed technical inspection.

Fortunately, some positive news was on the way. He won at Mid-Ohio, assisted by a slice of good fortune and excellent pit strategy, and again in Vancouver, where Unser's precise skills always have assumed paramount importance. Finally, after the season had been completed, an appeals court reinstated his Portland win.

Unser also came close to victory at Milwaukee and, especially, Michigan, where he led until the final few hundred yards before succumbing to a brilliant charge by Pruett. Detroit, too, could have fallen his way if the full-course cautions had been timed differently. In short, it seemed that whereas in 1994 everything worked in his favor, this time around the fickle hand of fate dealt him at least as many jokers as aces.

Unser's ability in the races remained undiminished. His biggest problem was that the PC24 rarely allowed him to qualify well; and even his unique blend of guile and aggression couldn't overcome that kind of handicap in the increasingly competitive Indy Car arena. Unser's frustration shone through occasionally, notably in Toronto, where his attempt to pass Rahal proved disastrous. Later, though, his spirits were raised by the prospect of winning his team's appeal against the perceived injustice in Portland. Unser, as ever, never failed to give of his best.

Al Unser Jr.

Date of birth: April 19, 1962

Residence: Albuquerque, New Mexico

Indy Car starts in 1995: 16

PPG Cup ranking: 2nd

Wins: 4; Poles: 0; Points: 161

3

Michael Andretti
Date of birth: October 5, 1962
Residence: Nazareth, Pennsylvania
Indy Car starts in 1995: 17
PPG Cup ranking: 4th
Wins: 1; Poles: 3; Points: 123

No one would have been surprised if Andretti had won at least a half-dozen races during the 1995 season. That he earned a solitary victory – after leading in 12 of the 17 events – might be considered a travesty of justice.

Andretti began the year impressively, taking advantage of a car honed by winter testing. He qualified on the pole three times in the first four races, each time on street circuits; and in the 12 official practice and qualifying sessions that were held at those events, he was headed only twice. But a variety of ills conspired to keep him out of Victory Lane. In Miami, a suspension component broke 20 laps after he had made minor contact with another car; in Surfers Paradise he made a mistake on the final lap, driving over his head in a vain effort to overcome a broken second gear; and in Long Beach he was again over-anxious. He crashed, too, at Indianapolis, after breathing the throttle in Turn Four just as Mauricio Gugelmin was slowing in front of him in preparation for a pit stop.

It could be argued that Andretti's trademark impetuosity cost him dear. Perhaps so. But only one of the mishaps was due to a glaring error; and looking at it from a slightly different perspective, with a modicum of good fortune, the consequences might not have been nearly so severe.

Later, engine problems cost him legitimate hopes of victory in successive races at Cleveland, Michigan and Mid-Ohio. Transmission woes took him out at Vancouver. Despite the setbacks, Andretti displayed a new-found tranquility in the face of adversity. Watch out for him in '96!

michael
ANDRETTI

4

Gil de Ferran

Date of birth: November 11, 1967

Residence: Indianapolis, Indiana

Indy Car starts in 1995: 17

PPG Cup ranking: 14th

Wins: 1; Poles: 1; Points: 56

Before the start of the season, many people were asking, 'Gil who?' No longer. Plucked out of Formula 3000 by perceptive veteran driver-turned-team owner Jim Hall, acting upon a recommendation from Adrian Reynard and Rick Gorne, de Ferran impressed the team from the first time he sat in the car. He was confident, communicative and congenial – but above all he was quick. De Ferran learned a great deal about the very different world of Indy Car racing during an extensive and productive test program during the winter, then caught everyone's attention at the season opener in Miami, where he took advantage of cooler conditions in the second qualifying session on Friday afternoon to secure the provisional pole in his bright yellow Pennzoil Reynard-Mercedes. Wow!

The problematic Reynard transmission voided his efforts in that first race, and again at Surfers Paradise after he had started sixth and fallen victim to a bogus jump-start call. He also looked good on his oval debut at Phoenix, until indulging in a quick spin after being caught out by his own enthusiasm. Then in Long Beach he was punted into the wall by Paul Tracy. Incredibly, his season continued in similar vein, a string of promising performances punctuated by problems. Through it all, de Ferran maintained his composure and his crew never lost faith in his ability. Finally, in the last two races, everything fell into place. De Ferran emerged with a second-place finish in Vancouver and followed that with a superb – and universally popular – victory at Laguna Seca. It was no more than he deserved.

gil **de FERRAN**

5

paul TRACY

The opening two races provided an accurate barometer of how Tracy's 1995 season would progress. In Miami he was blighted all weekend by an apparently insurmountable brake problem which caused him to run off the road numerous times, including a terminal excursion early in the race. Two weeks later, Tracy drove to a textbook victory in Australia. He had been content to bide his time after starting ninth, and then moved up the order as others fell by the wayside or ran into difficulty. It was a case of either feast or famine, it seemed.

Prior to the season some people had expected fireworks between Tracy and his Newman-Haas teammate, Andretti. In fact, they enjoyed a reasonably harmonious relationship, with absolutely no animosity between them. The biggest surprise was that Tracy was consistently outpaced by Andretti in qualifying, with the Canadian ahead just five times out of 17. Only once did he make it onto the front row of the grid. Tracy was usually at least a match for his teammate in the races, however, despite a distinct lack of testing which severely hindered his efforts to extract the maximum potential from his Lola chassis. He became increasingly frustrated, too, by a string of problems with the Ford/Cosworth XB Series II engines which thwarted at least a couple of potentially strong races.

His own impulsiveness also cost him on occasion, notably in Long Beach and Toronto, although he claimed another handsome victory in Milwaukee and added a trio of runner-up finishes, including a fine drive to round out the year at Laguna Seca.

Paul Tracy

Date of birth: December 17, 1968

Residence: Scottsdale, Arizona

Indy Car starts in 1995: 17

PPG Cup ranking: 6th

Wins: 2; Poles: 0; Points: 115

6

Bobby Rahal

Date of birth: January 10, 1953
Residence: New Albany, Ohio
Indy Car starts in 1995: 17
PPG Cup ranking: 3rd
Wins: 0; Poles: 0; Points: 128

Indy Car racing's Mr. Consistency lived up to his reputation during the 1995 season. But after adopting a 'back to basics' approach, which included ditching the Honda engine package (oops) and siding instead with the proven combination of Mercedes-Benz and Ilmor Engineering, Rahal was not satisfied with the results. Incredibly, for the third straight year, he failed to win either a race or even a pole. He led only two laps during the entire 17-race season: one at Long Beach and one at Indianapolis. He qualified among the top five only three times. Yet on race days he nearly always made progress, finishing second three times and third twice. He was looking good, too, in Long Beach until halted by a transmission failure.

Rahal's strongest run, as in 1994, came in Toronto, where he set fastest lap and pressured Andretti throughout the closing stages, although he was prevented from attempting a pass both by his own preservative instinct and the fact his engine was overheating alarmingly. Ironically, on one of the few occasions Rahal tried to assert himself, at Mid-Ohio, where he knew he needed to beat Villeneuve to maintain an outside chance at the title, a clash of wheels with his championship rival sent Rahal's Miller Genuine Draft Lola careening into the barriers.

His lengthy absence from Victory Lane – now numbering 50 races – clearly rankles with the always competitive Rahal, and for 1996 he has firm plans to set the record straight.

bobby

RAHAL

7

jimmy VASSER

With six races in the books, Vasser had just five PPG Cup points to his name – from a troubled eighth-place finish in Miami. Indeed, following the season opener, he failed to finish in five straight races, despite running among the top 10 on each occasion. Four times he was the victim of mechanical problems, while at Indianapolis, after moving into the lead of an Indy Car race for the first time in his career, he fell victim to an aggressive pass by Pruett and clouted the wall.

Vasser, of course, was disappointed to lose his chance of victory, yet in a way it proved to be a turning point, since he had demonstrated to himself, his team and the assembled throng that he was fully capable of mixing it with the big boys. He never looked back. Vasser remained a serious contender throughout the balance of the season, notching a career-best second in Detroit, where he was assisted by an inspired strategic call in the pits, and then, following an excellent drive and the provisional disqualification of Unser, being awarded – temporarily – his first victory in Portland.

Vasser, being a true sportsman, wasn't too concerned when the decision was later overturned. 'I was never a winner in my mind,' he said. Not quite. He nevertheless finished third at Road America and Cleveland, and was hindered by several more mechanical woes, notably in Vancouver when his front row grid placing was negated by a broken spark plug. By season's end he had served notice of his potential by achieving the third-best average starting position, 8.05, beaten only by Villeneuve and Andretti. His time will come.

Jimmy Vasser

Date of birth: November 20, 1965
Residence: Puyallup, Washington and San Francisco, California
Indy Car starts in 1995: 17
PPG Cup ranking: 8th
Wins: 0; Poles: 0; Points: 92

8

Gordon endured a dismal start to the year when a stuck throttle caused him to crash in Miami. He retired again in Australia, due to an electrical fault. His fortunes turned around at Phoenix where he scored a magnificent victory, then nose-dived again at Long Beach, forced out by an engine failure after running uncharacteristically far down the field. His year continued in a similarly topsy-turvy manner.

He qualified on the pole and finished fourth at Nazareth, then added a hard-earned fifth at Indianapolis, having driven impressively from the back of the field after the manifestation of an electrical problem before the start. He was fifth again in Milwaukee. Next was Detroit, where he displayed his customary verve by claiming another pole. Gordon struggled in the early part of the race, then vaulted back into contention by virtue of Derrick Walker's pit strategy. Gordon took care of the rest of the business, remaining cool under intense pressure and taking a second victory.

By midseason, he was firmly in contention for the PPG Cup championship. Everything was looking good. But then the wheels seemed to fall off. He qualified in midfield for the road course races at Portland and Road America, comfortably outpaced each time by rookie teammate Christian Fittipaldi. Then, after a wild charge at Cleveland brought a disappointing sixth instead of a potential podium finish, a broken suspension component pitched him heavily into the wall at Michigan and effectively brought his challenge to an end.

Robby Gordon

Date of birth: January 2, 1969
Residence: Orange, California
Indy Car starts in 1995: 16
PPG Cup ranking: 5th
Wins: 2; Poles: 2; Points: 121

robby
GORDON

Scott Pruett

Date of birth: March 24, 1960
Residence: Roseville, California
Indy Car starts in 1995: 17
PPG Cup ranking: 7th
Wins: 1; Poles: 0; Points: 112

Scott Pruett was a revelation in the early part of the season. He also claimed by far the most spectacular victory of the year, beating Unser in a tantalizing battle of wits on the final lap at Michigan International Speedway.

Pruett began the year with high hopes for his return to the Indy Car arena following an enforced hiatus. He struck a solid relationship with team manager/engineer Steve Newey and worked hard throughout 1994 in developing the new breed of Firestone Firehawk tires in preparation for the eagerly anticipated return of both Firestone and team owner Pat Patrick. Pruett duly exceeded all expectations by finishing fourth in his comeback in Miami, where he also set fastest lap of the race, and third in Surfers Paradise. He ran equally strongly on the oval at Phoenix until losing time with an unscheduled pit stop after making contact with Tracy. He then added a fine second at Long Beach. At that stage, against all the odds, a Firestone car was leading the PPG Cup standings!

Furthermore, with less than 20 laps to run in the Indianapolis 500, Pruett and fellow Firestone runner Scott Goodyear were locked in battle, comfortably out in front of the field . . . until an increasingly gusty wind caused Pruett to crash in Turn Two.

His championship challenge ultimately was blunted by a couple of mechanical problems, some disappointing performances on the road courses (due primarily to the tires), and an accident in New Hampshire. Nevertheless, Pruett showed that he and Firestone are back with a vengeance.

scott
PRUETT

10

teo FABI

For a man fired by Jim Hall at the end of the 1994 season and supposedly over the hill, Fabi did a heck of a job, particularly given the fact he was thrown in at the deep end with a brand-new team. As ever, his forte seemed to be in qualifying, especially on the ovals. He earned the pole at Milwaukee, just missed out at Nazareth, and also took second on the grid at Michigan. But he was just as fast on the road courses, fifth on the grid at Surfers, third in Detroit and Toronto, and fourth at Mid-Ohio and Laguna. For some reason, however, he seemed to be blighted by all manner of gremlins when it came to race day. In Australia, for example, moments after taking the lead, he was hobbled by a broken wastegate exhaust pipe; in Detroit he was involved in an incident in the pit lane; at Road America he made a mistake and ran off the road; in Cleveland, again having just taken the lead by virtue of a super-fast pit stop, he was stricken by another exhaust problem; in New Hampshire he lost valuable time in the pits due to an air-gun failure; in Vancouver he spun and then succumbed to an overheating engine; and finally at Laguna Seca he was almost taken out of the race by a backmarker. Jeez!

As ever, though, Fabi remained unflappable. He always managed to keep his Latin temperament in check. And in among the disappointments he claimed a strong third at Long Beach, adding fourth-place finishes at Milwaukee, Toronto and Michigan. It could have been so much better but it represented a solid beginning for the ambitious Forsythe team. Next year, perhaps, there will be even more to cheer about.

Teo Fabi

Date of birth: March 9, 1955

Residence: Milan, Italy

Indy Car starts in 1995: 17

PPG Cup ranking: 9th

Wins: 0; **Poles:** 1; **Points:** 83

THE FUN HAS

One of the most intriguing matchups of the 1995 PPG Indy Car World Series pitted Goodyear and Firestone against one another in the first Indy Car tire war in more than two decades. Firestone was returning to Indy Car racing after a 21-year absence, having been virtually synonymous with the sport throughout the 1920s, '30s, '40s, '50s and '60s when it won 43 straight Indianapolis 500s. On the other hand, Goodyear had used Indy Car racing as a springboard to a near-monopoly of the world's top racing series in the '70s, '80s and '90s, and brought an Indy Car winning streak of more than 300 races into the 1995 season.

Following its withdrawal from racing in 1974, Firestone saw its image as a leader in the performance tire market all but evaporate. But soon after Bridgestone of Japan purchased Firestone in 1990, the decision was made to get back into racing in order to revitalize the Firestone brand. In 1991 Firestone joined forces with the Indy Lights series as both the title sponsor and exclusive tire supplier. Two years later, Firestone announced it was embarking on a season-long test program with Patrick Racing and Scott Pruett in preparation for the 1995 PPG Indy Car World Series.

'Our return to racing is market driven,' said Rick Bangs, manager, Firestone consumer tire marketing. 'The Indy program is energizing and stressing the brand's marketing theme and we are using this as our core activity in promoting Firestone tires.'

With Comptech, Payton-Coyne and the newly organized Arciero-Wells and Tasman Motorsports teams coming aboard prior to the start of the 1995 campaign, Firestone had a capable, if small, cadre of teams in its stable.

Goodyear would continue supplying tires to a 'Who's Who' of Indy Car racing, including Galles, Newman-Haas, Penske and Rahal/Hogan Racing, winners of every PPG Cup championship in the 1990s. And Goodyear wasn't taking the challenge lightly.

'The one thing you learn, after you've been in a monopoly for a long time, is that you never want to underestimate anybody,' said Leo Mehl, general manager of Goodyear racing. 'And surely we don't underestimate [Firestone's] technology nor their drive and desire to represent what Goodyear now represents in the racing business.

'When Goodyear started its racing division in the early '60s we were the underdog everywhere. Personally, I prefer to be the established, experienced company with the winning tradition.'

While most observers agreed the competition would be a real shot in the arm to Indy Car racing's profile in the motor sports arena, there were also fears that an all-out tire war would have a negative impact on the sport. For more than two decades Goodyear had enjoyed a monopoly in Indy Car racing; not altogether a bad thing, considering every car at every race had equal tires. What's more, under no pressure to 'beat' anybody, Goodyear could develop tires at a methodical pace, always erring on the side of conservatism.

Naturally, there was concern that the tire companies might be tempted to stretch the 'safety' envelope in a quest for greater speed. After all, one had only to recall the summer of 1994 when Hoosier took on Goodyear in the Winston Cup series and tire reliability suffered even as speeds skyrocketed.

There were also worries that if either Goodyear or Firestone achieved a clear-cut advantage it would upset the delicate competitive balance of the PPG Cup series. Worse, a no holds-barred tire war might lead to a dramatic escalation in the price of tires, not to mention the specter of Indy Car starting grids divided into 'haves' and 'have nots' based on how closely teams were allied with their respective tire companies and whether they rated the trick tires of the weekend.

Happily, the fears were unfounded. Safety was never a problem. Although both companies experienced trouble with their tires blistering from time to time, there was not one instance of a catastrophic tire failure stemming from anything but a puncture caused by debris on the track or contact with another competitor.

'It's important to note from both sides there has not even been a hint of difficulty with regard to safety,' said Al Speyer, Bridgestone/Firestone motorsports manager.

What's more, Firestone and Goodyear – and perhaps most importantly, IndyCar – learned their lessons about the drawbacks of an all-out tire war, not just from the Indy Car tire wars of the 1960s and '70s but from the Goodyear versus Michelin battles in Formula 1 in the late 1970s and from the more recent Goodyear versus Hoosier contest in NASCAR.

'When we were in competition 20 years ago there were no rules,' said Mehl. 'IndyCar watched what happened in NASCAR, however, and developed some good rules. I think everybody can see what's going to happen if you don't have any control.

JUST BEGUN
by David Phillips

In the off-season IndyCar worked with Firestone and Goodyear to establish a sensible set of rules governing the competition that gave each company enough leeway to experiment with different tire compounds and constructions, without triggering a fiscal and technological free-for-all.

The IndyCar rules stipulated that each manufacturer had to provide enough tires and support to supply at least 50 percent of a 30-car field. Each company was permitted to bring one primary and one optional compound/construction tire to each event, with each competitor allotted 28 tires per weekend (apart from 500-mile races), plus four back-up tires that could be used only after a driver switched from the manufacturer's primary tire. Competitors were permitted to switch types and brands of tire at any time during practice but were restricted to a single type and brand in each qualifying session; and any change of tire type or brand from one qualifying session to the next voided any previous qualifying times.

As for the races themselves, competitors had to start the road races on one of the sets of tires used in qualifying. In the oval events they were required to start on the same set used in the one-car-at-a-time qualifying session. Once the race

started, competitors were permitted to change between primary and optional tires but were not permitted to switch brands.

The result was a season of intense, safe and fair competition that left both Goodyear and Firestone – not to mention IndyCar – with much to be proud of.

Firestone was on the pace from the get go, with Tasman's Andre Ribeiro posting second fastest time in the opening practice session of the season at Miami and Scott Pruett coming home a solid fourth and setting fastest race lap. Indeed, Pruett went on to third place in Australia and second at Long Beach, and entered the month of May at Indianapolis leading the PPG Cup points table.

For all the promise Firestone had shown, however, Goodyear still had won the first four poles and races – and had led every lap. Of course, it was not exactly front page news when Goodyear won races. After all, its winning streak had reached 308 by the time May rolled around.

'When you have the image we have, when you've been winning everything for such a long time, we know it's only news when Goodyear loses,' said Mehl.

Or nearly loses. Although Goodyear took the top two qualifying spots courtesy of the Menard-powered Lolas of Scott Brayton and Arie

Luyendyk, Firestone claimed the outside of the front row, ironically with a second Tasman entry driven by Scott Goodyear. And with 50 miles to go it looked like Goodyear – as in the tire – might have its worst nightmare realized as Goodyear – as in Scott – led the race by inches from Pruett. But a series of events worthy of *Ripley's Believe It or Not* saw Pruett crash, Scott Goodyear penalized for passing the pace car on a restart and Team Green's Jacques Villeneuve come through to save the day for the Goodyear Tire & Rubber Co.

Goodyear had things its way through June and much of July and, frankly, Firestone was off the pace at Milwaukee and Portland. At Michigan, however, Firestone returned to its Indianapolis form, earning pole in the hands of Parker Johnstone and his Comptech Reynard-Honda then leading handily, first with Johnstone and later with Ribeiro before mechanical problems knocked them out of the race. That only set the stage for a spectacular duel between Pruett and Al Unser Jr. in the closing laps which was finally decided in Firestone's favor on the last turn of the last lap, the victory margin a paltry 0.056 seconds.

'You cannot imagine the pride and excitement when the checkered flag came down at Michigan,' said Speyer. 'It was a very special moment for everyone in our company. For the people directly involved with our Indy Car program, it was a testament to their hard work and dedication.'

But if the competition was close at Michigan, there was no contesting the fact that Firestone had the edge at New Hampshire. There Ribeiro earned his first pole and, after biding his time in the first half of the race, passed Michael Andretti and drove away to a first Indy Car win for himself and Honda.

Goodyear rebounded with wins by Unser at Vancouver and Gil de Ferran at Laguna Seca, to capture first through sixth in the PPG Cup championship, nicely complementing a season that featured 15 wins, 15 poles and which saw Goodyear lead 1870 of 2194 laps.

'Goodyear's approach this year was to introduce new products at nearly every race,' said Mehl. 'We concentrated on compounds, molds and construction. Back when we were at it alone, our main emphasis was to provide a consistent, equal product for all competitors while trying to keep their tire expenses to a minimum.

'Considering we were competing against another major international tire company, we can't help but be very pleased with an Indy Car season in which we won the Indy 500, the PPG Indy Car World Series and 15 of 17 races.'

Firestone could not match Goodyear's numbers, of course, but nobody ever thought they would. Pruett finished seventh in the PPG points and Ribeiro 17th, with Firestone-shod cars responsible for two wins, two poles and 324 laps led.

'I doubt a year could ever be as rewarding as this year, we accomplished so much,' said Speyer. 'At the start, our goal was to be competitive and we far exceeded that expectation. We quickly developed the mind-set of not being satisfied with anything less than a checkered flag.

'We are very much looking forward to 1996. We've just gotten started. We are aggressively pursuing additional teams to run on our tires and have a concrete plan for the off-season and the next racing season. We're here for the long haul and the fun has just begun.'

Call it a tire war, a tire competition or just plain fun, Round Two of Firestone versus Goodyear begins on the weekend of March 3, 1996 at the new Homestead Motorsports Complex.

The fiercely contested tire war between Goodyear's Eagles *(top left)* and Firestone's Firehawks *(above)* has given Indy Car racing an extra dimension in 1995 and the generals commanding the rival armies, Leo Mehl *(left)* and Al Speyer *(above left)*, have worked with IndyCar to ensure that the sport has not been harmed.

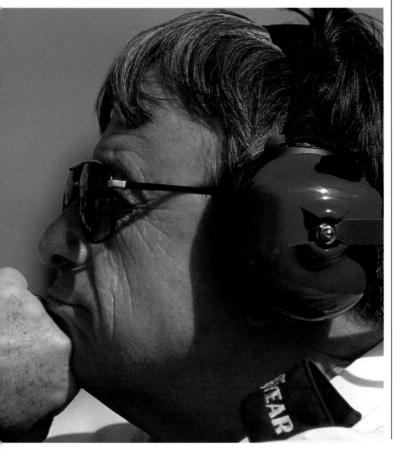

33

1995 A YEAR OF CHALLENGE

by Jeremy Shaw

COLORS

Since its foundation in 1883, PPG Industries has developed into a world leader in the production of a wide variety of high-class commodities for cars, homes, aircraft, commercial construction and chemical processing. It has become equally synonymous with auto racing as title sponsor of the PPG Indy Car World Series for the past 16 years.

PPG and Indy Car racing have prospered together since first joining forces in 1979. PPG sales topped $6.3 billion in 1994, while the company now boasts more than 31,000 employees and 90 production facilities in 16 countries.

PPG Cup race attendances, meanwhile, have blossomed more than 500 percent to an average in excess of 205,000. Television coverage has expanded to more than 150 countries around the globe, with a cumulative audience of 1.2 billion – or an average of 75 million viewers per race – during the 1994 season.

'We are proud of the tremendous growth in national and international exposure experienced by the PPG Indy Car World Series,' says Rich Zahren, Vice President–Automotive Products for PPG. 'Our support of Indy Car racing gives us an unparalleled opportunity to showcase the products of PPG and our automotive customers in new markets at home and abroad.'

Zahren also welcomes the new opportunities that will arise in 1996 as a result of the series paying its first-ever visit to South America for a race in Rio de Janeiro, Brazil, on March 17.

'PPG's OEM and Refinish Coatings businesses have recently strengthened our position in Brazil through new joint venture arrangements,' says Zahren, 'and this race will certainly provide many opportunities to increase our visibility.'

PPG Industries, like many companies involved in the sport, has utilized its title sponsorship as a means of broadening awareness of the company's products and expertise. For example, PPG showcases its technological leadership in automotive coatings via the PPG Pace Car program, which has grown to comprise a fleet of 34 cars, representing manufacturers all over the world. All cars competing in the PPG Indy Car World Series and IndyCar's official development series, the PPG-Firestone Indy Lights Championship, wear Deltron automotive refinish paint colors exclusively from PPG.

In 1995, PPG Industries provided a popular new twist to its support of Indy Car racing with the creation of the 'PPG Colorful Character' award.

'We take our business and racing very seriously, but this is a bit of fun,' says PPG Vice President–Refinish Tom Craig. 'The PPG Indy Car World Series is filled with some of the brightest, most talented, successful and colorful owners, drivers, mechanics, engineers and interesting personalities in all of motorsports. We want to recognize some of these rascals before they start writing their own books and doing the talk-show circuit.'

Father Phil DeRea, the universally loved and admired Catholic Chaplain of Indy Car racing – and a friend of the Andretti family for 40 years – was delighted to accept the first PPG Colorful Character award in April. Subsequent honorees include Lou Palmer, anchor of the Kmart Indy Car Radio Network; Leo Mehl, Goodyear's general manager of worldwide racing; Floyd Ganassi, patriarch of one the sport's premier teams; and Roger Bailey, president of the PPG-Firestone Indy Lights Championship.

The PPG Indy Car World Series provided superb entertainment in 1995. Race fans were treated to a season of wide-open racing and heart-stopping action; the stunningly liveried PPG pace cars added to the unrivaled spectacle.

TEAM-BY-TEAM *review*

A total of 56 drivers made an appearance during the 1995 PPG Indy Car World Series, of whom 34, representing 21 different teams, earned points. In the following pages, Editor Jeremy Shaw assesses some of the strengths and weaknesses of each team.

Photos: Michael C. Brown

Newman-Haas Racing

Base: Lincolnshire, Illinois
Drivers: Michael Andretti, Paul Tracy
Sponsors: Kmart, Texaco Havoline, Budweiser
Chassis: Lola T95/00
Engines: Ford/Cosworth XB
Tires: Goodyear
Wins: 3 (Tracy 2, Andretti 1); **Poles:** 3 (Andretti)
PPG Cup points: 238
Andretti 123 (4th), Tracy 115 (6th)

Newman-Haas Racing came out of the box strong, winning three poles from the first four races. Andretti, for a variety of reasons, failed to convert any of those poles into a victory, and in fact it was Tracy, newly recruited from Penske Racing, who broke the longest drought in the team's history – 18 races – by winning at Surfers Paradise.

The team was effectively reaping the benefit of an extensive winter test program, and soon enough the opposition began to catch up and then overhaul the quasi-factory Lola team. Curiously, especially given Tracy's reputation as a development driver, Newman-Haas undertook relatively little testing once the season was underway, and while they produced myriad new components and tweaks aimed at improving their cars, few of them were adequately tested. The team also suffered a spate of engine problems, especially in the latter part of the year. Once again, a lack of testing must be considered a contributory factor, although the failures continued even after the team opted to switch from the Ford/Cosworth XB Series II development engines to the tried-and-tested Series I versions.

Lee White replaced the departed Jim McGee as team manager, and after a few initial shocks he adapted well to the scene. Certainly, his call in Toronto gave Andretti the opportunity to score what was, criminally, to remain his only win of the year.

Despite three victories it was another largely frustrating season for high-profile team owners Paul Newman (seen conferring with Chip Ganassi and Roger Penske) and Carl Haas *(top right)*. The Newman-Haas Lolas looked very quick in the early-season races but that promise remained unfulfilled.

***Main picture:* Paul Tracy leads teammate Michael Andretti at Vancouver. Andretti *(top)* led more laps than any other driver but managed just one victory, despite the sage counsel of his father Mario *(top left)*. Tracy *(middle left)* was overshadowed in qualifying but showed unquenchable spirit on race day.**

Photos: Michael C. Brown

Marlboro Team Penske

Base: Reading, Pennsylvania
Drivers: Al Unser Jr., Emerson Fittipaldi
Sponsor: Marlboro
Chassis: Penske PC24
Engines: Mercedes-Benz IC108
Tires: Goodyear
Wins: 5 (Unser 4, Fittipaldi 1); Poles: 0
PPG Cup points: 228
Unser 161 (2nd), Fittipaldi 67 (11th)

By its own high standards, Penske Racing endured a disappointing year in 1995. But it was hardly disastrous. The failure to qualify at Indianapolis, of course, represented a major shock, especially after having dominated the event so convincingly one year ago, but the team still emerged with five victories, and defending series champion Unser was beaten only by Villeneuve in the final PPG Cup standings.

The biggest problem seemed to stem from the latest breed of Goodyear tires. It wasn't that the tires were bad, as the Penske team members continually were at pains to stress; it was just that the tires didn't seem to suit Nigel Bennett's PC24 design. At least such was the case in qualifying. It showed. Whereas last year the team claimed 10 poles, in 1995 they had none. Zippo. In fact, a Penske featured on the front row of the grid only three times, once with Unser in Detroit and twice with Fittipaldi on the ovals at Phoenix and Milwaukee. The races, however, were a different story. Fittipaldi twice established the fastest race lap, at Phoenix and Nazareth, where he won handsomely, while Unser was nearly always a factor among the leading group.

Nevertheless, starting from farther down the grid – Unser had an average starting position of 9.19, Fittipaldi 10.94 – always ensured an unnecessary handicap, and one which Fittipaldi, in particular, was unable to overcome. In the latter half of the season, the veteran Brazilian never qualified above 14th and managed no better than a pair of fifth-place finishes.

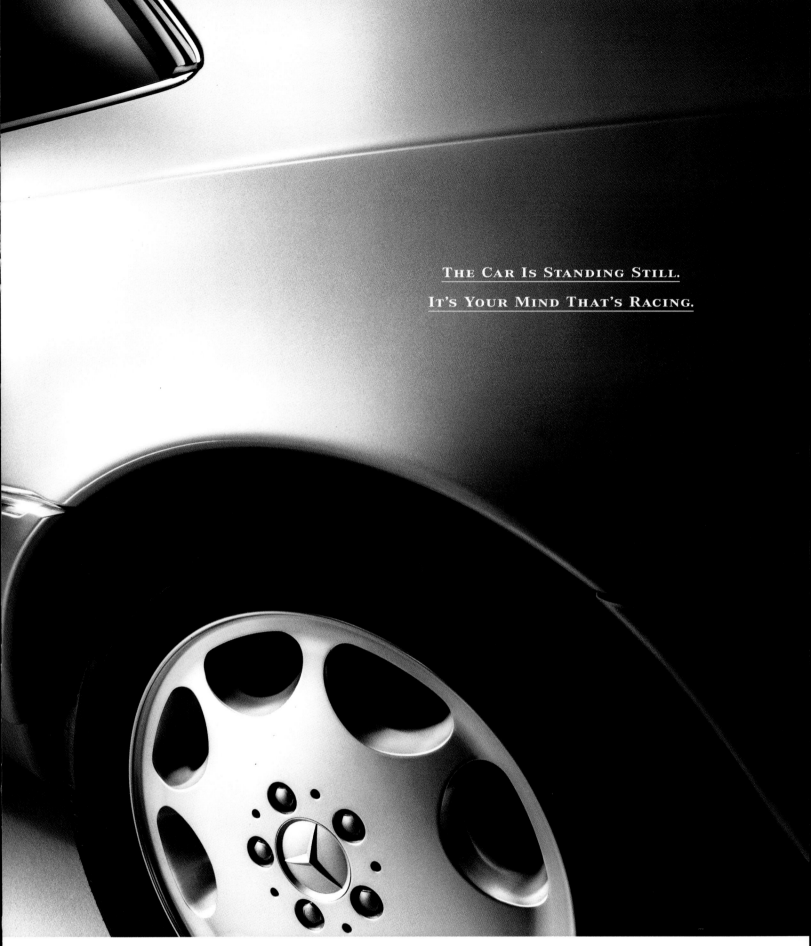

THE CAR IS STANDING STILL.

IT'S YOUR MIND THAT'S RACING.

The S-Class

For information and the dealer nearest you, please call 1-800-FOR-MERCEDES.

Rahal/Hogan Racing

Base: Hilliard, Ohio
Drivers: Bobby Rahal, Raul Boesel
Sponsors: Miller Genuine Draft, Duracell
Chassis: Lola T95/00
Engines: Mercedes-Benz IC108
Tires: Goodyear
Wins: 0; **Poles:** 0
PPG Cup points: 176
Rahal 128 (3rd), Boesel 48 (16th)

Much was expected of the Rahal/Hogan team in 1995, but neither the switch from Honda to Mercedes nor the decision to replace Mike Groff with Raul Boesel brought the hoped-for improvement in results.

Rahal and Boesel had begun the year among the favorites for honors, and sure enough they showed quite well in the first race. Boesel qualified third and finished sixth in Miami, despite a time-consuming pit stop for attention to a broken front wing, while Rahal finished third. It was a good start. But only twice more, at Portland and Toronto, did they claim top-six finishes together. Later, as Rahal continued to score points consistently, thanks to a combination of his usual heads-up style and reasonable reliability, Boesel was stricken by the lion's share of the bad luck, sidelined by a variety of problems whenever he looked set for a strong result.

Rahal maintained a shot at the PPG Cup title until the late stages. Ultimately, perhaps, it was a series of dismal performances on the one-mile ovals that blunted his efforts. By season's end, he and Carl Hogan were involved in a less than agreeable parting of the ways, and for 1996 they will run separate operations, with Rahal continuing his penchant for change by switching allegiance from Lola to Reynard chassis.

Photos: Michael C. Brown

Team owners Bobby Rahal *(top)* and Carl Hogan *(middle left)* have decided to end their partnership.

Rahal *(left)* again failed to score a win but, consistent and dependable as ever, he finished third in the PPG Cup standings.

Middle: Raul Boesel drove the second car with sponsorship from Duracell but the Brazilian *(above)* enjoyed little luck.

Robby Gordon was victorious at Phoenix *(below right)* and Detroit *(right)* but a huge crash at Michigan effectively ended his PPG Cup championship bid.

With highly regarded F1 driver Christian Fittipaldi signed to drive alongside Gordon, it seemed that Derrick Walker *(below)* was set to join the front rank of Indy Car team owners. The Walker Racing Reynards *(bottom)* were superbly presented but results didn't quite match the lofty expectations.

Walker Racing

Base: Indianapolis, Indiana
Drivers: Robby Gordon, Christian Fittipaldi (R)
Sponsors: Valvoline, Cummins, Marlboro, Chapeco, Bardahl
Chassis: Reynard 95I
Engines: Ford/Cosworth XB
Tires: Goodyear
Wins: 2 (Gordon); Poles: 2 (Gordon)
PPG Cup points: 175
Gordon 121 (5th), Fittipaldi 54 (15th)

After switching from Lola to Reynard chassis, undertaking by far its most ambitious winter test program ever, and then signing up the promising Christian Fittipaldi to drive alongside Robby Gordon, Derrick Walker's team looked set for its most successful season to date. And so it proved, although both Walker and Gordon had hoped for a more dramatic improvement.

The biggest setback came even before the first race, when race engineer Tim Wardrop announced his departure from the team. Walker's newly promoted chief engineer, Rob Edwards, had plenty of assistance from David Cripps, Damon Chandler, Diane Holl and electronics expert Ron Ruzewski, but they were all relatively inexperienced in the Indy Car arena; more importantly, they were unable to duplicate the interpretive skills of Wardrop, or the rapport he had previously established with Gordon.

Fittipaldi, after three seasons in Formula 1, adapted well to his new surroundings and impressed by finishing fifth on his debut in Miami. He outpaced Gordon all weekend, despite a bare minimum of testing. Fittipaldi overcame some initial fears to enjoy a career-best second at Indianapolis, thanks primarily to high attrition in the late stages, but rarely shone again. Gordon, meanwhile, had some good days and bad days. Consequently, his PPG Cup challenge faltered in the late stages.

VALVOLINE
THE WINNINGEST OIL OF THE 1995 INDY SEASON.

6592.531 MILES.
6 POLES.
6 VICTORIES.
INDY 500 VICTORY.
PPG INDYCAR CHAMPION.

ALSO AVAILABLE FOR RUSH HOUR GRIDLOCKS,
FAMILY VACATIONS, AND FRIDAY NIGHT CRUISING.

 PEOPLE WHO KNOW USE VALVOLINE.®

©1995 The Valvoline Company, Marketers of ZEREX and PYROIL

Although Team Green employed standard Reynard chassis *(below)*, the chemistry between Barry Green *(right)*, driver Jacques Villeneuve *(far right)* and the other members of the team gave it what proved to be a decisive edge over the opposition.

Team Green
Base: Indianapolis, Indiana
Driver: Jacques Villeneuve
Sponsors: Player's Ltd./Klein Tools/Raybestos
Chassis: Reynard 95I
Engines: Ford/Cosworth XB
Tires: Goodyear
Wins: 4; Poles: 6
PPG Cup points: 172 (1st)

Barry Green's organization worked wonders in 1995, showing absolutely no ill effects from a less than amicable split over the winter with former partner Jerry Forsythe. With brother Kim Green as team manager, Tony Cicale as chief engineer and Kyle Moyer as chief mechanic, Team Green comprised the perfect blend of youth and experience. The entire crew got along well together, including the driver, and each was an expert in his or her own field. Nothing was lacking. And in Villeneuve they possessed one of the most dynamic and ambitious young drivers Indy Car racing has been blessed with in years.

The team employed no special tricks. It relied upon standard Reynard 95I chassis, suitably customized and massaged, and was operated on an adequate but by no means extravagant budget. Villeneuve benefited instead from his own infectious enthusiasm, a well-structured test program and a superb relationship with Cicale, who was able to interpret Villeneuve's excellent technical feedback and translate it into results.

An open IndyCar test session at Mid-Ohio in June proved particularly beneficial. Villeneuve later described that test as a turning point, since it allowed the opportunity for some fine-tuning of the team's road course setup. More significantly, it seemed to give him an extra boost of confidence. From the seven subsequent races on street or road circuits, Villeneuve qualified on the pole six times and was second once.

His progress during the year was interrupted by a few mechanical glitches, notably in Australia and Long Beach by the fragile Reynard transmission, and at Portland by a broken shock absorber mounting. At Michigan he was halted – as were several others – by a right-rear wheel-bearing failure, although excellent work by the crew enabled him to return to the fray and earn useful 10th-place points. Remarkably, the team scored points in 15 out of 17 races, including each of the last 13.

54

The choice of professionals... since 1857

A generation before an automobile ever took to the road and more than half a century before the first Indy 500, tools manufactured by the earlier generations of the Klein family were the choice of master tradesmen. Like their counterparts of yesteryear, today's professionals, whose reputation and livelihood depend on the tools they use, still demand the quality found only in Klein tools.

Klein, the mark of quality since 1857, is still the most sought after and recognized name among professional tool users. Today, the professional, who takes pride in and realizes the importance of quality tools, can now select from more than 4,000 job-matched Klein tools.

As an IndyCar sponsor, Klein Tools is proud to be associated with and support the professionals of Team Green and Jacques Villeneuve in their pursuit of excellence in the 1995 PPG Indy Car World Series.

95268

Chicago, Illinois USA

We salute a group of true professionals...
Jacques Villeneuve,
Barry Green and his entire Team,
1995 PPG Indy Car World Series Champions.
It is our honor to have been part of the effort.

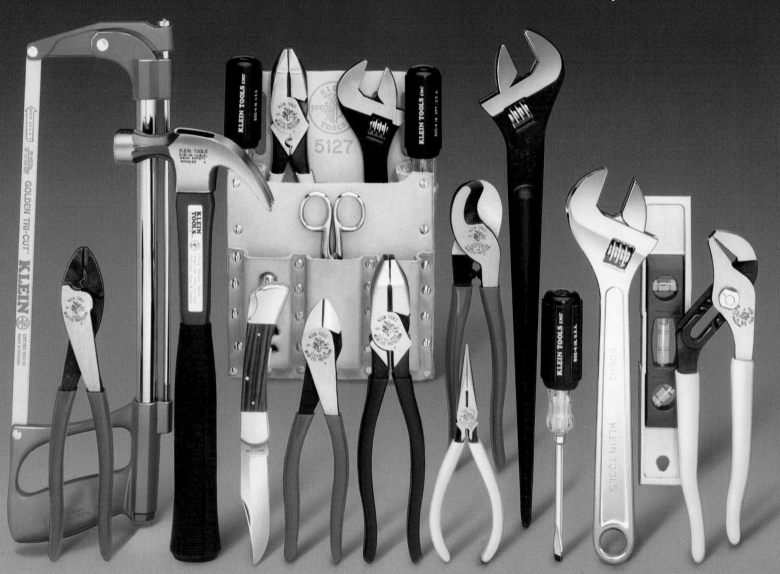

Chip Ganassi *(middle right)* placed his faith in young talent and was rewarded with a number of promising displays, if not the victories he had hoped for.

Right: Bryan Herta heads for fifth place at Mid-Ohio. Although Herta *(below right)* occasionally demonstrated impressive speed in qualifying, his efforts were hampered by unreliability and a difficult relationship with his race engineer, the hugely experienced Mo Nunn *(bottom)*.

Teammate Jimmy Vasser *(below far right)*, by contrast, formed an effective partnership with Julian Robertson *(below)* and was unlucky to end the season without recording his first Indy Car win with the Target/STP Reynard *(bottom right)*.

Target/Chip Ganassi Racing
Base: Indianapolis, Indiana
Drivers: Bryan Herta, Jimmy Vasser
Sponsors: Target, Scotch Video, STP
Chassis: Reynard 94I/95I
Engines: Ford/Cosworth XB
Tires: Goodyear
Wins: 0; Poles: 1 (Herta)
PPG Cup points: 122
Vasser 92 (8th), Herta 30 (20th)

It was perceived as a shrewd move by Ganassi to harness the talents of Herta and Vasser, two of North America's brightest young stars. For one reason or another, however, the team didn't appear to utilize its resources to the full. A disproportionate number of mechanical failures also served to restrict the drivers' accomplishments.

Vasser's deal was concluded relatively late, leaving him virtually no time for testing, and both drivers were beset by transmission troubles in the early part of the year. Herta then confirmed his promise by claiming the pole at Phoenix, in only his eighth Indy Car start. Later, though,

after a string of retirements, which included a couple of accidents – and one big crash at Indianapolis from which he was lucky to escape with no more than a heavy concussion – his race engineer, the mercurial Morris Nunn, began to question Herta's ability. The relationship went downhill from there, despite which Herta finished a fighting second (after starting third) at Cleveland and then qualified on the front row at both Mid-Ohio and Laguna Seca.

Vasser, meanwhile, developed an excellent rapport with race engineer Julian Robertson and began to reap the rewards, emerging as a consistent top-flight performer.

56

**Consider yourself fortunate.
Few people have seen the front end of the Team Target car.**

Thanks to the Target racing team and their crews for an awesome season and a top-ten finish.

Right: Mauricio Gugelmin started the year in style with second place at Miami but the Brazilian *(middle right)* endured a barren spell in the middle of the season.

Dominic Dobson *(below right)*, Tom Armstrong *(below far right)* and their partners can look back on a season of solid progress for the PacWest team.

Former PPG Cup champion Danny Sullivan *(bottom right)* was unable to recapture past glories at the wheel of the VISA Reynard *(bottom left)*. The nasty injury that curtailed Sullivan's season allowed Juan Manuel Fangio II *(below)* to demonstrate his considerable potential.

PacWest Racing Group
Base: Indianapolis, Indiana
Drivers: Danny Sullivan, Mauricio Gugelmin, Juan Fangio II
Sponsors: VISA Bank of America, Hollywood
Chassis: Reynard 95I
Engines: Ford/Cosworth XB
Tires: Goodyear
Wins: 0; Poles: 0
PPG Cup points: 118
Gugelmin 80 (10th), Sullivan 32 (19th), Fangio 6 (26th)

The team established in 1994 by Bruce McCaw, Tom Armstrong, Wes Lematta and Dominic Dobson made good strides in its sophomore season. The hiring of two seasoned professionals, Sullivan and Gugelmin, undoubtedly helped improve the image of this ambitious team, and before long it had concluded sponsorship arrangements with VISA Bank of America and Hollywood cigarettes.

The year started well with Gugelmin finishing second at the Miami season opener. Sullivan also ran among the top three until losing time with a slow pit stop and a spin. Gugelmin remained a top contender throughout the first half of the season. He led most laps at Indianapolis until strangely falling off the ulti-mate pace in the closing stages. Later, though, the team went off on a tangent in terms of car setup, seeking the proverbial 'unfair advantage,' and it wasn't until after Sullivan had been injured in a nasty (unrelated) crash at Michigan that the futility of that exercise was realized. Gugelmin suddenly returned to prominence, running strongly at Vancouver before being sidelined in someone else's accident, and follow-ing up with a third-place finish at Laguna Seca.

Sullivan, even prior to his acci-dent, endured a disappointing sea-son, although Fangio was most impressive on his debut at Mid-Ohio and ran equally well in his maiden Indy Car oval race at Loudon.

Photos: Michael C. Brown

Patrick Racing

Base: Indianapolis, Indiana
Driver: Scott Pruett
Sponsors: Firestone, Pennzoil, Nike Canada
Chassis: Lola T95/00
Engines: Ford/Cosworth XB
Tires: Firestone
Wins: 1; Poles: 0
PPG Cup points: 112 (7th)

After an absence of three years, Indy Car stalwart U.E. 'Pat' Patrick made an impressive return to the PPG Cup wars in cahoots with Firestone, which itself was making its first foray into the arena since 1974. The team benefited from an extensive development program throughout the 1994 season and over the ensuing winter, during which Pruett completed more than 12,000 miles of testing. Even so, few people expected him to be quite so competitive when the season opened in Miami. Pruett hung with the leaders all weekend and finished a close fourth, a frac-tion over two seconds behind the winner. He also was credited with fastest lap of the race. Patrick, Pruett and Firestone were back!

The team was a consistent performer throughout the season, with Pruett failing only five times to crack the top 10 in qualifying. If he lacked anything, it was perhaps the ability to put together one demon-quick lap in qualifying. Hence he sometimes started lower on the grid than he might have expected.

Nevertheless, for a first-year program, Patrick achieved a great deal, with much of the credit due to gener-al manager Jim McGee and team manager/race engineer Steve Newey. The crowning glory, of course, came at Michigan with Pruett's dazzling last-corner pass of Unser to claim his and Firestone's first victory.

Above: Reunited with team manager Jim McGee *(right),* Pat Patrick made a successful return to Indy Car racing, while driver Scott Pruett *(above left)* crowned a brave comeback from career-threatening injuries with an outstanding season at the wheel of the Firestone Lola *(below).*

Photos: Michael C. Brown

Seeking to emulate the success he had enjoyed more than a decade earlier, team owner Jerry Forsythe *(below left)* recreated his partnership with veteran driver Teo Fabi *(left)* and former March boss Robin Herd *(below)*. It is usually a mistake to try to recapture the past, but with experienced race engineer Lee Dykstra *(middle)* also joining the team, Fabi posted a number of strong qualifying performances, although he somehow failed to deliver on race day. Milwaukee *(bottom)*, where the Italian took pole position but finished fourth, was typical.

Forsythe Racing	
Base: Indianapolis, Indiana	
Driver: Teo Fabi	
Sponsors: Combustion Engineering, Indeck, ABB	
Chassis: Reynard 95I	
Engines: Ford/Cosworth XB	
Tires: Goodyear	
Wins: 0; Poles: 1	
PPG Cup points: 83 (9th)	

As part of his settlement with former partner Barry Green, Jerry Forsythe took over some of their joint assets, including the franchise earned by Villeneuve during the French-Canadian's rookie season, and set about re-establishing his own rival team for 1995. Tony Brunetti was responsible initially for putting together a crew, while Neil Micklewright later joined as vice president of operations.

Forsythe hired Fabi as his driver,

rekindling the partnership that first took the Indy Car world by storm in 1983. Robin Herd, designer of the March chassis with which Fabi and Forsythe won four races during their rookie season, also was brought back into the fold along with former March aerodynamicist Tino Belli, Herd's partner in the GenTech engineering company. By midseason, vastly experienced race engineer Lee Dykstra also was on the books.

An interesting array of Formula 1-type 'turning vanes' appeared on Fabi's car during the season, along with numerous other non-standard tweaks. The diminutive Italian responded with several strong performances, and even though his efforts on race day often seemed to be hindered in one way or another, Fabi still managed to top the categories for laps and miles completed during the season.

Galles Racing International

Base: Albuquerque, New Mexico
Drivers: Adrian Fernandez, Marco Greco
Sponsors: Tecate, Quaker State, Brastemp
Chassis: Lola T95/00
Engines: Mercedes-Benz IC108
Tires: Goodyear
Wins: 0; **Poles:** 0
PPG Cup points: 66 Fernandez (12th)

The loss of Al Unser Jr. at the end of 1993 has inevitably been a heavy blow to Rick Galles *(above left)* but young Mexican Adrian Fernandez *(left)* maintained his steady progress with the Tecate/Quaker State Lola *(below)* while Brazilian Marco Greco *(above)* performed respectably in the second-string entry.

In contrast to the Walker and PacWest teams, Rick Galles switched allegiance from Reynard to Lola during the off-season, although subsequent experience seemed to indicate that the Reynard might have been slightly the better car under most conditions.

Fernandez took time to adjust to the Lola's different characteristics but continued his steady progression and was regularly among the top 10. Prior to a couple of accidents during the New Hampshire weekend, the likable Mexican had earned points in eight consecutive races, including a fine third at Michigan and a fourth at Mid-Ohio. He was headed toward a top-five, too, at Cleveland, until retiring with an engine failure in the closing laps.

Greco competed in nine races for the team and showed signs of promise, but all too often his efforts were thwarted by a lack of empathy with his car's gearbox.

Photos: Michael C. Brown

Bettenhausen Motorsports
Base: Indianapolis, Indiana
Driver: Stefan Johansson
Sponsor: Alumax Aluminum
Chassis: Penske PC23/Reynard 94I
Tires: Goodyear
Engines: Mercedes-Benz IC108/Ford Cosworth XB
Wins: 0; **Poles:** 0
PPG Cup points: 60 (13th)

Tony Bettenhausen began the season full of optimism, armed with a pair of the all-conquering 1994-specification Penske PC23 chassis. Unfortunately, his team faced the same problems that confronted Roger Penske's operation: how to make the car work on the new breed of tires. There was an added difficulty posed by the fact the PPG Cup series has gained enormously in terms of competitiveness over the last few years. As Johansson pointed out regularly, he was generally as close, if not closer, to the ultimate pace than he had been with a similarly one-year-old chassis in 1994; but now there were more cars – and drivers – capable of running at the front.

Johansson drove as hard and well as ever during the 1995 season. He was desperately unlucky at Surfers Paradise, hobbled by a transmission failure with at least a second-place finish in his sights. He gained some recompense with a third at Nazareth and did well to make the field at Indy with a leased, year-old Reynard after Bettenhausen recognized the futility of trying to qualify the recalcitrant PC23. Ironically, Johansson bumped Emerson Fittipaldi from the field in the final moments.

Johansson's five top-six finishes, and the fact he scored more points than in '94, bore testimony to his efforts. Nice job.

Tony Bettenhausen *(below)* naturally hoped that the acquisition of a couple of the all-conquering Penske PC23s would enable his team to challenge for victory. Popular Swede Stefan Johansson *(above right)* led at Surfers Paradise *(top)* and shared the podium with eventual PPG Cup champion Jacques Villeneuve at Nazareth *(above)* but the cars were generally outpaced by the latest equipment. However, Johansson did have the satisfaction of leading Fittipaldi's '95 Penske at Mid-Ohio *(right)*.

Jim Hall's team took a major step forward with the imaginative decision to recruit top Formula 3000 driver Gil de Ferran *(below right)*. The talented Brazilian made a significant contribution to the development of the Pennzoil Reynard *(far right and opposite)* and proved to be a doughty racer. He even made the team owner *(right)* smile!

Below: De Ferran receives the congratulations of fellow countryman Christian Fittipaldi after scoring his long-overdue maiden Indy Car victory at Laguna Seca – a win which enabled him to snatch the Rookie of the Year award from Fittipaldi's grasp.

Hall Racing

Base:	Midland, Texas
Driver:	Gil de Ferran (R)
Sponsor:	Pennzoil
Chassis:	Reynard 95I
Engines:	Mercedes-Benz IC108
Tires:	Goodyear
Wins:	1; Poles: 1
PPG Cup points:	56 (14th)

Jim Hall's team made great strides in 1995, even though that might not be reflected in the final points tally. Rookie de Ferran proved a valuable addition to the team, for he brought a breath of fresh air, a positive approach and an impressive technical ability. He was also fast!

The 27-year-old Brazilian was involved in several incidents early in the year, usually not of his making, while the team let him down on occasion, notably at Road America (botched pit strategy) and Toronto (clutch problem). His Pennzoil Reynard was also hamstrung by a variety of engine and transmission failures.

De Ferran learned from his mistakes and gelled well with the team. Why, he even made Jim Hall smile on a regular basis! Hall, indeed, was beaming broadly when de Ferran sped home to victory at Laguna Seca, securing the team's first victory since John Andretti won on the team's debut in Australia in 1991. The result also clinched for de Ferran the coveted Jim Trueman Rookie of the Year Award.

Left: Experienced Canadian Scott Goodyear came agonizingly close to winning the Indy 500 for the Indy Car newcomers. Team owner Steve Horne stands over the car in pit lane.

Brazilian rookie Andre Ribeiro *(below)* confirmed the promise he had shown with the Tasman team in the PPG-Firestone Indy Lights series in 1994.

Bottom: The Honda-powered LCI International Reynard was particularly impressive on the ovals.

Steve Horne knows how to make an Indy Car team tick. He established a winning formula at Truesports more than a decade ago and showed he had lost none of his touch by dominating the PPG-Firestone Indy Lights Championship for two years with his newly formed Tasman team. In 1995 he stepped back into the PPG Cup fray and, with even a little bit of luck, might have added at least two more wins to the sensational runaway success claimed by rookie Ribeiro in New Hampshire.

His long-time chief lieutenant, Jeff Eischen, managed the operation with his usual rod of iron, with engineer Don Halliday providing the perfect foil as he continued the rapport he had established with Ribeiro during their season together in Indy Lights. Ribeiro showed what he – and the vastly improved Honda engines – were capable of by setting second fastest lap in the first session in Miami, although a series of

Tasman Motorsports Group		
Base: Hilliard, Ohio		
Drivers: Andre Ribeiro (R), Scott Goodyear		
Sponsors: LCI International, Marlboro, CNN, Motorola		
Chassis: Reynard 95I		
Engines: Honda Indy V8		
Tires: Firestone		
Wins: 1 (Ribeiro); **Poles:** 1 (Ribeiro)		
PPG Cup points: 39		
Ribeiro 38 (17th), Goodyear 1 (34th)		

incidents served to hinder his progress through the early races. His breakthrough came at Indianapolis.

Goodyear took center stage by qualifying on the front row and then had the race torn from his grasp following an incident involving the pace car shortly before the finish. Ribeiro, meanwhile, ran comfortably in his wake until hobbled by a broken throttle linkage. A small fire also cost the Brazilian a possible victory at Michigan.

The ultra-professional Tasman team created an excellent impression in its first year, thoroughly vindicating Horne's decision to side with Honda and Firestone. The 1996 season promises even more.

The relationship between Indy Car legend A.J. Foyt *(right)* and mercurial driver Eddie Cheever *(below right)* always seemed destined to end in tears. Cheever posted a few good early-season performances in the Copenhagen Lola *(below)* and nearly won at Nazareth, but after that it was downhill all the way.

Photos: Michael C. Brown

A.J. Foyt Enterprises

Base:	Houston, Texas

Base: Houston, Texas
Drivers: Eddie Cheever, Scott Sharp, Brian Till, Fredrik Ekblom (R)
Sponsors: Copenhagen
Chassis: Lola T95/00
Engines: Ford/Cosworth XB
Tires: Goodyear
Wins: 0; Poles: 0
PPG Cup points: 33 Cheever (18th)

Dick Simon Racing

Base: Indianapolis, Indiana
Drivers: Eliseo Salazar (R), Dean Hall, Arie Luyendyk, Carlos Guerrero (R), Lyn St. James, Davy Jones, Marco Greco
Sponsors: Cristal, Mobil 1, Copec, Subway, WavePhore, Herdez, Bufalo, McCormick, Whitlock Corp., Bryant Heating & Cooling, Jonathan Byrd's Cafeteria, Brastemp
Chassis: Lola T94/00 and T95/00
Engines: Ford/Cosworth XB
Tires: Goodyear
Wins: 0; Poles: 0
PPG Cup points: 25
Salazar 19 (21st), Guerrero 2 (29th), Greco 2 (30th), Hall 2 (31st)

Perhaps the biggest surprise was that Cheever stayed with the team until just two races remained on the schedule. Cheever, to his intense frustration, was never a serious contender in qualifying – due, he was convinced, to Foyt's insistence that no race engineer was necessary – but in the races he often moved steadily toward the front. He was unfortunate to miss out on a podium finish after running out of fuel on the final lap at Long Beach (although he still placed fourth), but that disappointment paled into insignificance at Nazareth. Foyt had taken a gamble on his fuel strategy, and as the laps ticked away it looked as though his team might emerge with its first triumph since 1981. Cruelly, though, a minor miscalculation caused Cheever to run out of fuel with only a couple of laps to go. He still placed fifth but it was of little consolation.

Indianapolis was an unmitigated disaster. Cheever was involved in the dramatic first-lap wreck and guest driver Sharp also collected the wall. The team never really recovered, although Cheever did post a good drive at Michigan, climbing into the top three before being felled by a gearbox dog-ring failure.

The defection of Raul Boesel and major supporter Duracell to Rahal/Hogan Racing left Dick and Dianne Simon without an established driver or sponsor. As such, they realized it would be a tall order to expect top results from Dean Hall, who had not raced for almost four years, and rookie driver Eliseo Salazar.

Nevertheless, thanks to Simon's guidance, the 40-year-old Salazar posted several strong performances on the ovals. He finished a fine fourth at Indianapolis – and probably would have been on the podium had he not been forced to lift off the gas during the chaotic final restart. He showed well, too, at Nazareth, Michigan and New Hampshire.

After Hall's promised sponsorship evaporated, Mexican rookie Carlos Guerrero joined the fray and also drove well on occasion, although all too often his efforts were punctuated by accidents.

Greco claimed his best result of the year, 11th, at Portland, in the

Chilean rookie Eliseo Salazar *(middle)* showed well on the ovals with the Cristal/Mobil 1/ Copec Lola *(bottom left)* and his fourth place at Indianapolis represented the high spot of the season for Dick Simon *(far left)* and his team. Mexico's Carlos Guerrero *(left)* displayed promise but his Herdez/Viva Mexico! Lola *(below)* was involved in rather too many accidents, while Lyn St. James *(bottom)* did her usual steady job.

Regular drivers Alessandro Zampedri *(middle right)* and Eric Bachelart *(bottom right)* performed dependably for team owner Dale Coyne and his new partner Walter Payton *(right)*. Zampedri's ninth place at Vancouver with the Mi-Jack car *(below right)* was particularly creditable.

Payton-Coyne Racing
Base: Plainfield, Illinois
Drivers: Alessandro Zampedri, Eric Bachelart, Buddy Lazier, Ross Bentley, Franck Freon
Sponsors: Mi-Jack, Agfa
Chassis: Lola T94/00
Engines: Ford/Cosworth XB
Tires: Firestone
Wins: 0; Poles: 0
PPG Cup points: 23
Zampedri 15 (22nd), Bachelart 8 (23rd)

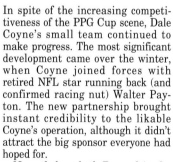

first of two outings with the team, but Simon's finest hour came on Bubble Day at Indianapolis, when, in stark contrast to Penske Racing, he contrived to qualify all four of his drivers – Salazar, Guerrero, Jones and St. James. The bad news, however, was that three cars were eliminated by accidents during the day, including two on the first lap. In all, during a very difficult year, Simon's cars were involved in no fewer than 29 wrecks. Ouch!

In spite of the increasing competitiveness of the PPG Cup scene, Dale Coyne's small team continued to make progress. The most significant development came over the winter, when Coyne joined forces with retired NFL star running back (and confirmed racing nut) Walter Payton. The new partnership brought instant credibility to the likable Coyne's operation, although it didn't attract the big sponsor everyone had hoped for.

Nevertheless, both Zampedri, who had shown great promise in his rookie season, and Bachelart, returning to the Indy Car scene after an absence of more than two years, produced several impressive performances in their year-old Lolas. The pair finished a worthy seventh (Bachelart) and eighth in Long Beach, while Zampedri added two more top-10 finishes at Cleveland and Vancouver despite a minimalist budget.

Lazier, who substituted for Bachelart on a few occasions when the Belgian was otherwise committed to a Peugeot touring car program, showed especially good form at Nazareth and Michigan. The youngster from Colorado, like his teammates, really did deserve an opportunity in a properly funded car.

Christian Danner took a fine seventh place at Miami in the Project Indy team's '93 Lola-Ford after an engine problem sidelined its new '94 Reynard *(below)*. Other drivers to turn out for the team during the season included little-known Austrian Hubert Stromberger *(middle)* and Frenchman Franck Freon *(bottom)*.

Project Indy

Base: Brownsburg, Indiana
Drivers: Christian Danner, Buddy Lazier, Franck Freon, Johnny Parsons, Hubert Stromberger (R), Jeff Wood, Mimmo Schiattarella (R)
Sponsors: No Touch, Van Dyne, Marcelo Group
Chassis: Lola T93/00 and Reynard 94I
Engines: Ford/Cosworth XB
Tires: Goodyear
Wins: 0; Poles: 0
PPG Cup points: 6 Danner (24th)

Team Menard

Base: Indianapolis, Indiana
Drivers: Arie Luyendyk, Scott Brayton, Buddy Lazier
Sponsors: Glidden Paints, Quaker State
Chassis: Lola T95/00
Engines: Menard/Buick V6
Tires: Goodyear
Wins: 0; Poles: 1 (Brayton)
PPG Cup points: 7
Luyendyk 6 (25th), Brayton 1 (33rd)

John Menard might not yet have achieved his goal of winning the Indianapolis 500, but he took one big step in the right direction as two of his cars, driven by the experienced Brayton and Luyendyk, qualified on the front row for the 79th running of 'The Greatest Spectacle in Racing.' If the rumors were to be believed,

Menard spent in the region of $6 million on this one race. His investment included a full-time engine development program which brought improved power and reliability from the trusty V6 engines, thanks primarily to an exotic and exclusive fuel management system produced by TAG Electronics.

The Lola-Menards still proved excessively thirsty by comparison to the 'conventional' four-valve engines, however, and various minor glitches restricted Luyendyk to a seventh-place finish. Brayton, who never really featured in the race, took 17th. A third car, driven by the deserving Lazier, retired early.

Without a regular Indy Car drive, 1990 Indy 500 winner Arie Luyendyk *(top)* was recruited to the Menard effort. The Dutchman's teammate Scott Brayton *(left and below)* took pole but did not feature among the leaders in the race.

Team co-owner Christian Danner crowned an otherwise disappointing year for the ambitious but desperately under-financed Project Indy operation by taking an excellent seventh in the opening round at Miami. The result was achieved in the team's trusty '93 Lola rather than the newly acquired ex-Villeneuve Reynard.

An unrequited sponsorship deal left the team in a difficult situation and it was to Andreas Leberle's credit that he managed to attend as many races as he did. The veteran Johnny Parsons didn't quite make the cut at Indianapolis, thanks primarily to a crash just prior to the final weekend of qualifications, while Buddy Lazier hopped into the car at ludicrously short notice on a couple of occasions. Unfortunately, the resources simply were not available to attain the results of which this team was undoubtedly capable.

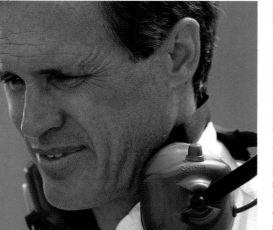

Parker Johnstone repaid the confidence of Comptech owners Doug Peterson *(left)* and Don Erb by taking pole position at Michigan with the Motorola Cellular Reynard-Honda and leading the race until wheel bearing problems intervened *(below left)*. At Laguna Seca *(bottom left)* it seemed that he was coming to terms with the car's handling on road courses.

The Reynard overseen by Frank Arciero *(right)* was immaculately prepared but Hiro Matsushita *(below right)* shows little sign of developing into a championship contender.

Veteran Roberto Guerrero *(bottom right)* scored a PPG Cup point for Pagan Racing with 12th place at Indianapolis.

Comptech Racing

Base: El Dorado Hills, California
Driver: Parker Johnstone
Sponsor: Motorola Cellular
Chassis: Reynard 95I
Engines: Honda Indy V8
Tires: Firestone
Wins: 0; **Poles:** 1
PPG Cup points: 6 (27th)

Arciero-Wells Racing

Base: Rancho Santa Margarita, California
Driver: Hiro Matsushita
Sponsors: Panasonic, Duskin, YKK
Chassis: Reynard 94I and 95I
Engines: Ford/Cosworth XB
Tires: Firestone
Wins: 0; **Poles:** 0
PPG Cup points: 5 (28th)

The new association between the Arciero family, long-time Indy Car entrants, and Cal Wells, best known previously for his extremely successful exploits in the world of off-road racing, made a very favorable impression in its first year. The team was always immaculately presented and its car enjoyed an enviable record of reliability in spite of the generally lackluster displays by driver Hiro Matsushita.

The Japanese, now in his sixth season, showed best at Indianapolis, where he qualified a strong 10th in a brand-new Reynard 95I chassis and finished 10th after a steady if unspectacular afternoon. Next year, however, Arciero-Wells has more ambitious plans centered upon employment of the brand-new Toyota engine.

Photos: Michael C. Brown

After dipping a toe in the Indy Car waters in 1994, Comptech undertook an extensive test and development program on behalf of Honda during the winter, then returned to the fray for a limited program of seven races commencing in Detroit. Johnstone, who had been with Comptech owners Doug Peterson and Don Erb for more than eight years, quickly developed an affinity for the ovals. He qualified, sensationally, on the pole at Michigan and led convincingly until hobbled by a wheel-bearing failure.

Johnstone found it more difficult to make an impression on the road courses. He nevertheless scored points on his second and third outings, at Road America and Cleveland, then looked far more comfortable in the last couple of races, when his task was eased by the addition of experienced race engineers John Bright and Tim Wardrop to the ambitious Comptech team.

Pagan Racing

Base: Indianapolis, Indiana
Drivers: Dennis Vitolo, Roberto Guerrero
Sponsors: Charter America, Carlo Environmental, Upper Deck, General Components
Chassis: Reynard 94I
Engines: Mercedes-Benz IC108
Tires: Goodyear
Wins: 0; **Poles:** 0
PPG Cup points: 1 Guerrero (32nd)

Jack and Allan Pagan decided to run a couple of races in preparation for the Indianapolis 500, firstly with Vitolo in Miami and then with Guerrero in Phoenix. It proved to be a wise move as he qualified comfortably on the first weekend at Indy in an ex-Ganassi team Reynard modified to accept an up-to-date Mercedes engine from Ilmor Engineering. Guerrero ran well in the race, too, finishing 12th despite losing a couple of laps during the confusion that erupted during an early full-course caution.

Midget star Stan Fox *(left)* was grievously injured in an appalling first-lap crash at Indianapolis but happily appears to be on the road to recovery.

Michael Greenfield *(below left)*, Scotland's Jim Crawford *(bottom left)* and former motocross star Jeff Ward *(below)* all ran at Indianapolis but joined Al Unser Jr. and Emerson Fittipaldi on the sidelines on race day.

Reynard

Production base: Bicester, England
Number of cars built in 1995: 25
Wins: 8 (Villeneuve 4, Gordon 2, Ribeiro 1, de Ferran 1);
Poles: 13 (Villeneuve 6, Gordon 2, Herta 1, Fabi 1, de Ferran 1, Johnstone 1, Ribeiro 1)

No points but trying . . .

Impressively, in addition to Team Menard, which competed only at Indianapolis, all 20 teams that contested at least one additional PPG Cup race earned points toward the championship. As usual, of course, a few other teams chose to run only at The Speedway, but only Beck Motorsports and Hemelgarn Racing made it into the show.

Greg Beck, who previously had worked on an occasional basis for Dick Simon, concluded a deal to continue his association with sophomore entrant Hideshi Matsuda. The Japanese once again was impressive, qualifying solidly despite a minimum of track time in a previously unraced '94 Lola-Ford acquired from Patrick Racing. Matsuda finished 15th in the well-prepared car.

Hemelgarn Racing did not enjoy such good fortune. Midget star Stan Fox made his annual pilgrimage to

the 2.5-mile superspeedway and qualified comfortably in a brand-new Reynard, only to crash catastrophically on the first lap. Miraculously, the well-liked and respected Fox was able to escape the carnage alive, albeit with a serious head injury, and in the ensuing months he appeared to be making great strides toward a full recovery. Wonderful news.

SuperModified star Davey Hamilton also attempted to qualify a second Hemelgarn Reynard, only for a broken wheel to pitch him heavily into the wall during the first week of practice. Hamilton sustained a broken ankle, although that didn't deter him from making a tenacious but ultimately unsuccessful bid to make the field on the final weekend.

Franck Freon came agonizingly close to making the cut in an aged '92 Lola-Menard/Buick, fielded by the ever-optimistic Steve Erickson's Autosport Racing Team, while former motocross star Jeff Ward, with absolutely no prior Indy Car experience, gave a similarly good account of himself despite failing to qualify a year-old Lola entered by Jeff Sinden and Joe Kennedy.

Michael Greenfield tried hard but to no avail in a '93 Lola powered by his father Peter's ingenious Greenfield GC209T engine, but Jim Crawford never had a prayer of extracting sufficient speed from Grant Adcox's under-powered '92 Lola-Buick. Finally, Dick Simon, Tero Palmroth and the sadly unemployed Mike Groff all took some laps at Indianapolis, for a variety of reasons, but none of them had serious plans for participation. Not this time, anyway.

Chief designer Malcolm Oastler utilized extensive experience gained during Reynard's first season as an Indy Car constructor in finalizing the specifications for the 95I. Aesthetically, the new car looked quite similar to its predecessor, at least so far as the chassis was concerned. Special emphasis was placed on the aerodynamic configuration, which Reynard admitted had been compromised on the original car due to time constraints. Consequently, the 94I had not lived up to expectations. It was far too pitch-sensitive and the drivers and race engineers experienced great difficulty in determining a setup that would provide consistent handling. Right away, the 95I proved

superior in that department, as exemplified by the final statistics.

The gearbox and transmission also was subjected to extensive development in conjunction with Xtrac. Early in the year, especially, the selector mechanism proved extremely troublesome, although eventually those problems were overcome.

Overall, the '95 Reynard could be described as 'user-friendly.' It appeared to work with equal effectiveness whether mated to Goodyear tires or Firestones, or to the variety of engine configurations on offer. The supply of parts, however, continued to prove elusive for some teams, and that aspect was due to be extensively improved in time for the 1996 season.

Lola

Production base: Huntingdon, England
Number of cars built in 1995: 27
Wins: 4 (Tracy 2, Andretti 1, Pruett 1);
Poles: 4 (Andretti 3, Brayton 1)

Penske

Production base: Poole, England
Number of cars built in 1995: 6
Wins: 5 (Unser 4, E. Fittipaldi 1);
Poles: 0

Photos: Michael C. Brown

The defection of the Walker and PacWest teams to Reynard last winter, allied to the poor results achieved during 1994, galvanized the staff at Lola Cars into producing a significantly improved alternative. In large part, John Travis and the crew were successful.

The new car looked substantially different when compared to a T94/00, especially in the sidepod and nose areas. The sidepods on the newer car reached higher up the cockpit sides than previously, while the lower front suspension pickups were raised by as much as three inches in order to improve the air flow into, around and underneath the sidepods.

Interestingly, the Lola seemed especially susceptible to temperature changes, frequently performing better during the relative cool of the morning practice sessions than during qualifying later in the day.

As ever, Lola's customer support and parts supply, handled by Carl A. Haas Automotive, was excellent, and for 1996 it seems the split between Lola and Reynard customers will remain similar, with Team Rahal's switch to Reynard being offset by the fellow Hilliard, Ohio-based Tasman team's move to Lola.

Nigel Bennett was always going to have a tough task in improving upon his PC23 design, which had been so utterly dominant in 1994. The new car, as usual for Bennett and his staff, represented a logical development, and both Unser and Fittipaldi expressed their satisfaction after an initial test in the PC24 at Firebird. It wasn't until they arrived at the first race in Miami that anyone realized there was a problem.

First, as Bennett had anticipated, Lola and Reynard had improved their cars dramatically over the winter, minimizing the advantage Penske had previously enjoyed. But that didn't explain why the Penskes were so far from the pace.

Immediately after the race, all hands were called on deck to address the PC24's apparent shortcomings. A back-to-back test with a PC23 chassis was hastily convened at Firebird, and the same problems surfaced. Uh-oh. Fortunately, significant progress was made and thereafter the cars were much more competitive.

Eventually it became apparent that the latest Goodyear Eagle radial tires, to which Penske was contractually obligated, did not suit the PC24 nearly as well as the opposition. The reasons behind that reality continued to elude the Penske engineers – otherwise they would surely have fixed the problem. Nevertheless, the tire characteristics, which included a slightly taller profile and a more flexible sidewall, clearly upset the Penske's stability and drivability, especially in qualifying trim.

There was an additional problem, too, at Indianapolis, where no amount of fine-tuning would allow the drivers to carry sufficient speed through the corners. The only solution was to carry more downforce – but then they were too slow on the straightaways. The quandary proved insurmountable. The Penskes, almost unbelievably, failed to qualify.

Ford/Cosworth
Production base: Northampton, England; Torrance, California
Wins: 10; Poles: 13

The crowning glory of Ford and Cosworth's championship-winning season came at Indianapolis, where they finally broke arch rival Ilmor Engineering's streak of success that had extended, with a variety of engines, since 1988.

Four different teams contributed to the achievement of Ford's 10 race wins, and it was interesting to note that seven of those triumphs were claimed by regular 'customer' teams, such as Team Green, which employed 'standard' XB Series I equipment and enjoyed generally excellent reliability.

For much of the season, meanwhile, the manufacturer's two 'favored' teams, Newman-Haas and Target/Chip Ganassi Racing, were engaged in development of a Series II version of the successful XB engine, which has been in existence since 1992. The Series II, which featured revised cylinder heads and a new inlet system, showed well on the dyno and in initial testing, but several difficulties were encountered and numerous failures occurred. The Ganassi team emerged winless from the season – and promptly announced it will switch allegiance to Honda for 1996 – while of the three Newman-Haas wins, only one, in Toronto, was earned with the Series II.

Mercedes-Benz
Production base: Brixworth, England
Wins: 6; Poles: 1

In terms of outright horsepower the Mercedes-Benz IC108 engine, developed by Ilmor Engineering, seemed to be lacking slightly by comparison to the Ford/Cosworth and Honda alternatives. The deficit was most readily apparent on the super-speedways at Indianapolis and Michigan, where none of the Mercedes-powered cars was able to match the ultimate pace. On the road courses, however, where tractability and torque assumed greater importance, all three engine manufacturers appeared to be more closely matched – especially in race configuration.

As ever, the Penske team utilized engines maintained exclusively in its own shop in Reading, Pennsylvania, while the Rahal/Hogan, Hall and Galles 'customer' engines were all supplied via VDS Engines in Midland, Texas.

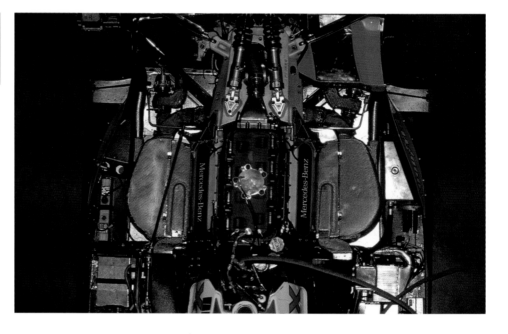

Honda
Production base: Santa Clarita, California
Wins: 1; Poles: 2

The biggest strides in terms of engine development, by far, were made by Honda Performance Development. The original HRX engine was markedly improved over the winter, featuring a new inlet system, with a totally redesigned plenum chamber, and revised cylinder heads. After much on-track testing by the Comptech team, it proved immediately competitive in Tasman's Reynard chassis at Miami, although Andre Ribeiro's inexperience saw to it that the promise was never truly realized.

Then, for Indianapolis, Honda introduced the all-new HRH, which benefited from many of the lessons learned on the HRX and, for the first time, incorporated an aluminum (rather than cast-iron) block. Scott Goodyear, in a second Tasman entry, qualified on the front row of the grid – ahead of all the other four-valve entries – and looked set for an historic victory until being assessed a stop-and-go penalty in the closing moments.

The Honda soon became competitive on all kinds of tracks. It was also astonishingly reliable: the Tasman team never once performed an unscheduled engine change during the season. The sophisticated Honda electronics caused a few problems from time to time, but their effectiveness was illustrated by the barely perceptible full-throttle shifts, which at the end of the season were noticeably faster than those attained by the Ford and Mercedes teams.

Honda might have only one Indy Car victory to its name right now, but that number seems set to rise substantially in 1996.

104

PPG World Championship Victories

Emerson Fittipaldi marked Ilmor's 100th win at Nazareth, 23 April 1995.

1 Long Beach, Mario Andretti 2 Cleveland, Emerson Fittipaldi 3 Toronto, Emerson Fittipaldi 4 Pocono, Rick Mears 5 Elkhart Lake, Mario Andretti 6 Phoenix, Mario Andretti 7 Long Beach, Al Unser Jr 8 Indy 500, Rick Mears 9 Milwaukee, Rick Mears 10 Portland, Danny Sullivan 11 Cleveland, Mario Andretti 12 Toronto, Al Unser Jr 13 Meadowlands, Al Unser Jr 14 Michigan 500, Danny Sullivan 15 Mid-Ohio, Emerson Fittipaldi 16 Elkhart Lake, Emerson Fittipaldi 17 Nazareth, Danny Sullivan 18 Laguna Seca, Danny Sullivan 19 Miami, Al Unser Jr 20 Phoenix, Rick Mears 21 Long Beach, Al Unser Jr 22 Indy 500, Emerson Fittipaldi 23 Milwaukee, Rick Mears 24 Detroit, Emerson Fittipaldi 25 Portland, Emerson Fittipaldi 26 Cleveland, Emerson Fittipaldi 27 Toronto, Michael Andretti 28 Michigan 500, Michael Andretti 29 Pocono, Danny Sullivan 30 Elkhart Lake, Danny Sullivan 31 Nazareth, Emerson Fittipaldi 32 Laguna Seca, Rick Mears 33 Phoenix, Rick Mears 34 Long Beach, Al Unser Jr 35 Indy 500, Arie Luyendyk 36 Milwaukee, Al Unser Jr 37 Detroit, Michael Andretti 38 Portland, Michael Andretti 39 Cleveland, Danny Sullivan 40 Meadowlands, Michael Andretti 41 Toronto, Al Unser Jr 42 Michigan 500, Al Unser Jr 43 Denver, Al Unser Jr 44 Vancouver, Al Unser Jr 45 Mid-Ohio, Michael Andretti 46 Elkhart Lake, Michael Andretti 47 Nazareth, Emerson Fittipaldi 48 Laguna Seca, Danny Sullivan 49 Surfers Paradise, John Andretti 50 Long Beach, Al Unser Jr 51 Phoenix, Arie Luyendyk 52 Indy 500, Rick Mears 53 Milwaukee, Michael Andretti 54 Detroit, Emerson Fittipaldi 55 Portland, Michael Andretti 56 Cleveland, Michael Andretti 57 Meadowlands, Bobby Rahal 58 Toronto, Michael Andretti 59 Michigan 500, Rick Mears 60 Denver, Al Unser Jr 61 Vancouver, Michael Andretti 62 Mid-Ohio, Michael Andretti 63 Elkhart Lake, Michael Andretti 64 Nazareth, Arie Luyendyk 65 Laguna Seca, Michael Andretti 66 Surfers Paradise, Emerson Fittipaldi 67 Phoenix, Bobby Rahal 68 Long Beach, Danny Sullivan 69 Indy 500, Al Unser Jr 70 Detroit, Bobby Rahal 71 New Hampshire, Bobby Rahal 72 Michigan 500, Scott Goodyear 73 Cleveland, Emerson Fittipaldi 74 Elkhart Lake, Emerson Fittipaldi 75 Mid-Ohio, Emerson Fittipaldi 76 Nazareth, Bobby Rahal 77 Long Beach, Paul Tracy 78 Indy 500, Emerson Fittipaldi 79 Detroit, Danny Sullivan 80 Portland, Emerson Fittipaldi 81 Cleveland, Paul Tracy 82 Toronto, Paul Tracy 83 Elkhart Lake, Paul Tracy 84 Vancouver, Al Unser Jr 85 Mid-

in 156 IndyCar World Series Races

Ohio, Emerson Fittipaldi 86 Laguna Seca, Paul Tracy 87 Phoenix, Emerson Fittipaldi 88 Long Beach, Al Unser Jr 89 Indy 500, Al Unser Jr 90 Milwaukee, Al Unser Jr 91 Detroit, Paul Tracy 92 Portland, Al Unser Jr 93 Cleveland, Al Unser Jr 94 Mid-Ohio, Al Unser Jr 95 Loudon, Al Unser Jr 96 Vancouver, Al Unser Jr 97 Nazareth, Paul Tracy 98 Laguna Seca, Paul Tracy 99 Long Beach, Al Unser Jr 100 Nazareth, Emerson Fittipaldi 101 Portland, Al Unser Jr 102 Mid-Ohio, Al Unser Jr 103 Vancouver, Al Unser Jr 104 Laguna Seca, Gil de Ferran

ILMOR ENGINEERING LTD

Racing Engines

A WINNING

Jacques Villeneuve contested only two seasons of PPG Indy Car World Series competition before moving onward to Formula 1, but he left an indelible impression.

During 1995, the 24-year-old French-Canadian displayed all the hallmarks of a worthy champion. He was fast and aggressive, yet his speed was balanced with consistency. Villeneuve knew when to bide his time. He developed into an awesome qualifier, claiming six poles in the last nine races. He performed well under pressure. Mistakes were few and far between – and never came in clutch situations.

But it wasn't always so. In 1994, during his ultimately successful rookie campaign, he developed a reputation early in the season as being rather wild. He was not noted as an especially good qualifier; in fact, he didn't claim his first pole until Portland this past June.

The man most commonly credited with developing Villeneuve's skills these past three years is vastly experienced team manager/owner Barry Green, who, along with Jerry Forsythe, his partner for the first two years, was responsible for plucking Villeneuve from the Japanese Formula 3 Championship and procuring long-term sponsorship from Player's Ltd. Indeed the entire Team Green organization has worked hard to nurture Villeneuve's skills, starting in the Player's Ltd. Toyota Atlantic Championship in 1993, but no one has worked with him as closely, or had such a profound effect on his maturation, as chief engineer Tony Cicale.

The combination of Villeneuve and Cicale seems to have been a match made in heaven (with Barry Green also playing a pivotal role). The young Villeneuve, clearly, had talent to throw away. He was ambitious and willing to learn. And in Cicale he found the perfect teacher. A former school-master who himself was no slouch behind the wheel of a race car, Cicale had carved an enviable reputation during the past 15 years or so as a gifted and imaginative aerodynamicist and, latterly, an especially astute race engineer.

When the Forsythe-Green team was founded, prior to the 1993 season, Cicale had almost dropped out of the racing scene. He had quit the Newman-Haas team in 1991 after many successful years, working mostly with Mario Andretti, and was enjoying his new-found leisure time. Wind-surfing had usurped auto racing as his abiding passion, and Cicale was pursuing the sport with his customary verve and vigor – and competitiveness. But Green's offer captivated his interest.

'I had never, ever worked with a

COMBINATION

young, inexperienced driver,' notes Cicale. 'All the drivers I worked with were very, very experienced, competent people, like Mario and Michael Andretti, Geoff Brabham, Kevin Cogan and Alan Jones and on and on and on. So I thought it would be kind of interesting, A) to do Formula Atlantic, which was a nice type of car to start with; and B) to work with very non-experienced drivers.'

Cicale found the venture satisfying and enjoyable. His drivers, Villeneuve and Claude Bourbonnais, didn't claim the championship, as had been expected, but they won most of the races. It was a rewarding exercise.

'I liked the series, I liked the cars,' he recalls. 'I enjoyed working with Jacques, and I think what I enjoyed most was, for the first time in a long time, I started to get some personal satisfaction. I felt that my input really did make a difference, where working with a lot of the experienced drivers, I'm sure my input made a difference there too, but I just didn't feel that it was important or vital. But working with Jacques and Claude in the first year, I really felt I was contributing to their growth in racing. And to me, that brought a huge amount of personal satisfaction, which made me happy. I definitely had more fun than I'd had in racing in a long time.'

Cicale is a captivating individual. He resembles the archetypal boffin, studious and bespectacled. He is most at ease in his small office/lounge within the Team Green transporter, where he can usually be found poring over computer data or conferring with Villeneuve and/or data analyst Scott Graves. But Cicale isn't all business. He chats easily and smiles often. He speaks quietly but deliberately, with authority and confidence, and no trace of arrogance.

'The combination that Jacques and I seemed to develop just worked,' he says matter-of-factly. 'We philosophically progressed in exactly the same fashion. I can honestly say that in three years of working with him, we never, ever, ever had an unkind word for each other and we always, I think, 100 percent respected each other and we always listened very carefully to one another.

'Philosophically, we both felt the same things. Not only about racing but about many, many things. About how you go about racing. And what are the critical things in racing? What are you really doing it for? And when you should stop developing the car and when you should go testing and when you shouldn't go testing and all kinds of things. We just meshed in so many ways, which is why I think our relationship was

very special. There were no areas of conflict whatsoever.'

Cicale leaves no doubt as to his admiration for the young man, both in terms of his skill and as a human being. When asked to name Villeneuve's greatest gifts, Cicale has no hesitation: 'He's very intelligent. He's a very, very, very bright young man. That's number one. I think number two is he's a very positive person, which in some ways is different to me, but I like being around very positive people; and because I was around Jacques I became much more positive. So, consequently, when we didn't have the car right or we went in the wrong direction, we either made light of it or made a joke of it, but we never got down on ourselves.

'We always said, "Well, OK, tomorrow we'll do something different and it will be better." We had just a lot of positive energy, a lot of positive thoughts. Stupid as that sounds, we were just very positive on what we felt we could both do together. I was confident that Jacques would be able to do a good lap time and Jacques was confident that I would be able to get the car right, for him, so that he could do a good lap time. And I think it was the confidence that both of us had in each other that ultimately made it work.

'Many times we just forced it to work. There was a lot of artistic manipulation rather than scientific manipulation, which I think is what racing is really all about. It's a lot more artistic than scientific. In a lot of ways. Not necessarily the design side but certainly the race engineering side is a very artistic, manipulative endeavor, and it's very, very important that the driver and the engineer both have a huge amount of confidence in each other – and of course that the team allows the driver and the engineer to progress in the way that they feel comfortable, which is very important to me. Barry and the rest of the team allowed us to do that.

'We didn't like to be influenced by anyone from the outside. Jacques and I didn't care what anybody else had [on their car]. We didn't care if Robby [Gordon] was on pole and we were 18th on the grid with a totally different setup. We just stuck to our plan. And the team allowed us to do that. They had confidence that we would come up with a program that would ultimately be competitive. And that was very, very important.'

Cicale, rightly, is proud of Team Green's achievements this year. He quickly points out, too, that Villeneuve had the benefit of no special equipment. He used the standard Ford/Cosworth XB engine package and a stock Reynard 95I chassis.

'I've always thought that race

engineers are too much in a hurry to change something they really don't understand in the first place,' he says. 'They spend an awful lot of time, an awful lot of money and an awful lot of resources re-doing what they're not really sure is wrong. In fact, I find that it takes me at least two-thirds to three-quarters of the season to really understand what the strengths and weaknesses of the car might be, and to really get a direction for how you would like to develop the car.

'My philosophy has always been, first, understand what you have. Because there's a *huge* amount of permutations that are supplied with the standard car. I mean, we have three different front wheelbases, two different rear wheelbases, three different front and rear wing configurations, four or five different rear geometries, three or four different front geometries, two or three different front rockers – besides all the spring and damper combinations, all the aero data that has to be absorbed and accumulated and understood.'

Instead, Cicale concentrated on learning as much about the car as he could, then optimizing it to suit Villeneuve's style.

'We really weren't interested in trying to develop the car into some state-of-the-art missile that would require a huge amount of funding and a huge amount of testing,' he says. 'Just concentrate on the basics.'

The strategy worked perfectly. Villeneuve scored points in all bar two of the races and was consistently quick, especially in the second half of the season. Only Al Unser Jr. and, briefly, Bobby Rahal, both acknowledged paragons of dependability, were able to keep pace as he charged toward the title.

Villeneuve himself points to a midseason test at Mid-Ohio as providing a turning point in his season. And certainly the statistics appear to concur with that perception. Prior to the June test, Villeneuve had never qualified on the pole. He did so at the next race, Portland, and repeated the feat in five of the next eight races.

'Yes, the infamous Mid-Ohio test,' says Cicale with a chuckle. 'You know, really, it was a combination of factors. Yes, we did have a good test. Yes, we learned a couple of things about the car that may have made it a little bit nicer, a little bit more comfortable to drive; but I think more than anything else, he just gained in confidence.

'He and I talked at Mid-Ohio about his aspirations in Formula 1. That is when, really, I think, his whole outlook changed. Even though he had not yet done the Formula 1

test [with Williams-Renault], I think, deep down, he was saying, "You know, if I could be on pole, maybe I could pull this off. Maybe I can get the Formula 1 drive." So I think the seed was planted at that Mid-Ohio test and it developed through the natural course of events – some physical, some mental and some just good fortune.

'You know, Jacques is a funny character. He always continues to surprise me. The Toronto and Vancouver races this year provided a good example. He loves being smooth [in the car]. He loves carrying speed into a corner and through a corner. He tends to try and build momentum through a corner, which is why the Portlands and Road Americas tend to suit him. He doesn't really like the street circuits, because typically you have to be nasty and aggressive with the car to go quickly; and he managed to win the pole in both races without being nasty and aggressive on the car. Also, having not shown well in those races last year, he wanted to prove that he could go well on street circuits.

'It's the same with his qualifying. I never really thought, up until Portland, that he was ever going to be a particularly good qualifier. I thought he would be a little bit like Al Jr., and if the car was really spectacular he would be on the front row or on the pole, but I never thought he was going to be an inherently good qualifier, like Michael [Andretti], for example. But now I've totally changed my mind. He's a spectacular qualifier. He has the ability to go out and get the maximum out of the car in a very short period of time.

'He kind of comes up to what you think is his limit, and you'll say, "Jacques, you sure that's your limit? You sure you can't brake another 50 feet deeper or get on the throttle a little bit sooner or turn a little bit later?" And he'll say, "OK. I'll do it." And he'll go out and he'll just do it!

'It's pretty amazing. I have to give him a lot credit for the success of this season. Yes, we had a good team; yes, we had a good relationship; but I think in many ways he is truly spectacular. And I think he'll be very, very successful in Formula 1.'

TONY CICALE INTERVIEW

FACTS & FIGURES

The drivers assembled for a group photo before the final race of the season. *Back row, l to r:* Tracy, Fangio, Greco, Ekblom, Villeneuve, Johnstone, Boesel, Zampedri, Gordon, Matsushita, Schiattarella, Vasser, de Ferran and Christian Fittipaldi. *Front row:* Ribeiro, Gugelmin, Herta, Emerson Fittipaldi, Andretti, Unser, Rahal, Pruett, Fernandez, Salazar, Carlos Guerrero and Fabi.

Right: Triumphant PPG Cup champion Jacques Villeneuve holds aloft his trophy in celebration.

Lap Leaders *(Number of races led)*

1	Michael Andretti	478	(12)
2	Al Unser Jr.	419	(7)
3	Jacques Villeneuve	280	(10)
4	Andre Ribeiro	164	(2)
5	Gil de Ferran	127	(4)
6	Emerson Fittipaldi	116	(2)
7	Teo Fabi	103	(6)
8	Paul Tracy	91	(6)
9	Mauricio Gugelmin	70	(4)
10	Robby Gordon	69	(4)
11	Scott Pruett	66	(2)
12	Parker Johnstone	52	(1)
13	Scott Goodyear	42	(1)
14	Eddie Cheever	40	(2)
15	Bryan Herta	30	(1)
16	Jimmy Vasser	20	(1)
17	Christian Fittipaldi	10	(1)
18	Arie Luyendyk	7	(1)
19	Stefan Johansson	6	(1)
20	Bobby Rahal	2	(2)
	Raul Boesel	2	(1)

Nations Cup

1	United States	290
2	Canada	219
3	Brazil	201
4	Italy	90
5	Mexico	68
6	Sweden	60
7	Chile	19
8	Belgium	8
9	Germany	6
	Netherlands	6
	Argentina	6
12	Japan	5
13	Colombia	1

Manufacturers Championship

1	Ford	310
2	Mercedes-Benz	272
3	Honda	40
4	Menard	6

Constructors Cup

1	Reynard	286
2	Lola	264
3	Penske	197

Jim Trueman Rookie of the Year

1	Gil de Ferran	57
2	Christian Fittipaldi	55
3	Andre Ribeiro	38
4	Eliseo Salazar	19
5	Juan Fangio II	6
6	Carlos Guerrero	2

Position	Driver	Car	Tires	Miami	Surfers Paradise	Phoenix	Long Beach	Nazareth	Indianapolis	Milwaukee	Detroit	Portland	Road America	Toronto	Cleveland	Michigan	Mid-Ohio	New Hampshire	Vancouver	Laguna Seca	Points total
1	**Jacques Villeneuve** (CDN)	Team Green *Player's Ltd.* Reynard 95I-Ford	GY	**1**	20	**5**	25	**†2**	**1**	**6**	**9**	P20	**P†1**	**P3**	**1**	**10**	**P3**	**4**	**P12**	**P11**	**172**
2	**Al Unser Jr.** (USA)	Marlboro Team Penske Penske PC24-Mercedes	GY	**15**	**6**	**8**	**†1**	**13**	NQA	**†2**	**5**	**†1**	28	26	18	**2**	**1**	**3**	**†1**	**6**	**161**
		Marlboro Team Penske Reynard 94I-Mercedes	GY	–	–	–	–	–	NQA	–	–	–	–	–	–	–	–	–	–	–	
		Marlboro Team Penske Lola T95/00-Mercedes	GY	–	–	–	–	–	NQ	–	–	–	–	–	–	–	–	–	–	–	
3	**Bobby Rahal** (USA)	Rahal/Hogan *Miller Genuine Draft* Lola T95/00-Mercedes	GY	**3**	**2**	21	21	**6**	**3**	**13**	24	**3**	**5**	**2**	**4**	**8**	26	**10**	**5**	**7**	**128**
4	**Michael Andretti** (USA)	Newman-Haas *Kmart/Texaco Havoline* Lola T95/00-Ford	GY	P†20	P†9	**2**	**P9**	22	25	**3**	**4**	**4**	27	**†1**	**7**	25	†19	**2**	21	**4**	**123**
5	**Robby Gordon** (USA)	Walker *Valvoline/Cummins Special* Reynard 95I-Ford	GY	13	14	**1**	22	**P4**	**5**	**5**	**P†1**	**8**	26	**5**	**6**	NS	**8**	**9**	**3**	**15**	**121**
6	**Paul Tracy** (CDN)	Newman-Haas *Kmart/Budweiser* Lola T95/00-Ford	GY	27	**1**	**4**	28	26	24	**1**	**8**	18	**2**	**8**	26	23	**2**	23	**8**	**2**	**115**
7	**Scott Pruett** (USA)	Patrick Racing *Firestone* Lola T95/00-Ford	FS	**4**	**3**	**9**	**2**	**8**	19	**12**	**3**	**13**	**7**	25	16	**1**	**11**	24	**6**	**5**	**112**
8	**Jimmy Vasser** (USA)	Ganassi *Target/STP* Reynard 95I-Ford	GY	**8**	24	23	23	24	22	**9**	**2**	**2**	**3**	17	**3**	**7**	**9**	**6**	27	**8**	**92**
9	**Teo Fabi** (I)	Forsythe Racing *Combustion Engineering/Indeck* Reynard 95I-Ford	GY	16	**13**	**7**	**3**	**7**	**8**	**P4**	**7**	23	**9**	**4**	19	**4**	**17**	**12**	19	**9**	**83**
10	**Mauricio Gugelmin** (BR)	PacWest Racing Group *Hollywood* Reynard 95I-Ford	GY	**2**	**4**	**13**	**5**	**17**	**†6**	**14**	**15**	**7**	24	**12**	23	**11**	**6**	**11**	20	**3**	**80**
11	**Emerson Fittipaldi** (BR)	Marlboro Team Penske Penske PC24-Mercedes	GY	24	18	**†3**	20	**1**	NQA	23	**10**	21	**15**	**10**	25	**5**	21	**5**	**7**	**16**	**67**
		Marlboro Team Penske Penske PC23-Mercedes	GY	–	–	–	–	–	NQA	–	–	–	–	–	–	–	–	–	–	–	
		Marlboro Team Penske Lola T95/00-Mercedes	GY	–	–	–	–	–	NQ	–	–	–	–	–	–	–	–	–	–	–	
12	**Adrian Fernandez** (MEX)	Galles *Tecate/Quaker State* Lola T95/00-Mercedes	GY	**11**	26	**12**	**18**	**9**	21	**10**	**6**	**9**	**6**	**7**	12	**3**	**4**	26	22	**10**	**66**
13	**Stefan Johansson** (S)	Bettenhausen *Alumax Aluminum* Penske PC23-Mercedes	GY	22	17	24	**6**	**3**	W	W	**11**	6	**10**	**14**	**8**	**6**	23	25	**4**	**14**	**60**
		Bettenhausen *Alumax Aluminum* Reynard 94I-Ford	GY	–	–	–	–	–	**16**	–	–	–	–	–	–	–	–	–	–	–	
		Bettenhausen *Alumax Aluminum* Penske PC22-Mercedes	GY	–	–	–	–	–	–	**21**	–	–	–	–	–	W	–	–	–	–	
14	***Gil de Ferran** (BR)	Hall Racing *Pennzoil Special* Reynard 95I-Mercedes	GY	25	16	**11**	27	19	29	**8**	**16**	**10**	21	16	P†14	12	24	**7**	**2**	**†1**	**56**
15	***Christian Fittipaldi** (BR)	Walker *Marlboro/Chapeco Special* Reynard 95I-Ford	GY	**5**	25	**10**	14	20	**2**	**7**	**17**	**12**	**8**	**9**	24	**9**	25	**8**	24	24	**54**
16	**Raul Boesel** (BR)	Rahal/Hogan *Duracell Charger* Lola T95/00-Mercedes	GY	**6**	**8**	**6**	**16**	**10**	20	**11**	NS	**5**	22	**6**	20	24	20	**18**	**10**	**12**	**48**
17	***Andre Ribeiro** (BR)	Tasman Motorsports *LCI International* Reynard 95I-Honda	FS	21	23	26	**12**	**11**	**18**	25	18	**14**	**4**	**13**	27	†21	27	**P†1**	23	26	**38**
18	**Eddie Cheever** (USA)	A.J. Foyt *Copenhagen Racing* Lola T95/00-Ford	GY	**14**	**7**	**14**	4	5	31	W	25	25	**17**	**11**	22	19	**10**	**17**	–	–	**33**
		A.J. Foyt *Copenhagen Racing* Lola T94/00-Ford	GY	–	–	–	–	–	–	26	–	–	–	–	–	–	–	–	–	–	
19	**Danny Sullivan** (USA)	PacWest Racing Group *VISA* Reynard 95I-Ford	GY	**9**	**5**	27	**10**	**18**	**9**	**17**	**12**	22	25	18	**5**	16	–	–	–	–	**32**
20	**Bryan Herta** (USA)	Ganassi *Target/Scotch Video* Reynard 95I-Ford	GY	**10**	W	P20	26	23	**13**	W	27	26	**14**	27	**2**	16	**5**	**19**	**16**	25	**30**
		Ganassi *Target/Scotch Video* Reynard 94I-Ford	GY	–	15	–	–	–	–	24	–	–	–	–	–	–	–	–	–	–	
21	***Eliseo Salazar** (RCH)	Simon *Cristal/Mobil 1/Copec* Lola T95/00-Ford	GY	17	**10**	**15**	W	**12**	**4**	**16**	20	**15**	**18**	21	**10**	18	**13**	**13**	**13**	NQ	**19**
		Simon *Cristal/Mobil 1/Copec* Lola T94/00-Ford	GY	–	–	–	24	–	–	–	–	–	–	–	–	–	–	–	–	–	
22	**Alessandro Zampedri** (I)	Payton-Coyne *The Mi-Jack Car* Lola T94/00-Ford	FS	23	**19**	**19**	**8**	**15**	**11**	**22**	26	**16**	**20**	23	**9**	13	**14**	**14**	**9**	**20**	**15**
23	**Eric Bachelart** (B)	Payton-Coyne *The Agfa Car* Lola T94/00-Ford	FS	19	22	**18**	**7**	–	28	–	23	**19**	**11**	22	21	–	**16**	–	–	–	**8**
24	***Juan Manuel Fangio II** (RA)	PacWest Racing Group *VISA* Reynard 95I-Ford	GY	–	–	–	–	–	–	–	–	–	–	–	–	–	**7**	**15**	28	**13**	**6**
25	**Christian Danner** (D)	Project Indy *Rial/No Touch/Van Dyne* Reynard 94I-Ford	GY	W	–	–	–	–	–	–	22	–	–	–	–	–	–	–	–	–	**6**
		Project Indy *Rial/No Touch/Van Dyne* Lola T93/00-Ford	GY	**7**	–	–	–	–	–	–	–	–	–	–	–	–	–	–	–	–	
26	**Arie Luyendyk** (NL)	Simon *Marlboro/WavePhore* Lola T95/00-Ford	GY	–	–	25	–	–	–	–	–	–	–	–	–	–	–	–	–	–	**6**
		Team Menard *Glidden/Quaker State* Lola T95/00-Menard	GY	–	–	–	–	–	**7**	–	–	–	–	–	–	–	–	–	–	–	
27	**Parker Johnstone** (USA)	Comptech *Motorola Cellular* Reynard 95I-Honda	FS	–	–	–	–	–	–	–	19	–	**12**	–	**11**	P22	28	–	**11**	**17**	**6**
28	**Hiro Matsushita** (J)	Arciero-Wells *Panasonic/Duskin/YKK* Reynard 94I-Ford	FS	26	**11**	22	**19**	NQ	–	–	–	–	–	–	–	–	–	–	–	–	**5**
		Arciero-Wells *Panasonic/Duskin/YKK* Reynard 95I-Ford	FS	–	–	–	–	–	**10**	**19**	**14**	**17**	**13**	19	**13**	20	**15**	**22**	**17**	**22**	
29	***Carlos Guerrero** (MEX)	Simon *Herdez/Viva Mexico!* Lola T95/00-Ford	GY	–	–	–	**11**	–	33	**15**	W	24	W	24	**17**	26	**18**	**16**	**15**	**18**	**2**
		Simon *Herdez/Viva Mexico!* Lola T94/00-Ford	GY	–	–	–	–	**14**	–	–	21	–	**19**	–	–	–	–	–	–	–	
30	**Marco Greco** (BR)	Galles *Brastemp* Lola T95/00-Mercedes	GY	–	–	–	**13**	**21**	NQ	–	**13**	–	–	20	**15**	–	**22**	20	25	**23**	**2**
		Simon *Brastemp/Int. Sports* Lola T95/00-Ford	GY	–	–	–	–	–	–	–	–	**11**	**23**	–	–	–	–	–	–	–	
31	**Dean Hall** (USA)	Dick Simon Racing *Subway* Lola T95/00-Ford	GY	**12**	**12**	**17**	**17**	**16**	NQA	–	–	–	–	–	–	–	–	–	–	–	**2**
32	**Scott Goodyear** (CDN)	Tasman Motorsports *LCI/Motorola/CNN* Reynard 95I-Honda	FS	–	–	–	–	–	**14**	–	–	–	–	–	–	–	**12**	–	**14**	–	**1**
33	**Roberto Guerrero** (USA)	Pagan *Upper Deck/General Components* Reynard 94I-Mercedes	GY	–	–	**16**	–	–	**12**	–	–	–	–	–	–	–	–	–	–	–	**1**
34	**Scott Brayton** (USA)	Team Menard *Quaker State/Glidden* Lola T95/00-Menard	GY	–	–	–	–	–	**P17**	–	–	–	–	–	–	–	–	–	–	–	**1**
	Buddy Lazier (USA)	Project Indy *Phos/Conrad Jupiters* Reynard 94I-Ford	GY	–	21	–	–	–	–	–	–	–	–	**15**	–	–	–	–	–	–	**0**
		Project Indy *Phos/Conrad Jupiters* Lola T93/00-Ford	GY	–	W	–	–	–	–	–	–	–	–	–	–	–	–	–	–	–	
		Payton-Coyne *The Agfa Car* Lola T94/00-Ford	FS	–	–	–	–	25	–	**18**	–	–	–	–	–	**14**	–	21	–	–	
		Team Menard *Glidden/Quaker State* Lola T95/00-Menard	GY	–	–	–	–	–	27	–	–	–	–	–	–	–	–	–	–	–	
	***Hideshi Matsuda** (J)	Beck Motorsports *Taisan/Zunne Group* Lola T94/00-Ford	FS	–	–	–	–	–	**15**	–	–	–	–	–	–	–	–	–	–	–	**0**
	***Franck Freon** (F)	Project Indy *No Touch/Van Dyne/Phos* Reynard 94I-Ford	GY	–	–	–	**15**	–	–	–	–	–	–	–	–	–	–	–	–	–	**0**
		Autosport Racing Team *Earl's* Lola T92/00-Menard	FS	–	–	–	–	–	NQ	–	–	–	–	–	–	–	–	–	–	–	
		Payton-Coyne *The Agfa Car* Lola T94/00-Ford	FS	–	–	–	–	–	–	–	–	–	–	–	–	–	–	–	–	NQ	
	***Hubert Stromberger** (A)	Project Indy *No Touch/Van Dyne/Marcelo* Reynard 94I-Ford	GY	–	–	–	–	–	–	–	–	–	**16**	–	–	–	NQ	–	–	–	**0**
	Lyn St. James (USA)	Simon *Whitlock Auto Supply* Lola T95/00-Ford	GY	–	–	–	–	–	32	W	–	–	–	–	–	17	–	–	–	–	**0**
		Simon *Whitlock Auto Supply* Lola T94/00-Ford	GY	–	–	–	–	–	–	**20**	–	–	–	–	–	–	–	–	–	–	
	***Mimmo Schiattarella** (I)	Project Indy *No Touch/Van Dyne/Marcelo* Reynard 94I-Ford	GY	–	–	–	–	–	–	–	–	–	–	–	–	–	–	–	**18**	**21**	**0**
	Dennis Vitolo (USA)	Pagan *Charter America/Carlo* Reynard 94I-Mercedes	GY	18	–	–	–	–	–	–	–	–	–	–	–	–	–	–	–	–	**0**
	***Fredrik Ekblom** (S)	A.J. Foyt *Copenhagen Racing* Lola T95/00-Ford	GY	–	–	–	–	–	–	–	–	–	–	–	–	–	–	–	–	**19**	**0**
	Davy Jones (USA)	Simon *Jonathan Byrd/Bryant Heating* Lola T95/00-Ford	GY	–	–	–	–	–	23	–	–	–	–	–	–	–	–	–	–	–	**0**
	Scott Sharp (USA)	A.J. Foyt *Copenhagen Racing* Lola T95/00-Ford	GY	–	–	–	–	–	26	–	–	–	–	–	–	–	–	–	–	–	**0**
	Brian Till (USA)	A.J. Foyt *Copenhagen Racing* Lola T95/00-Ford	GY	–	–	–	–	–	–	–	–	–	–	–	–	–	–	–	26	–	**0**
	Stan Fox (USA)	Hemelgarn *Delta Faucet/Bowling* Reynard 95I-Ford	FS	–	–	–	–	–	30	–	–	–	–	–	–	–	–	–	–	–	**0**
	***Davey Hamilton** (USA)	Hemelgarn *Delta Faucet/Alfa Laval* Reynard 94I-Ford	FS	–	–	–	–	–	NQ	–	–	–	–	–	–	–	–	–	–	–	**0**
	***Jeff Ward** (USA)	Arizona Motor Sports *Executive Air* Lola T94/00-Ford	FS	–	–	–	–	–	NQ	–	–	–	–	–	–	–	–	–	–	–	**0**
	Johnny Parsons (USA)	Project Indy *James Dean/Van Dyne* Reynard 94I-Ford	GY	–	–	–	–	–	NQ	–	–	–	–	–	–	–	–	–	–	–	**0**
	Mike Groff (USA)	Ganassi *Target/Scotch Video* Reynard 95I-Ford	GY	–	–	–	–	–	NQA	–	–	–	–	–	–	–	–	–	–	–	**0**
	Jim Crawford (GB)	Adcox *Rain-X/Indiana Buick Dealers* Lola T92/00-Buick	FS	–	–	–	–	–	NQA	–	–	–	–	–	–	–	–	–	–	–	**0**
	***Michael Greenfield** (USA)	Greenfield Industries Lola T93/00-Greenfield	FS	–	–	–	–	–	NQA	–	–	–	–	–	–	–	–	–	–	–	**0**
	Tero Palmroth (SF)	Simon Lola T92/00-Buick	GY	–	–	–	–	–	NQA	–	–	–	–	–	–	–	–	–	–	–	**0**
	Dick Simon (USA)	Simon *Jonathan Byrd/Bryant Heating* Lola T95/00-Ford	GY	–	–	–	–	–	NQA	–	–	–	–	–	–	–	–	–	–	–	**0**
	Jeff Wood (USA)	Project Indy *No Touch/Van Dyne/Marcelo* Reynard 94I-Ford	GY	–	–	–	–	–	–	–	–	–	–	W	–	–	–	–	–	–	**0**
	Ross Bentley (CDN)	Payton-Coyne *The Agfa Car* Lola T94/00-Ford	FS	–	–	–	–	–	–	–	–	–	–	–	–	–	–	–	NQ	–	**0**

Bold type indicates car still running at finish
* rookie
† led most laps
P pole position
W withdrawn
NQ did not qualify
NQA did not attempt to qualify
NS did not start

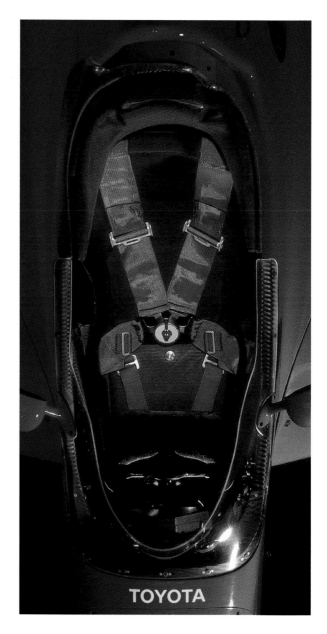

We've radically changed
our position on Indy car racing.

Toyota is moving from avid fan to active participant.
Within the next year, we'll face our toughest challenge ever, Indy car competition.
But with a proud heritage of Indy car event sponsorships, combined
with IMSA GTO and GTP championships, it's quite possible that from this
new seat, we could see even more checkered flags.

TOYOTA *motorsports*

OUR MINDS ARE ALWAYS RACING

MIAMI

Jacques Villeneuve reaffirmed the immense promise he displayed during his 1994 rookie campaign by earning a classical victory in the season-opening Marlboro Grand Prix of Miami, presented by Toyota.

The 23-year-old wasn't the fastest contender at any stage during the weekend. He didn't need to be. Instead, after qualifying eighth in his Player's Ltd. Reynard-Ford/Cosworth, Villeneuve maintained a steady pace in the 90-lap contest. He made not the hint of a mistake and moved up stealthily as other potentially faster combinations fell by the wayside.

Even more crucially, Team Green performed two spectacularly fast pit stops, which enabled Villeneuve to move into the lead with 35 laps remaining. The Canadian took care of the rest of the business, holding off a determined challenge from the PacWest Reynard-Ford of Mauricio Gugelmin to win by just over one second.

'We had a bit of a rough start to the weekend,' admitted team owner Barry Green, alluding to some electrical problems which plagued Villeneuve until the final qualifying session, 'but the guys just stayed focussed. I'm so proud of them.'

Gugelmin was equally delighted to finish second in his Reynard-Ford, the best Indy Car result to date both for himself and the emerging PacWest team.

Bobby Rahal snared the other podium position after a typically sensible drive in his Miller Genuine Draft Lola-Mercedes, while Scott Pruett ensured a fine debut for Firestone by finishing a close fourth in Patrick Racing's Lola-Ford.

Indy Car racing's return to Florida was a huge success, a sell-out crowd enjoying an incident-filled race. Mauricio Gugelmin *(far left)* gave the ambitious PacWest team its best result to date with second place while teammate Danny Sullivan *(left)* made an impressive return to the series after a year on the sidelines. However, slick pitwork helped the Player's Ltd. Reynard-Ford of Jacques Villeneuve *(below)* to victory.

Marlboro

SURGEON GENERAL'S WARNING: SMOKING CAUSES LUNG CANCER, HEART DISEASE, AND EMPHYSEMA.

Photos: Michael C. Brown

Christian Fittipaldi took fifth place after an eventful Indy Car debut at the wheel of Derrick Walker's strikingly liveried Reynard-Ford.

A bold tactical gamble early in the race helped popular German Christian Danner (below left) to a seventh-place finish in Project Indy's two-year-old Lola.

QUALIFYING

Michael Andretti arrived in Miami intent on proving wrong the many preseason prognosticators who suggested the 1995 PPG Indy Car World Series would be among the most competitive ever seen.

Andretti, who won the season-opening event one year earlier in Surfers Paradise, celebrated his return to Newman-Haas Racing in exactly the same manner in which he had departed at the end of the 1992 season – by winning the pole. The #6 Kmart/Texaco Havoline Lola-Ford/Cosworth was fastest in all but one of the four sessions of practice and qualifying, although Andretti had to come from behind during the critical final half-hour after Raul Boesel posted a strong time early on with Rahal/Hogan's Duracell Lola-Mercedes.

'I knew I had to go for it,' related Andretti after clinching the 28th pole of his career, the most among active drivers. 'The car's just working really well for me.'

Gugelmin also dug deep into his reserves of talent to nip fellow Brazilian Boesel in the closing moments, and by earning a place on the front row, he assured himself of his best ever starting position in an Indy car.

'My crew told me another Brazilian was faster, so that motivated me,' said the personable Gugelmin with a broad smile. 'We had a good winter test program. We found a good balance for this type of circuit.'

Boesel, who lives within easy reach of the Bicentennial Park temporary circuit, the scene of his only IMSA GTP victory for Tom Walkinshaw's Jaguar team in 1991, slipped to third on the grid. Nevertheless, he was reasonably content, having switched to the backup car after damaging his primary Lola on Friday afternoon.

Yet another Brazilian, rookie Gil de Ferran, occupied the other second row position with veteran owner Jim Hall's Pennzoil Reynard-Mercedes. De Ferran, indeed, had been the sensation on Friday, taking advantage of significantly cooler conditions late in the afternoon to claim the provisional pole.

'I'm really pleased,' he said. 'I expected to be competitive, to be honest, because I think we were well prepared for coming here, so I would have been disappointed if we were off the pace. But I hardly expected to be on pole position.'

It didn't last, although de Ferran certainly had provided the perfect riposte to those uninformed critics who questioned Hall's tactics in employing a rookie from the European Formula 3000 series instead of someone with experience of the altogether different North American racing scene.

Paul Tracy didn't exactly cover himself with glory during practice and qualifying. In fact, the former Penske star crashed no fewer than three times – on the same corner – on Friday in a dreadful debut for the Newman-Haas team.

'The car's good,' he lamented. 'I just kept knocking bits off it – getting over-anxious.'

Tracy, in his defence, had complained of a persistent brake problem.

Veteran Danny Sullivan, by contrast, celebrated his return to the Indy Car ranks after an enforced one-year hiatus by qualifying a strong sixth in the second PacWest Reynard, followed by another impressive debutante, Christian Fittipaldi, who completely eclipsed his highly touted Walker Racing teammate, Robby Gordon.

RACE

Mario Andretti might have retired from active Indy Car competition at the end of the 1994 season but he certainly hasn't bowed out of the spotlight completely. Event promoter Ralph Sanchez saw to that by inviting Andretti to serve as Grand Marshal for the Marlboro Grand Prix of Miami.

Mario was happy to oblige, and he was especially proud to see eldest son Michael on the pole.

Both men recognized the importance of starting from the front row on the tortuous Bicentennial Park layout, and Michael's primary focus under sunny skies and in front of a sell-out crowd was to ensure a good getaway when the pace car pulled off.

'It's very tough to pass here,' noted Michael. 'The race will be all about track position. You can dictate more what will happen if you're in front.'

True to his word, Andretti accelerated clear of the 27-car field into Turn One. Gugelmin dutifully tucked in behind, while de Ferran showed his youthful aggression by charging around the outside of Boesel going into the long, 180-degree right-hander.

Boesel was further demoted by Tracy, although on lap two the Canadian braked just a fraction too late for the tight Biscayne Boulevard chicane. Tracy missed his turn-in point and from there on was little more than a passenger as his Kmart/Budweiser Lola clipped the tire barrier hard on the left side of the chicane, then ricocheted with equal force into the wall on the other side of the road.

It was the end of a dismal weekend for Tracy. The mishap also spelled bad news for a close-following Boesel, who fell to seventh place immediately and later dropped almost to the tail of the field when he stopped for repairs to his Lola's nose-wing.

The full-course caution proved but a minor inconvenience to Andretti, who quickly moved clear at the front of the pack once the green flags waved again at the beginning of lap seven. Gugelmin continued to lead the chase, although de Ferran's challenge faltered when the Pennzoil Reynard suffered a transmission problem. Sullivan emerged in third, having profited most from the Tracy incident by moving past not only Christian Fittipaldi, who continued to run well in his Marlboro/Chapeco Reynard-Ford, but also Villeneuve and the stricken Boesel.

By lap 20, Andretti had demonstrated his superiority and extended his lead over the PacWest duo to almost 10 seconds. Clearly he was in a class of his own. Fittipaldi, meanwhile, had made an unscheduled pit stop after his Reynard's handling deteriorated rapidly.

Fittipaldi claimed to have picked up a puncture, due to a nudge from the close-following Villeneuve. The Canadian, however, vehemently denied any contact had been made. His view was supported by the fact the Walker team found no evidence of any lack of air pressure. The most logical explanation was that the Brazilian had simply over-used his first set of tires – a phenomenon also encountered by several more seasoned campaigners.

Fittipaldi's hopes took another nose dive when, as he exited his pit stall, he inadvertently ran over one of his discarded wheels, which had been left just a little too close to the car. It was a harmless incident, although Christian was obliged to pit again for a mandatory stop-and-go penalty.

The middle stages of the race were broken up by a series of full-course cautions, most of them caused by plain overexuberance among some of the less experienced drivers.

The interruptions were to have dire repercussions for Andretti. He had continued to hold the upper hand, despite what appeared to be a minor scrape with a slower car immediately following one of the pace car periods; but then, on lap 49, Andretti unexpectedly pulled onto pit road. A suspension piece weakened by the earlier impact had broken.

The demise of clearly the fastest car left an open scramble for the top spot on the victory podium. Gugelmin, of course, still held the inside track, on the point for the first time in his short Indy Car career.

Close behind, however, was Villeneuve, having slipped ahead of Sullivan during the first round of pit stops, which had been made, under caution, on lap 26. Pruett and Rahal rounded out the top five after 50 laps, with Jimmy Vasser (Target/STP Reynard-Ford), a recovering Fittipaldi, Gordon and Teo Fabi (Combustion Engineering/Indeck Reynard-Ford) also within nine seconds of the leader in what was turning out to be a fascinating race.

The vast crowd remained riveted by the action. The yellow flags were unfurled again just a half-dozen laps after Andretti's retirement. The timing was perfect for everyone to make their second – and decisive – scheduled pit stops.

'Our first pit stop was really great,' observed Villeneuve. 'The second one was even better. I don't think we ever had such a good pit stop like that all last year. The pit boxes in front of me and behind me were clear, so I was able to get in and out very fast as soon as the fuel was done.'

Gugelmin's stop also was good, but not fast enough to prevent Villeneuve from emerging in the lead. And try as he did in the final 35 laps, there was no way to redress the balance.

'We were both running flat out, so it was tough,' said Gugelmin. 'I was hoping for a mistake. The circuit was breaking up a little bit, and off-line was terrible, so we couldn't do anything. But I'm pretty happy. Second place is good. I think this team is really going places.'

The pit stops also proved crucial for Rahal, who had qualified a lowly 11th after failing to find an optimal setup on his Lola. Race day was better, whereupon an excellent second stop saw him leapfrog past both Pruett and Sullivan to claim third.

Pruett was another to post a solid

Bad news and good news

A thoughtful Michael Andretti trudges away from the Kmart/Texaco Havoline Lola with which he had dominated the race for 48 laps.

After enduring a desperately disappointing season with Honda power in 1994, Bobby Rahal *(below)* made an encouraging start to the new campaign, earning a place on the podium with the Miller Genuine Draft Lola-Mercedes.

performance, the Californian delighting his team owner, Pat Patrick, and the entire Bridgestone/Firestone contingent by finishing close behind Rahal. Pruett also was credited with fastest lap.

'I think we made a real good statement,' said Pruett, who, like the tire giant, was making his Indy Car comeback. 'We struggled a little in practice, and we could have been a little bit better on the pit stops, but for our first race I think we did a great job.'

Fittipaldi also drove well to make up ground after his early delays. A brief hiccup on lap 64 allowed Vasser to make up one position, although Fittipaldi regained the advantage 15 tours later when the American began to slip backward as his rear tires lost adhesion.

Fittipaldi then closed in on his own teammate, Gordon, who had struggled all weekend in the Valvoline/Cummins Reynard. Worse, Gordon was having to contend with an intermittently sticking throttle, which finally led to him crashing out of a well-earned fifth place just seven laps shy of the finish. The car was badly damaged during the high-speed wreck in Turn Seven, and

Michael Andretti looked set for victory after pulling out almost a 10-second lead inside the first 20 laps and then rebuilding his advantage despite the intrusion of several full-course caution periods. It was on the second restart, however, that things started to go wrong, with Andretti trapped behind a couple of slower competitors when the green flags were waved.

One of them, he thought, was Christian Fittipaldi. Not so. Instead it was debutante Eliseo Salazar, who never really came to grips with Dick Simon's similarly liveried Lola.

'If I had known it was him, I wouldn't even have attempted to pass,' rued Andretti. 'I thought it was Christian and I knew I could trust him, so I committed myself to passing on the inside . . . and then I thought, uh-oh, he hasn't seen me and I had to back out.'

Too late. Contact was inevitable. Andretti's on-board camera revealed a light brush both with Salazar's right-rear wheel and, on the other side, with the wall, although no damage was immediately apparent. Andretti was able to continue in the lead.

'I was holding my breath and I thought maybe I'd got away with one and it's going to be my day,' he said.

No such luck. Twenty laps later, the lower wishbone on the right-front suspension gave way. His day was done.

Andretti was obviously disappointed, but in marked contrast to his mood following other mishaps in the past, he preferred to reflect upon the positive aspects of his weekend.

'The car was so good,' he declared. 'I mean, it was a walk in the park, it really was. I was short-shifting. It was nice; it was fun. I didn't even build up a sweat. That's a good sign. This team's really working well together and I feel good about the rest of the year. Real good.'

Gordon was fortunate to emerge without personal injury.

Thus did Fittipaldi clamber back to fifth at the checkered flag, having

held off a determined challenge from Boesel.

'It wasn't a bad result for such an eventful race,' noted Fittipaldi, who was one among very few drivers to execute any clean passing maneuvers. 'The car was excellent, but being fast is only part of it; I had to worry about passing too. It's good to know that we're very competitive.'

An unusually high rate of attrition allowed Christian Danner to finish a fine seventh for the under-funded Project Indy team, of which he is a part-owner. Danner had begun the weekend at the wheel of a newly acquired year-old Reynard, but switched to his backup, a trusty '93 Lola, when an engine problem manifested itself on Friday.

Smart strategy during the early stages of the race saw Danner, who qualified 21st, stay out on course when virtually everyone else made their first pit stops. The ploy elevated Danner to eighth, and he made full use of the improved track position to maintain a top-10 placing for most of the afternoon.

Vasser limped home in eighth place, the last driver on the lead lap, followed by Sullivan, who lost another position during his second pit stop and then fell a lap behind when he ran off the road while trying just a bit too hard to make up for lost ground.

SNIPPETS

• The PPG Cup series' first appearance in Florida since 1988, when promoter Ralph Sanchez hosted the last of four annual events at Tamiami Park, was a huge success. All tickets, including general admission, were sold out several days before the race.

The Bicentennial Park venue, adjacent both to the downtown area and the Port of Miami, has been in existence since 1983, when Sanchez first hosted a round of the IMSA Camel GT series, although for the Indy cars the circuit was run in the opposite direction.

• Rookie Andre Ribeiro *(above right)* showed very promising form in the Tasman Motorsports Group's LCI Reynard-Honda. The Brazilian graduate of Indy

Lights was second fastest in the opening session on Friday, having topped the timing charts until being nipped by Andretti in the closing stages. Ultimately, however, Ribeiro's inexperience told as he crashed both in qualifying and the race.

• IndyCar President Andrew Craig succeeded in broadening the appeal of the

PPG Cup series by confirming the formation of a new Manufacturers Championship, Nations Cup and Constructors Championship, with points to be accumulated following each race.

• Team owner Chip Ganassi could be forgiven for his rueful look after qualifying, having noted that the two drivers who drove for him in

1994, Michael Andretti and Mauricio Gugelmin, would start the new season on the front row of the grid. Ganassi's new charges, Jimmy Vasser *(below)* and Bryan Herta, who missed almost all the first session due to a faulty fuel injector, lined up a disappointing 12th and 20th, although both rebounded to earn top-10 placings in the race.

• Canadian fans enjoyed a banner weekend in Miami. In addition to Villeneuve's fine victory in the feature event (which was backed by Marlboro) countrymen Greg Moore and Patrick Carpentier also triumphed in the respective PPG-Firestone Indy Lights and Player's Toyota Atlantic Championship openers. All three, ironically, were sponsored by Player's.

• An indication of the level of competitiveness in Miami was given by the official EDS fastest lap report, which showed 17 drivers within one second of each other during the 90-lap race. Intriguingly, the race winner, Villeneuve, ranked only 13th at 1m 06.657s, compared to Pruett's best of 1m 05.892s.

• Christian Danner had not expected to contest the season opener, although after some projected sponsorship deals fell through for other potential drivers, the likeable German garnered support from his former entrant in Formula 1, Gunter Schmid (Rial Wheels), who now lives in Miami, to secure Project Indy's position on the starting grid. Marlboro Germany and Hawaiian Tropic also chipped in to help.

Photos: Michael C. Brown

PPG INDY CAR WORLD SERIES • ROUND 1
MARLBORO GRAND PRIX OF MIAMI PRESENTED BY TOYOTA

BICENTENNIAL PARK, MIAMI, FLORIDA

MARCH 5, 90 LAPS – 164.610 MILES

Place	Driver (Nat.)	No.	Team Sponsors Car-Engine	Tires	Q Speed	Q Time	Q Pos.	Laps	Time/Status	Ave.	Pts.
1	Jacques Villeneuve (CDN)	27	Team Green *Player's Ltd.* Reynard 95I-Ford	GY	103.254	1m 04.257s	8	90	1h 59m 16.863s	82.801	20
2	Mauricio Gugelmin (BR)	18	PacWest Racing Group Reynard 95I-Ford	GY	104.263	1m 03.635s	2	90	1h 59m 17.885s	82.789	16
3	Bobby Rahal (USA)	9	Rahal/Hogan *Miller Genuine Draft* Lola T95/00-Mercedes	GY	102.729	1m 04.585s	11	90	1h 59m 18.214s	82.785	14
4	Scott Pruett (USA)	20	Patrick Racing *Firestone* Lola T95/00-Ford	FS	102.792	1m 04.546s	10	90	1h 59m 18.893s	82.778	12
5	*Christian Fittipaldi (BR)	15	Walker *Marlboro/Chapeco Special* Reynard 95I-Ford	GY	103.318	1m 04.217s	7	90	1h 59m 21.945s	82.742	10
6	Raul Boesel (BR)	11	Rahal/Hogan *Duracell Charger* Lola T95/00-Mercedes	GY	104.175	1m 03.689s	3	90	1h 59m 22.093s	82.741	8
7	Christian Danner (D)	64	Project Indy *Rial/No Touch/Van Dyne* Lola T93/00-Ford	GY	100.353	1m 06.115s	21	90	1h 59m 32.583s	82.620	6
8	Jimmy Vasser (USA)	12	Ganassi *Target/STP* Reynard 95I-Ford	GY	102.700	1m 04.603s	12	90	2h 00m 11.309s	82.176	5
9	Danny Sullivan (USA)	17	PacWest Racing Group Reynard 95I-Ford	GY	103.467	1m 04.125s	6	89	Running		4
10	Bryan Herta (USA)	4	Ganassi *Target/Scotch Video* Reynard 95I-Ford	GY	101.482	1m 05.379s	20	87	Running		3
11	Adrian Fernandez (MEX)	10	Galles *Tecate/Quaker State* Lola T95/00-Mercedes	GY	102.077	1m 04.998s	17	86	Running		2
12	Dean Hall (USA)	99	Dick Simon Racing *Subway* Lola T95/00-Ford	GY	95.171	1m 09.715s	26	86	Running		1
13	Robby Gordon (USA)	5	Walker *Valvoline/Cummins Special* Reynard 95I-Ford	GY	102.673	1m 04.621s	14	83	Accident		
14	Eddie Cheever (USA)	14	A.J. Foyt *Copenhagen Racing* Lola T95/00-Ford	GY	99.700	1m 06.548s	22	81	Running		
15	Al Unser Jr. (USA)	1	Marlboro Team Penske Penske PC24-Mercedes	GY	103.012	1m 04.408s	9	79	Running		
16	Teo Fabi (I)	33	Forsythe *Combustion Engineering/Indeck* Reynard 95I-Ford	GY	101.732	1m 05.218s	18	72	Exhaust header		
17	*Eliseo Salazar (RCH)	7	Dick Simon *Cristal/Mobil 1/Copec* Lola T95/00-Ford	GY	99.442	1m 06.720s	23	71	Engine fire		
18	Dennis Vitolo (USA)	21	Pagan *Charter America/Carlo* Reynard 94I-Mercedes	FS	95.089	1m 09.774s	27	55	Engine		
19	Eric Bachelart (B)	19	Payton-Coyne *The Agfa Car* Lola T94/00-Ford	FS	98.347	1m 07.463s	24	54	Suspension damage		
20	Michael Andretti (USA)	6	Newman-Haas *Kmart/Texaco Havoline* Lola T95/00-Ford	GY	104.892	1m 03.254s	1	49	Suspension damage		2
21	*Andre Ribeiro (BR)	31	Tasman Motorsports *LCI International* Reynard 95I-Honda	FS	102.540	1m 04.705s	15	47	Accident		
22	Stefan Johansson (S)	16	Bettenhausen *Alumax Aluminum* Penske PC23-Mercedes	GY	102.683	1m 04.614s	13	46	Transmission		
23	Alessandro Zampedri (I)	34	Payton-Coyne *The Mi-Jack Car* Lola T94/00-Ford	FS	101.620	1m 05.290s	19	34	Accident		
24	Emerson Fittipaldi (BR)	2	Marlboro Team Penske Penske PC24-Mercedes	GY	102.336	1m 04.834s	16	24	Engine		
25	*Gil de Ferran (BR)	8	Hall Racing *Pennzoil Special* Reynard 95I-Mercedes	GY	104.038	1m 03.773s	4	14	Transmission		
26	Hiro Matsushita (J)	25	Arciero-Wells *Panasonic/Duskin* Reynard 94I-Ford	FS	97.204	1m 08.257s	25	10	Fuel pressure		
27	Paul Tracy (CDN)	3	Newman-Haas *Kmart/Budweiser* Lola T95/00-Ford	GY	103.997	1m 03.798s	5	1	Accident		

* denotes Rookie driver

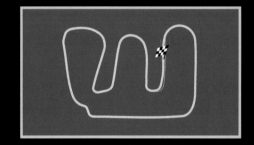

Caution flags: Laps 1–5, accident/Tracy; laps 24–26, accident/Fernandez and Ribeiro; laps 28–30, accident/Vitolo; laps 36–41, accident/Zampedri; laps 54–58, accident/Ribeiro; laps 72–74, tow/Sullivan; laps 80–82, accident/Gordon. *Total:* seven for 28 laps.

Lap leaders: Michael Andretti, 1–48 (48 laps); Mauricio Gugelmin, 49–55 (7 laps); Jacques Villeneuve, 56–90 (35 laps). *Totals:* Andretti, 48 laps; Villeneuve, 35 laps; Gugelmin, 7 laps.

Fastest race lap: Scott Pruett, 1m 05.892s, 99.927 mph, on lap 15.

Championship positions: 1 Villeneuve, 20; 2 Gugelmin, 16; 3 Rahal, 14; 4 Pruett, 12; 5 C. Fittipaldi, 10; 6 Boesel, 8; 7 Danner, 6; 8 Vasser, 5; 9 Sullivan, 4; 10 Herta, 3; 11 Fernandez and Andretti, 2; 13 Hall, 1.

EDS

SURFERS PARADISE

The aura of unpredictability that traditionally seems to permeate the only overseas round of the PPG Cup series held true as Paul Tracy's Kmart/Budweiser Lola-Ford/Cosworth emerged triumphant in Surfers Paradise, on the Gold Coast of Queensland, Australia.

This year, thankfully, the 65-lap contest was completed comfortably within the hours of daylight, but for most of the afternoon it was Tracy's Newman-Haas teammate, Michael Andretti, who looked set to claim victory – for the second year running.

Andretti did just about everything right. He qualified on pole for the second time in as many races and established a clear margin over the pursuing pack. Just as in Miami, Andretti seemed to be in control. Then he lost the use of second gear.

Andretti nevertheless refused to yield to the handicap, and, amazingly, prior to the final lap, he relinquished only one position, to Tracy, who had driven steadily rather than spectacularly after starting on the fifth row of the grid.

'I tried to be real easy and not make a mistake,' said Tracy after scoring the ninth win of his career and his first for Newman-Haas. 'I made a fool of myself in Miami, which really didn't help me to establish myself with my crew or my sponsors. This win certainly gives me a lot of confidence.'

Andretti's luck ran out completely when he crashed less than a mile from the finish line, allowing Bobby Rahal (Miller Genuine Draft Lola-Mercedes) and Scott Pruett (Firestone Lola-Ford) to move up into second and third.

Paul Tracy *(below left)* bounced back from a confidence-sapping weekend in Miami to score his first win for Newman-Haas.

Left: Clearly delighted to be back on the podium, a jubilant Tracy tells Scott Pruett how he took the lead, while Bobby Rahal looks as though he's heard it all before.

QUALIFYING

Andretti picked up from where he left off in Miami by continuing to outpace his rivals during practice and qualifying for IndyCar Australia. He was fastest in all but one of the four sessions on Friday and Saturday.

'My hat's off to the Kmart/Caltex team,' said Andretti after securing the pole. 'They're just giving me a great car.'

Tracy underscored the effectiveness of the Newman-Haas team's Lola T95/00 when, on Saturday morning, he became the only driver other than Andretti to head the timing charts. Curiously, however, come final qualifying later in the day, the Canadian was unable to match his earlier best of 1m 36.697s, which was to stand as the fastest lap of the weekend.

'Everything went wrong,' lamented Tracy after setting ninth fastest time. 'I got blocked on every good lap on my first set of tires. No one would let me come through. Then I had a bad second set of tires.'

Countryman Jacques Villeneuve endured his share of disappointment on Friday, the Miami winner completing only 22 laps due to a persistent gearbox selector problem on his #27 Player's Ltd. Reynard-Ford. The trouble was rectified by the following morning, only for Villeneuve to lose more time in qualifying due to a miscue on the suspension setup. He returned to the track with only a few minutes remaining, and promptly vaulted into contention by annexing a place on the front row of the grid.

'The last three laps you go to the limit, you go crazy a little bit,' explained the French-Canadian in his own inimitable way. 'You use the curbs and sometimes it pays off.'

Certainly it did this day.

Miami had been an unmitigated disaster for Marlboro Team Penske, yet nobody truly expected Al Unser Jr. or Emerson Fittipaldi to be off the pace for long. Sure enough, following a hastily arranged additional test session, the pair of markedly improved Mercedes-powered PC24s qualified solidly on row two.

'We've been working with the Marlboro cars and trying to get 'em working for us,' said Unser after clinching third on the grid. 'We're happy with the performance that the car is giving us. I'm just so proud of my guys for showing they're true champions by overcoming our problems.'

Teo Fabi, uniquely, chose to con-

centrate on Goodyear's 'option' tire, featuring a harder tread compound that clearly worked well on his Combustion Engineering/Indeck Reynard. The Italian duly wound up fastest of the Reynard contingent, demoting provisional front row qualifier Gil de Ferran to sixth on the grid after the Brazilian's Pennzoil Reynard-Mercedes suffered an engine failure early in final qualifying.

Stefan Johansson also posted a good performance, seventh in his Alumax Penske PC23-Mercedes and easily fastest of those running year-old equipment, while Jimmy Vasser wound up eighth despite his Target/STP Reynard grinding to a halt with transmission woes, just as it had in every previous session, too.

RACE

Clear blue skies and warm temperatures on race morning helped to attract another record crowd to the challenging Surfers Paradise street circuit. Some cloud cover had begun to move in as the prerace ceremonies were commenced, and indeed rain showers were forecast for later in the afternoon, although fortunately they did not materialize until after the race had been concluded.

Queensland Premier Wayne Goss issued the command to start engines, and at the green flag, Andretti and Villeneuve jockeyed for position out in front as the 26-car field accelerated toward the Queensland chicane for the first time.

Villeneuve nosed briefly ahead of his rival, only for Andretti to brake deeper into the first corner and reclaim the advantage. Unser followed in third until an optimistic attempt to pass Villeneuve around the outside line at Marlboro Corner allowed de Ferran and Fabi to nip through as the PPG Cup champion almost made contact with the concrete wall on the exit.

Farther around a dramatic opening lap, de Ferran ducked out of Villeneuve's slipstream on The Esplanade, then proceeded to bound high and not-so-handsomely over the curbs at the Marlboro Esses as he muscled through into second place.

'It wasn't a pass, it was an avoidance maneuver,' claimed de Ferran. 'He braked early and I really didn't expect him to brake. I was right on his gearbox, so I ducked left as fast as I could, but it was the first lap and the tire pressures were low and the car bottomed out [under braking], so I couldn't stop in time for the corner.'

Transmission failures handicap Reynards

One year after celebrating a magnificent victory on its Indy Car debut, Reynard Racing Cars commenced an inquest into why a plague of transmission problems caused several of its customers to fall out of contention on the same Surfers Paradise street circuit. Indeed the only Reynards to finish among the top 10 were the two PacWest cars of Mauricio Gugelmin and Danny Sullivan, who, ironically, overcame myriad dramas on Saturday to claim fourth and fifth by virtue of some judicious tweaks as well as a sympathetic technique adopted by the drivers.

Early testing of the 95I chassis had revealed the potential for excessive wear of the ring and pinion, although that was alleviated by a minor alteration to the profile of the gear-teeth. Prior to the season opener in Miami, all existing components were modified in a mere 15 days by the British transmission specialists, Xtrac, which had manufactured the entire drivetrain system to a design specified by Reynard.

Some additional deficiencies within the gear-selector mechanism were detected at Miami, although it wasn't until after Surfers Paradise that the true extent of the problem became apparent. Representatives from Xtrac and Reynard met immediately following the race in Australia, and while the failures were initially blamed upon substandard production, it was subsequently ascertained that the true cause lay with the selector mechanism itself. In effect, even as it allowed a gear to be engaged, the system was simultaneously attempting to disengage the gear, which resulted in a disproportionate wearing of the dog-rings.

Right: As the waves of the South Pacific Ocean roll onto the beach, Mauricio Gugelmin leads Bobby Rahal and Robby Gordon through the spectacular Foster's Chicane. The layout had been modified for this year's race in order to reduce speeds and improve safety.

Life begins at 40. Indy Car newcomer Eliseo Salazar brought one of Dick and Dianne Simon's Lolas home in 10th place.

In effect, it was a rookie error. De Ferran was fortunate that his car escaped damage.

Nevertheless, his tenure in second place was brief, for his initial start was adjudged to have been too lively. He was assessed a stop-and-go penalty for improving his position prior to the start line.

Before de Ferran had a chance to serve his sentence, the caution flags flew for the first time when Adrian Fernandez's attempts to relieve Pruett of 10th place ended with Rick Galles' Tecate/Quaker State Lola-Mercedes parked firmly against the barriers.

The order behind the pace car saw Andretti leading from de Ferran, Fabi, Unser and Villeneuve, who had slipped a couple of places on lap two, firstly to Fabi after he had locked up his brakes into the Queensland Chicane, and then to Unser, who, impressively, tried exactly the same outside-line pass as on the opening lap, and this time pulled it off.

Villeneuve soon regained the lost ground, however, when both de Fer-

ran and Unser were shown the black flag. The defending series champion had passed Fabi moments before the green flag was waved to signify the restart. That's a no-no. An irate Unser then compounded his delay by overtaking de Ferran on the exit of the pits – and in so doing he exceeded the pit lane speed limit. Another stop-and-go penalty dropped him to 24th place.

Once the race finally settled down, Andretti held a clear cushion over Fabi, with Villeneuve, Vasser, Tracy and Emerson Fittipaldi, who had made a poor start, all running equally spaced a second or so apart.

Vasser, predictably, was the first to fall by the wayside, due to yet another transmission failure on lap 19. Villeneuve later succumbed to a similar problem, while Fittipaldi dropped out of contention when, surprisingly, he forgot to activate his speed control button as he left the pits after taking routine service. Like his teammate earlier,

Fittipaldi was assessed a stop-and-go penalty.

Andretti continued to control the proceedings, and on lap 40 he turned what was to stand as the fastest lap of the race, despite having switched to the harder Goodyear tires at his first pit stop. Next time around, however, Andretti caused a stir when he pitted again. It was too early for routine service. In fact, a glitch with the refueling equipment meant that Andretti had resumed after his first stop without a full tank of methanol. Hence the second halt on lap 41. It was but a minor inconvenience, since Andretti would have no problem in completing the distance without the need for an extra stop.

Andretti's earlier-than-planned pit stop allowed Fabi to inherit the lead, although, sadly, it never showed on the official charts as the veteran Italian was forced into the pits on the very next lap. His Reynard's wastegate exhaust system had broken.

'The car was very good and we were positioned to do very well,' said a disappointed Fabi. 'I think our strategy of using the harder compound tires would have paid off if we hadn't had problems.'

Johansson duly inherited the lead for Tony Bettenhausen's Alumax team. The Swede had moved ahead of Tracy under somewhat bizarre circumstances on lap 31, when official starter Jim Swintal gave every indication he was about to signal a full-course caution. Johnny Rutherford even took the PPG Pace Car out onto the track, only to be told moments later by Race Control that his services would not be required. Tracy had recognized the probability of an impending caution and relaxed his guard for a moment, allowing Johansson to take advantage before the yellow flags were withdrawn and the Canadian realized his mistake.

Tracy gained his revenge during the second round of pit stops, emerging from the pits on lap 48 ahead of his rival and now in second place behind Andretti, who, of course, had

Photos: Michael C. Brown

The misfortunes that befell a number of the faster runners helped Hiro Matsushita *(right)* and Dean Hall *(far right)* claim point-scoring finishes.

Gearbox problems cost pole-sitter Michael Andretti *(below)* victory in a race he had dominated and his misery was compounded when he crashed out of second place on the last lap as he battled to stay ahead of Bobby Rahal.

stopped seven laps earlier. Andretti, however, was running at a reduced pace, handicapped by a broken second gear.

'It was the worst gear to lose,' he reflected, 'because I use it on every corner but one.'

Andretti continued to lead, but Tracy was closing inexorably. Johansson followed in a highly competitive third place, until, unfortunately, he became the latest victim of an unusually high rate of attrition. Once again, it was a broken gearbox that took him out of contention.

'I feel like someone tore my heart out,' said a distraught Bettenhausen. 'We were doing everything we wanted to do. Stefan was taking care of the equipment. We were the first Penske to lead this year and the first Mercedes to lead. It doesn't pay but at least it gives us a lot of hope for the future.'

Johansson's demise shifted the focus back onto the battle for the lead. Andretti was a sitting duck, especially after a late caution period allowed Tracy to close onto his tail. After biding his time for a lap, Tracy moved alongside Andretti on The Esplanade before assuming the lead for the first time.

'He knew that I was going to make a move on him,' said Tracy. 'He knew that he had a problem and he gave me the room.'

After taking the lead, it was just a matter of reeling off the remaining eight laps before taking the checkered flag.

'Coming into the race, I was a little worried about our [starting] position, but after the warmup I knew we had a great car,' continued Tracy. 'We only ran 10 minutes in that session because I didn't want to wear out the car. It was just a case of saving the bits – less miles on the

motor, gearbox and brakes was key at the end of the race.

'In the early stages, I just wanted to make sure I didn't make any mistakes. It was just a question of saving the equipment and not doing anything stupid.

'You know, I wasn't too fond of this place the last couple of years. I didn't have much luck here, it seemed. But I sure like it now!'

Andretti wasn't quite so sure. The pole-sitter modified his driving style, to take account of the lack of second gear, and drove brilliantly to keep the third-placed Rahal at bay. Until the last lap. Going into the fast Foster's Chicane, striving to eke out enough of an advantage to see him home, Andretti left his braking a fraction too late, locked up his rear tires and finally ran out of room on the exit. The impact ripped off his car's right-rear corner.

'I was trying really hard,' said a

crest-fallen Andretti, 'and it caught up to me.'

Rahal picked his way through the wreckage to claim his second podium finish in as many races, while Pruett withstood a late challenge from Mauricio Gugelmin's Hollywood Reynard to finish third in Pat Patrick's Firestone Lola.

'We had a nice clean race and stayed out of trouble,' summarized Pruett. 'The car just ran like clockwork.'

Danny Sullivan profited from the attrition to finish fifth in the second PacWest car. It was a solid reward for a weekend of hard graft by his crew following a spate of transmission problems. Unser also persevered, claiming sixth after his early delays, to be followed by Eddie Cheever (Copenhagen Lola-Ford) and Raul Boesel (Duracell Lola-Mercedes), who completed the unlapped finishers.

Michael C. Brown

SNIPPETS

• A very disappointing performance in Miami resulted in Marlboro Team Penske completely rearranging its agenda prior to Surfers Paradise. Thus, while three cars were dispatched on the scheduled charter flight from Indianapolis, one PC24 was diverted on a special mission to Firebird Raceway, Arizona, where Emerson Fittipaldi conducted three days of intensive testing. One of last year's PC23s also was used for comparison purposes. The session confirmed designer Nigel Bennett's belief in the new car, which was then taken by road to Los Angeles and flown separately to Queensland.

• Immediately following the national anthems during the prerace ceremonies, a flypast by four F-16 fighter planes served as a spectacular tribute to popular local driver Gregg 'Harry' Hansford, who one week earlier had been tragically killed in an accident during a sedan race at Phillip Island.

• Brazilian rookies Gil de Ferran and Christian Fittipaldi both appeared to have a shot at the pole on Saturday afternoon, only for their hopes to be shattered by blown engines. Their individual reactions were somewhat at variance. While Fittipaldi (below) threw his steering wheel out of the car in disgust and strode back to the pits in a rage, de Ferran (below right) calmly radioed to his crew, then assisted the marshals in moving his stricken Pennzoil Reynard to a safe location. Class act.

• The fast Foster's Chicane, adjacent to the South Pacific Ocean on Main Beach Parade (see previous spread), was modified for this year's race, with the approach tightened considerably in an attempt to slow down the action. In addition, the tire wall at the exit was moved farther back. 'They did a good job,' praised pole-winner Michael Andretti. 'They definitely achieved their aim, which was to make it safer. Now you don't have that concrete wall staring you in the face.' The changes ensured that the front-runners negotiated the left-right-left-right sequence in third gear instead of fourth.

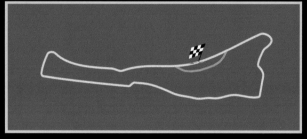

• Robby Gordon's progress in the waning minutes of the final qualifying session was thwarted by an incident with Alessandro Zampedri. An irate Gordon duly 'flipped the bird' to the Italian, and the gesture was recorded for posterity by his on-board camera. Gordon's mood darkened still further when he learned of a $5000 fine levied by the IndyCar officials for 'unsportsmanlike conduct.'

• Michael Andretti's performance in qualifying on the pole extended his record of starting on the front row each time he has visited the Gold Coast. Michael was on the pole in 1991, while in both 1992 and 1994 he qualified second fastest. 'I like the course layout,' he said, 'because you can really attack it and it pays you back on lap times.'

PPG INDY CAR WORLD SERIES • ROUND 2

INDY CAR AUSTRALIA

SURFERS PARADISE STREET CIRCUIT, QUEENSLAND, AUSTRALIA

MARCH 19, 65 LAPS – 182.260 MILES

Place	Driver (Nat.)	No.	Team Sponsors Car-Engine	Tires	Q Speed	Q Time	Q Pos.	Laps	Time/Status	Ave.	Pts.
1	Paul Tracy (CDN)	3	Newman-Haas *Kmart/Budweiser* Lola T95/00-Ford	GY	103.320	1m 37.700s	9	65	1h 58m 26.054s	92.335	20
2	Bobby Rahal (USA)	9	Rahal/Hogan *Miller Genuine Draft* Lola T95/00-Mercedes	GY	102.886	1m 38.113s	13	65	1h 58m 33.037s	92.244	16
3	Scott Pruett (USA)	20	Patrick Racing *Firestone* Lola T95/00-Ford	FS	102.944	1m 38.057s	11	65	1h 58m 37.760s	92.183	14
4	Mauricio Gugelmin (BR)	18	PacWest Racing Group *Hollywood* Reynard 95I-Ford	GY	103.213	1m 37.802s	10	65	1h 58m 39.601s	92.159	12
5	Danny Sullivan (USA)	17	PacWest Racing Group Reynard 95I-Ford	GY	102.234	1m 38.738s	19	65	1h 58m 45.188s	92.087	10
6	Al Unser Jr. (USA)	1	Marlboro Team Penske Penske PC24-Mercedes	GY	104.093	1m 36.975s	3	65	1h 59m 01.331s	91.879	8
7	Eddie Cheever (USA)	14	A.J. Foyt *Copenhagen Racing* Lola T95/00-Ford	GY	102.440	1m 38.539s	17	65	1h 59m 03.314s	91.853	6
8	Raul Boesel (BR)	11	Rahal/Hogan *Duracell Charger* Lola T95/00-Mercedes	GY	101.642	1m 39.313s	21	65	1h 59m 10.580s	91.760	5
9	Michael Andretti (USA)	6	Newman-Haas *Kmart/Caltex Havoline* Lola T95/00-Ford	GY	104.313	1m 36.770s	1	64	Accident		6
10	*Eliseo Salazar (RCH)	7	Dick Simon *Cristal/Mobil 1/Copec* Lola T95/00-Ford	GY	101.064	1m 39.881s	23	64	Running		3
11	Hiro Matsushita (J)	25	Arciero-Wells *Panasonic/Duskin* Reynard 94I-Ford	FS	98.720	1m 42.253s	26	62	Running		2
12	Dean Hall (USA)	99	Dick Simon Racing *Subway* Lola T95/00-Ford	GY	99.368	1m 41.586s	25	61	Running		1
13	Teo Fabi (I)	33	Forsythe *Combustion Engineering/Indeck* Reynard 95I-Ford	GY	103.921	1m 37.135s	5	60	Running		
14	Robby Gordon (USA)	5	Walker *Valvoline/Cummins Special* Reynard 95I-Ford	GY	102.716	1m 38.275s	15	59	Electrical		
15	Bryan Herta (USA)	4	Ganassi *Target/Scotch Video* Reynard 94I-Ford	GY	102.373	1m 38.604s	18	58	Suspension		
16	*Gil de Ferran (BR)	8	Hall Racing *Pennzoil Special* Reynard 95I-Mercedes	GY	103.699	1m 37.343s	6	54	Accident		
17	Stefan Johansson (S)	16	Bettenhausen *Alumax Aluminum* Penske PC23-Mercedes	GY	103.382	1m 37.642s	7	53	Transmission		
18	Emerson Fittipaldi (BR)	2	Marlboro Team Penske Penske PC24-Mercedes	GY	103.963	1m 37.096s	4	52	Electrical		
19	Alessandro Zampedri (I)	34	Payton-Coyne *The Mi-Jack Car* Lola T94/00-Ford	FS	101.822	1m 39.138s	20	51	Running		
20	Jacques Villeneuve (CDN)	27	Team Green *Player's Ltd.* Reynard 95I-Ford	GY	104.165	1m 36.908s	2	38	Transmission		
21	Buddy Lazier (USA)	64	Project Indy *Phos/Conrad Jupiters* Reynard 94I-Ford	GY	100.692	1m 40.250s	24	32	Transmission		
22	Eric Bachelart (B)	19	Payton-Coyne *The Agfa Car* Lola T94/00-Ford	FS	102.448	1m 38.532s	16	31	Transmission		
23	*Andre Ribeiro (BR)	31	Tasman Motorsports *LCI International* Reynard 95I-Honda	FS	101.603	1m 39.352s	22	23	Transmission		
24	Jimmy Vasser (USA)	12	Ganassi *Target/STP* Reynard 95I-Ford	GY	103.370	1m 37.653s	8	19	Transmission		
25	*Christian Fittipaldi (BR)	15	Walker *Marlboro/Chapeco Special* Reynard 95I-Ford	GY	102.815	1m 38.180s	14	11	Transmission		
26	Adrian Fernandez (MEX)	10	Galles *Tecate/Quaker State* Lola T95/00-Mercedes	GY	102.942	1m 38.059s	12	3	Accident		

* denotes Rookie driver

Caution flags: Lap 1, no-start; laps 4–6, accident/Fernandez; laps 26–27, tow/Hall and Lazier; laps 55–56, accident/de Ferran. **Total:** four for 8 laps.

Lap leaders: Michael Andretti, 1–41 (41 laps); Stefan Johansson, 42–47 (6 laps); Andretti, 48–57 (10 laps); Paul Tracy, 58–65 (8 laps). **Totals:** Andretti, 51 laps; Tracy, 8 laps; Johansson, 6 laps.

Fastest race lap: Michael Andretti, 1m 37.564s, 103.464 mph, on lap 40.

Championship positions: 1 Rahal, 30; **2** Gugelmin, 28; **3** Pruett, 26; **4** Villeneuve and Tracy, 20; **6** Sullivan, 14; **7** Boesel, 13; **8** C. Fittipaldi, 10; **9** Unser and Andretti, 8; **11** Cheever and Danner, 6; **13** Vasser, 5; **14** Herta and Salazar, 3; **16** Matsushita, Fernandez and Hall, 2.

EDS

PHOENIX

Robby Gordon was cursing his luck some 60 laps into the Slick 50 200, presented by LCI International. The 26-year-old Californian had started out well, moving quickly from ninth to fifth before losing the delicate balance on Derrick Walker's Valvoline/ Cummins Reynard-Ford/Cosworth and falling a lap behind the leaders.

But Gordon wasn't done. The car's handling characteristics were transformed by a judicious wing change during his first pit stop. Within a few more laps Gordon had swept around the outside of Paul Tracy in Turn Four to regain the lead lap. He was on his way once more toward the front.

An action-packed event saw 11 lead changes among five different drivers. First, pole-sitter Bryan Herta controlled the early stages before Tracy and Newman-Haas teammate Michael Andretti took up the running. Emerson Fittipaldi was the next to show his hand, and as the race ran toward its climax, the 1989 PPG Cup champion looked set to score the first win of the season both for himself and Marlboro Team Penske.

Then it was Fittipaldi's turn to curse. His Mercedes-Benz/Ilmor engine was running desperately low on fuel. With only six laps remaining, the veteran Brazilian was forced to relinquish his advantage by making a quick splash-and-go pit stop.

Gordon, meanwhile, had shown his customary verve by charging back up the order. He was assisted by the fact Andretti's crew erroneously believed that their man was still a lap ahead of the #5 Reynard. By the time the Newman-Haas team realized its mistake, Gordon was already past and away. A dramatic first-ever Indy Car victory was assured.

Robby Gordon scored the first Indy Car win of his career in swashbuckling style, charging back through the field after going a lap down in the early stages.

Emerson Fittipaldi *(inset)* looked set to take victory until a splash-and-dash pit stop cost him the lead with just six laps remaining.

QUALIFYING

The intensely competitive nature of this year's PPG Cup series was exemplified perfectly during practice at Phoenix International Raceway. Three different drivers emerged on top of the timing sheets during as many sessions of practice, while no fewer than 23 were within a fraction over one second of pace-setter Jacques Villeneuve, who on Saturday morning became the first driver officially to dip below the elusive 20-second barrier. It was clear the qualifying times would be extremely close.

Villeneuve repeated his earlier feat during an exciting single-car qualifying session with Team Green's Play-er's Ltd. Reynard-Ford, only for Emerson Fittipaldi to move onto the provisional pole with a fine 19.957 in his Marlboro Penske-Mercedes.

'The car was much better than this morning,' said Fittipaldi, beaming broadly as he climbed from his car. 'We made some good changes and they came together just right.'

Indy Car sophomore Bryan Herta remained undaunted by the veteran's achievement. A few minutes later, as Fittipaldi was still receiving congratulations from his crew, the talented youngster turned a sensational 19.785 in Chip Ganassi's Target/Scotch Video Reynard-Ford.

'The good news is I'm on pole,' said Herta once he had gathered his breath. 'The bad news is I have to sweat it out while 22 other guys try to knock me off.'

The even better news was that no one was able to do so. 'I was a bit surprised at the lap time,' admitted the 24-year-old after securing his first Indy Car pole. 'I knew it had to be in the 19s, because I was much faster through Turns Three and Four than in the morning, when I ran a 20-flat, but I wasn't expecting a 19.7.

'[Race engineer] Morris [Nunn] put a half-turn of front wing in the car right before we went out to qualify. It was just what we needed. That was the key. Here, you can't push the car unless it's really good, and it was the team that gave me the opportunity to take the pole because they gave me a good car.'

Newman-Haas duo Tracy and Andretti headed the Lola contingent in fourth and fifth, while Scott Pruett also ran strongly in Patrick Racing's Firestone-shod Lola-Ford. Herta's teammate, Jimmy Vasser, overcame a little too much understeer for his liking to claim seventh on the grid in Chip Ganassi's Target/STP Reynard-Ford.

Gil de Ferran took the honor of being fastest rookie, 10th in the Pennzoil Reynard-Mercedes, after Andre Ribeiro was unable to match the pace he had shown during practice with Steve Horne's LCI Reynard-Honda.

As so often in oval racing, pit stops played a crucial role in the outcome of the race. As Bobby Rahal rolls to a halt at his pit, the eventual winner, Robby Gordon, pulls away after receiving service. Ahead of him, Mauricio Gugelmin and Dean Hall head down pit road.

when Ribeiro's progress through the field was arrested when he lost control and crashed in Turn Two.

A lengthy caution period was necessary while the debris was cleared, during which Al Unser Jr.'s surge from 17th on the grid to eighth was halted by an electrical problem. The #1 Marlboro Penske lost three laps in the pits while repairs were effected.

Herta makes his mark

Bryan Herta first came to the notice of the Indy Car team owners in 1993, when he cruised to a clear Firestone Indy Lights Championship victory with Steve Horne's Tasman Motorsports Group. Prior to that, however, Herta had parlayed a successful grounding in kart racing to win a Formula Ford title, which he followed by taking the Barber Saab Pro Series crown in 1991.

Herta was unable to make a direct graduation into the Indy Car arena, but when A.J. Foyt sought a replacement for Davy Jones prior to the Indianapolis 500 in 1994, Herta was his choice. It was an astute move.

Herta drove to a fine ninth-place finish on his debut, then added strong point-scoring performances at Milwaukee and Detroit. His career was off to a flying start.

Tragically, Herta then crashed heavily during practice for the race in Toronto, sustaining a broken pelvis and right thigh which kept him out of action until the end of the season.

Foyt promised to have a car ready for Herta as soon as he was fully recuperated, but in the meantime Herta was offered a drive with Chip Ganassi's Target/Scotch Video-backed team. It was, he decided, an opportunity too good to miss.

Herta repaid the confidence shown in him by winning the pole at Phoenix in only his eighth Indy Car start, and his third for Ganassi. It was also the first Indy Car pole ever for Reynard Racing Cars.

'The team's really working well together,' said Herta, whose pole helped to atone for a disappointing start to the season. 'Jimmy [Vasser] and I have a good rapport and we both have similar driving styles. We looked at what Team Penske did last year and we saw that we needed to work together to get the most out of our cars.'

Herta also paid tribute to his vastly experienced race engineer, Morris Nunn *(bottom)*.

'I defer to Morris' experience a lot of the time,' said Herta, who has established an excellent reputation for his technical feedback. 'I try to give him as much information as I can, and then I leave it up to him to make the decisions.'

In all, no fewer than 18 drivers broke Paul Tracy's existing track record, set during qualifying in 1994.

RACE

Any nerves Herta might have felt prior to the start were kept well under control as he led the 27-car field confidently into Turn One. Fittipaldi tucked in dutifully behind, while the Newman-Haas twins, Tracy and Andretti, quickly moved past Villeneuve, who later confessed to his crew that he had 'forgotten' to shift gears! Villeneuve lost some more momentum when he was almost squeezed into the wall by Tracy.

Herta continued to lead until he

was forced to move off line while seeking to lap an unwilling Eddie Cheever in A.J. Foyt's Copenhagen Lola-Ford. Tracy took advantage by nipping around the outside in Turns One and Two on lap 28; but the Canadian wasn't able to find a way past Cheever either. Next time around, Herta was able to redress the balance.

Andretti and Fittipaldi joined in the fun to make a tight four-way battle for the lead, and before long it was Andretti who took over the point, using his greater experience to execute a couple of typically brave maneuvers amid heavy traffic.

The yellow warning lights flashed on soon afterward for the first time

Michael C. Brown

Herta also hit trouble, literally, when he ran over one of the Penske team's air hoses during his subsequent pit stop. The mandatory stop-and-go penalty relegated him to the back of the lead pack. Herta continued to run strongly, only for his Target/Scotch Reynard later to fall off the pace when a piece of debris penetrated the undertray and robbed the car of its downforce.

'It's terribly disappointing,' said Herta, 'but it's also very encouraging because I know how things might have been.'

Tracy and Andretti battled mightily for the lead for more than 20 laps after the restart. Villeneuve, Fittipaldi and an impressive Pruett also were in close contention. Rookie de Ferran was running strong, too, closing onto the tail of Pruett and soon to be followed by Gordon, who had unlapped himself and quickly carved his way through the midfield. Indeed, between laps 69 and 81, Gordon rose spectacularly from 12th to seventh. At that stage he was easily the fastest man on the track.

'I've got to give credit to [engineers] Rob Edwards and Damon Chandler,' said Gordon. 'We had a great car at the start of the race, and then the car went loose. I knew we were in big trouble, but we got lucky when Ribeiro crashed and we were able to make an adjustment in the pits. We took a load of front wing out of the car. Then the car was great. I could go anywhere on the track I wanted.'

The race continued at a fast pace, and when Tracy began to lag slightly, due to a touch too much understeer, Fittipaldi slipped past to challenge Andretti for the lead. The proximity of the two front-runners varied according to how often they encountered lapped cars until finally, on lap 105, Fittipaldi was able to find a way past.

Another caution then enabled all of the leaders to make pit stops. Once again there was a slight shuf-fling of the order. The Newman-Haas crew had failed to call Andretti in fast enough, so he was obliged to complete one extra lap before bringing the #6 Kmart/Havoline car onto pit lane for service. By the time he resumed, Andretti had fallen to fifth behind Fittipaldi, Tracy, Pruett and Villeneuve. Gordon, in sixth, also remained on the lead lap. Everyone else, led by Raul Boesel (Duracell Lola-Mercedes) and de Ferran, who, unfortunately, had made a pit stop right before the yellow, was at least one lap down.

Pruett's hopes of a maiden Indy Car victory were dealt a cruel blow when he was controversially penalized for passing Mauricio Gugelmin, who was already several laps down, on the exit of the pits. The Patrick team's vehement protestations fell on deaf ears, so Pruett was obliged to make a stop-and-go on lap 135. He fell from third to sixth.

The penalty elevated Gordon one more position. Then he passed Villeneuve for fourth. Next ahead of him was Andretti.

Tracy, meanwhile, having relieved Fittipaldi of the lead in a character-istically bold maneuver on the previous restart, soon had to bow to the Penske's superior balance. Fittipaldi proceeded to take charge of the race. Inside 15 laps he had pulled out a lead of over six seconds. Later, following another brief caution when de Ferran spun in Turn Two – incredibly without making any serious contact – Fittipaldi once again stretched out a seemingly secure advantage.

By now, most of the leaders were well into fuel-saving mode. Having pitted on lap 114 (and Andretti on 115), they faced the necessity of running 86 miles on a tankful in order to reach the finish line. Otherwise they would have to make an additional pit stop. It would be a close-run thing.

Interestingly, however, the Ford/Cosworth runners were able to make the distance without undue drama. Fittipaldi's Mercedes/Ilmor was not.

'We did all the calculations over and over again,' said Fittipaldi's race engineer Tom Brown, 'but each time we came up with the same result: He wasn't going to make it.'

The team hoped and prayed for one more caution period, which could have made all the difference. There was none. Finally, on lap 194, with just six to go, Fittipaldi bowed to the inevitable. He was stationary for only a few seconds as the crew pumped in a handful of gallons, but the delay dropped him to third place, without enough time to make up the deficit.

'I don't know why we were burning more fuel, because the car was working so well,' said Fittipaldi, still smiling despite the intense frustration. 'I was surprised I had to come in [to the pits] again. I was expecting the others to come in for fuel as well. It's a shame, because today I had one of the best cars I've ever had; but I'm very pleased because we are back in business again. We were very competitive today. All the testing has paid off and the car is very strong.'

The late pit stop by Fittipaldi should have secured Andretti in the catbird seat. Unfortunately, his crew had failed to convey the news that Gordon, who had been inching closer in his mirrors, was about to engage in a battle for position.

Andretti thought he was ensconced in a clear second place, under no pressure from behind. Thus, when he encountered a group of slower cars with less than 10 laps to go, Andretti's first concern was to negotiate the traffic cleanly.

'I didn't know that Robby was breathing down my neck for position,' related Andretti. 'I thought he was still a lap behind because we had lapped him earlier. I was being cautious – a little too cautious. I got caught up in the marbles behind a couple of slow cars and he got by me.'

Ironically, in the Newman-Haas pit area, Michael's father, Mario, had been all too aware of the true situation. But his frantic warnings went unheeded. Mario was unable to convey the message to his son. And, boy, was he mad!

Only when Fittipaldi ducked into the pits two laps later did the enormity of the situation sink in. Gordon was now in the lead. Andretti remained in second.

'It's a little frustrating,' said Michael, with admirable restraint. 'We need to work on our communication a little bit.'

Andretti drove as if his life depended on it for the final few laps, closing to within 0.788 seconds at the finish line, but he wasn't able to prevent Gordon from claiming a magnificent come-from-behind victory – his first in an Indy car.

'I can't believe it finally happened,' said an elated Gordon. 'The first one is always the hardest to win. This win takes a lot of pressure off me and it's just great for the team and our sponsors.'

Behind Andretti and Fittipaldi, Tracy brought his understeering car home fourth, having fought off the advances of both Pruett and Villeneuve in the closing stages. Pruett, though, after a fine performance, was forced to pit on lap 176 following contact with the rear of Tracy's car in Turn One. The impact bent a steering arm on the #20 Firestone car, but Pruett doggedly returned to the fray a couple of laps down and earned valuable PPG Cup points by finishing ninth.

'The car was fabulous all day,' said Pruett. 'I just wish Paul had given me a little more room. I'm disappointed with the turn of events. The car was good enough to finish in the top two, if not to win. But we are now tied for second in the points. That's pretty encouraging.'

Al Unser Jr. monitors progress in his mirror as his well-drilled pit crew services his Penske-Mercedes. The reigning PPG Cup champion lost three laps while an electrical fault was rectified and could finish no higher than eighth.

SNIPPETS

• Newman-Haas Racing appeared at Phoenix with a distinctive front wing setup for its pair of Lolas. The concept was developed by aerodynamicist Dr. Mark Handford following extensive (and exclusive) work in the wind-tunnel at Farnborough, England. The wings resembled those introduced several years ago on the very effective Formula 1 Tyrrell 019, which is hardly surprising, since Handford also played a large part in that car's design.

• The race morning warmup practice was interrupted when Stefan Johansson crashed heavily in Turn Four. The Swede had been struggling to find a consistent balance on his Alumax Penske PC23 and was taken by surprise when the rear end suddenly snapped away from him. Johansson, fortunately, emerged shaken but unhurt. He was able to take up his position on the grid after his crew hastily prepared the spare car.

• Popular former PIR winners Roberto Guerrero *(above)* and Arie Luyendyk made a welcome return to the PPG Cup series. Guerrero drove a consistent race to finish 16th in Pagan Racing's Reynard 94I-Mercedes, which bore allegiance to Upper Deck and General Components, while Arie Luyendyk, with backing from Marlboro and WavePhore, was classified an unrepresentative 25th in one of Dick and Dianne Simon's Lola-Fords.

• Having set the pre-season testing pace at PIR, during which he recorded an unofficial 19.77, Robby Gordon was perplexed on Saturday morning after being unable to find a good balance on his Reynard. A faulty tire pressure gauge was discovered as the cause of his problems.

• The latest Series II version of the Ford/Cosworth XB engine made a very promising public debut. The Newman-Haas and Target/Chip Ganassi teams were entrusted with the latest powerplants, with Bryan Herta securing the pole at a new track record average speed of 181.952 mph. The SII had undergone a mere 400 miles of testing prior to the race weekend, and hence was used only during practice and qualifying.

• Rahal/Hogan teammates Bobby Rahal and Raul Boesel were among the very fastest during practice on Friday but, curiously, they never featured strongly again. The pair were disappointed to qualify only eighth (Boesel) and 14th (Rahal), while both struggled with ill-handling cars in the race.

Rahal *(below)* also lost his lead in the PPG Cup point standings when his Mercedes engine expired during the race.

• Robby Gordon became the sixth driver to score the first Indy Car win of his career at Phoenix, joining Gary Bettenhausen (1968), George Follmer (1969), Swede Savage (1970), Kevin Cogan (1986) and Roberto Guerrero (1987).

PPG INDY CAR WORLD SERIES • ROUND 3
SLICK 50 200
PRESENTED BY LCI INTERNATIONAL

PHOENIX INTERNATIONAL RACEWAY, PHOENIX, ARIZONA

APRIL 2, 200 LAPS – 200.000 MILES

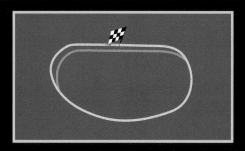

Place	Driver (Nat.)	No.	Team Sponsors Car-Engine	Tires	Q Speed	Q Time	Q Pos.	Laps	Time/Status	Ave.	Pts.
1	Robby Gordon (USA)	5	Walker *Valvoline/Cummins Special* Reynard 95I-Ford	GY	178.808	20.133s	9	200	1h 29m 33.930s	133.980	20
2	Michael Andretti (USA)	6	Newman-Haas *Kmart/Texaco Havoline* Lola T95/00-Ford	GY	179.511	20.055s	5	200	1h 29m 34.719s	133.960	16
3	Emerson Fittipaldi (BR)	2	Marlboro Team Penske Penske PC24-Mercedes	GY	180.386	19.957s	2	200	1h 29m 38.878s	133.857	15
4	Paul Tracy (CDN)	3	Newman-Haas *Kmart/Budweiser* Lola T95/00-Ford	GY	179.565	20.049s	4	200	1h 29m 42.776s	133.760	12
5	Jacques Villeneuve (CDN)	27	Team Green *Player's Ltd.* Reynard 95I-Ford	GY	180.056	19.994s	3	200	1h 29m 43.706s	133.737	10
6	Raul Boesel (BR)	11	Rahal/Hogan *Duracell Charger* Lola T95/00-Mercedes	GY	178.863	20.127s	8	198	Running		8
7	Teo Fabi (I)	33	Forsythe *Combustion Engineering/Indeck* Reynard 95I-Ford	GY	176.728	20.370s	16	198	Running		6
8	Al Unser Jr. (USA)	1	Marlboro Team Penske Penske PC24-Mercedes	GY	176.638	20.381s	17	197	Running		5
9	Scott Pruett (USA)	20	Patrick Racing *Firestone* Lola T95/00-Ford	FS	178.958	20.117s	6	197	Running		4
10	*Christian Fittipaldi (BR)	15	Walker *Marlboro/Chapeco Special* Reynard 95I-Ford	GY	174.789	20.596s	19	195	Running		3
11	*Gil de Ferran (BR)	8	Hall Racing *Pennzoil Special* Reynard 95I-Mercedes	GY	178.770	20.138s	10	195	Running		2
12	Adrian Fernandez (MEX)	10	Galles *Tecate/Quaker State* Lola T95/00-Mercedes	GY	178.248	20.197s	12	195	Running		1
13	Mauricio Gugelmin (BR)	18	PacWest Racing Group *Hollywood* Reynard 95I-Ford	GY	178.422	20.177s	11	194	Running		
14	Eddie Cheever (USA)	14	A.J. Foyt *Copenhagen Racing* Lola T95/00-Ford	GY	176.514	20.406s	18	194	Running		
15	*Eliseo Salazar (RCH)	7	Dick Simon *Cristal/Mobil 1/Copec* Lola T95/00-Ford	GY	170.916	21.063s	23	192	Running		
16	Roberto Guerrero (USA)	21	Pagan *Upper Deck/General Components* Reynard 94I-Mercedes	GY	168.539	21.360s	25	190	Running		
17	Dean Hall (USA)	99	Dick Simon Racing *Subway* Lola T95/00-Ford	GY	171.963	20.935s	22	189	Running		
18	Eric Bachelart (B)	19	Payton-Coyne *The Agfa Car* Lola T94/00-Ford	FS	168.527	21.361s	26	188	Running		
19	Alessandro Zampedri (I)	34	Payton-Coyne *The Mi-Jack Car* Lola T94/00-Ford	FS	166.389	21.636s	27	185	Running		
20	Bryan Herta (USA)	4	Ganassi *Target/Scotch Video* Reynard 95I-Ford	GY	181.952	19.785s	1	170	Handling		1
21	Bobby Rahal (USA)	9	Rahal/Hogan *Miller Genuine Draft* Lola T95/00-Mercedes	GY	177.085	20.329s	14	160	Engine		
22	Hiro Matsushita (J)	25	Arciero-Wells *Panasonic/Duskin* Reynard 94I-Ford	FS	168.919	21.312s	24	143	Handling		
23	Jimmy Vasser (USA)	12	Ganassi *Target/STP* Reynard 95I-Ford	GY	178.946	20.118s	7	131	Transmission		
24	Stefan Johansson (S)	16	Bettenhausen *Alumax Aluminum* Penske PC23-Mercedes	GY	177.185	20.318s	13	112	Accident		
25	Arie Luyendyk (NL)	22	Simon *Marlboro/WavePhore* Lola T95/00-Ford	GY	173.945	20.696s	20	71	Handling		
26	*Andre Ribeiro (BR)	31	Tasman Motorsports *LCI International* Reynard 95I-Honda	FS	176.948	20.345s	15	38	Accident		
27	Danny Sullivan (USA)	17	PacWest Racing Group Reynard 95I-Ford	GY	173.228	20.782s	21	21	Brakes		

* denotes Rookie driver

Caution flags: Laps 39–55, accident/Ribeiro; laps 113–120, accident/Johansson and Villeneuve; laps 155–159, spin/de Ferran. **Total:** three for 30 laps.

Lap leaders: Bryan Herta, 1–27 (27 laps); Paul Tracy, 28 (1 lap); Herta, 29–31 (3 laps); Michael Andretti, 32–56 (25 laps); Tracy, 57–71 (15 laps); Andretti, 72–104 (33 laps); Emerson Fittipaldi, 105–113 (9 laps); Andretti, 114–115 (2 laps); Fittipaldi, 116–121 (6 laps); Tracy, 122–131 (10 laps); Fittipaldi, 132–194 (63 laps); Robby Gordon, 195–200 (6 laps). **Totals:** Fittipaldi, 78 laps; Andretti, 60 laps; Herta, 30 laps; Tracy, 26 laps; Gordon, 6 laps.

Fastest race lap: Emerson Fittipaldi, 21.240s, 169.492 mph, on lap 164.

Championship positions: 1 Tracy, 32; **2** Villeneuve, Rahal and Pruett, 30; **5** Gugelmin, 28; **6** Andretti, 24; **7** Boesel, 21; **8** Gordon, 20; **9** E. Fittipaldi, 15; **10** Sullivan, 14; **11** C. Fittipaldi and Unser, 13; **13** Fabi, Cheever and Danner, 6; **16** Vasser, 5; **17** Herta, 4; **18** Salazar and Fernandez, 3; **20** de Ferran, Matsushita and Hall, 2.

EDS

LONG BEACH

Al Unser Jr.'s name has become synonymous with success in the Toyota Grand Prix of Long Beach. Unser won the event a record-breaking four straight years with Galles Racing, from 1988 to 1991, and in fact he might easily have taken five in a row had his own teammate, Danny Sullivan, not tipped him into a spin while Unser was leading with only a few laps remaining in 1992.

A brush with Nigel Mansell cost Unser another shot at the win in 1993, while last year he reconfirmed his superiority on the California streets by claiming the first of eight victories during the season for Marlboro Team Penske. Unser thereby secured his place in the record books as the first driver in the 16-year history of CART/IndyCar to win five races at the same venue.

Now make that six. Out of the last eight. 'It's great to be back,' said Unser, whose 1995 season had begun poorly with only a sixth and an eighth to show from the first three events. 'We knew from the first few races that the Lolas and Reynards had caught up to us, so the whole Marlboro Team Penske has been working really hard.'

Michael Andretti, who started once again from the pole, fell to ninth after making a couple of errors, and Scott Pruett rose from sixth to second during the dramatic closing stages. Pruett thereby gained the lead in the PPG Cup standings for the first time in his career.

Michael C. Brown

Maintaining his remarkable record of success on the Long Beach street circuit, Al Unser Jr. gave Marlboro Team Penske its first win of the season.

QUALIFYING

There are no prizes for guessing who set the pace during practice and qualifying. Michael Andretti continued the trend he had established during the first three races by being fastest in all four sessions with Newman-Haas Racing's Kmart/Texaco Havoline Lola-Ford/Cosworth.

'We're pretty happy with the car,' said Andretti after taking the provisional pole Friday. 'I think we could've gone a bit faster on the second set of tires. I had set my time on my third run on the first set and then we made a change to the car when we put on the second set. It wasn't so good. Hopefully we can improve it for tomorrow.'

Working with race engineer Peter Gibbons, Andretti did indeed tune the car more to his liking. But so did several other drivers, including teammate Paul Tracy, who moved to the top of the charts midway through the final half-hour qualifying session. Andretti, though, was by far the most consistent performer. Virtually all of his laps were in the 52-second bracket; in the closing moments he reclaimed the pole at 52.482.

'The car is comfortable and you don't have to overextend to drive the car,' he said. 'It's nice to have the pole, but it's tomorrow that counts.'

Tracy wound up less than one-tenth of a second slower on the all-Newman-Haas front row, with rookie Gil de Ferran posting another sensational performance in claiming third with Jim Hall's Pennzoil Reynard-Mercedes.

'It's quite satisfying because I've been trying to learn the circuit and improve the car,' said de Ferran. 'That says a lot for my crew. About 70 percent of our decisions have been good ones, which, believe me, is quite good.'

A broken valve-spring restricted Unser's progress on Friday, so he did well to claim fourth in the final session.

'He's not happy-happy,' suggested race engineer Terry Satchell, 'but he's a lot happier than he was yesterday. If we'd been able to fine-tune the car on Friday we'd be in a lot better shape.'

Brazilian Mauricio Gugelmin maintained his street circuit form by qualifying fifth in the Hollywood/PacWest Reynard-Ford, closely followed by Bobby Rahal, whose Miller Genuine Draft Lola-Mercedes ensured five different chassis-engine combinations among the top six. All

but Rahal improved upon Tracy's year-old track record of 52.780, with the top 15 within one second of Andretti's new standard. Talk about competitive!

RACE

Gugelmin served notice of his intentions by being fastest in the morning warmup at 53.258. Andretti, meanwhile, was hobbled by an electrical problem. His engine was changed in time for the race.

Under a characteristically sunny California sky, the first attempt at a start was aborted when Tracy jumped on the throttle just a fraction too soon. One extra lap was completed at reduced speed, whereupon the record-sized crowd roared its approval as Andretti acknowledged

Jim Swintal's green flags and headed the 28-car field along Shoreline Drive. The race was on.

The amazing de Ferran made a superb getaway and actually nosed ahead of both Newman-Haas drivers on the 180 mph straightaway. But his inexperience caught up with him under braking, with Andretti diving deeper into the corner on the inside line and Tracy also making a successful pass on the outside.

'If I had known where to brake, I could have led the race,' said the Brazilian. 'But I braked early, and Michael and Tracy went by on both sides of me.'

Andretti and Tracy thereby regained the advantage. De Ferran was obliged to tuck in behind, followed by Unser, Gugelmin and Teo Fabi, whose Combustion Engineer-

ing/Indeck Reynard-Ford slipped past Rahal in the initial drag race.

The first change among the leaders came on lap five, when Unser performed an audacious pass on de Ferran through the tricky Turn One-Two-Three complex. The maneuver began when Unser dived for the inside under braking at the end of Shoreline Drive. De Ferran wasn't prepared to give up the position without a fight, however, so he held his line to assure himself of the preferred approach to the left-handed Turn Two. Unser then displayed his own determination by braving it out around the outside . . . which gave him the favored line into the tight right-hander at Turn Three. There, finally, Unser was able to complete the pass.

Interestingly, an identical attempt

to out-fox Nigel Mansell had cost Unser a chance of the win in 1993. Mansell on that occasion squeezed his rival into the wall. Unser's suspension was broken in the impact. This time, by contrast, de Ferran chose to give Unser j-u-s-t enough room.

De Ferran was impressed: 'It was fun racing with him. He gave me plenty of room. It was good, clean racing.'

Unser then set his sights on Tracy, and on lap 15 he executed another perfectly judged pass into Turn One.

By now the leaders had begun to lap some of the backmarkers, and next time around at the Turn Eight hairpin Tracy found himself blocked in behind a slower car. De Ferran took full advantage and was able to draw alongside on the fastest part of

The closing stages saw a lively battle for second place. Eddie Cheever (Copenhagen Lola-Ford) holds off Teo Fabi's Combustion Engineering/Indeck Reynard and the Firestone Lola of Scott Pruett.

Below: No margin for error as Gil de Ferran forces his way past the Hollywood Reynard of Mauricio Gugelmin. Jim Hall's new recruit drove superbly until a collision with Paul Tracy ended his race after 16 laps.

'It was in a particularly narrow place on the track and I knew there was no room for two of us.'

The resultant full-course caution permitted the first opportunity for pit stops. Several drivers, however, elected not to stop, including Fabi and Pruett, who duly moved to the front of the pack.

The most significant overtaking maneuver of the day came on the restart, when Unser towed up alongside Andretti on Shoreline Drive – on the outside line – and proceeded to take over third place with a magnificent example of late-braking. A half-dozen laps later, when the yellow flags flew again to warn of Bryan Herta's crash in Turn Seven, Unser assumed the lead as both Fabi and Pruett ducked into the pit lane for fuel and fresh tires.

Shortly afterward, Andretti, who complained that his newly fitted Ford/Cosworth engine was down on power, also came under attack from a hard-charging Gugelmin. The Brazilian mirrored Unser's earlier outside-line pass on Shoreline Drive, although when Andretti attempted to retaliate under braking for Turn One, his nose wing just nicked the right-rear tire on Gugelmin's Hollywood Reynard. Gugelmin did manage to take the place, only for the tire to lose all its air pressure as he accelerated out of the Turn Eight hairpin on the very next lap. It was a cruel misfortune. If the tire had punctured moments earlier, Gugelmin would have been able to duck into the pits and minimize his delay. Instead, he was forced to drive a complete lap at much-reduced speed before the offending wheel

could be changed. By the time he resumed, Gugelmin was a lap down in 19th place.

Unser and Andretti continued their duel for the lead through the middle portion of the race. They were rarely separated by more than a couple of car lengths until lap 54, when Andretti thought he saw an opportunity to take advantage of a slower car on Seaside Way. The two leaders ran either side of Dean Hall's Subway Lola-Ford, whereupon Andretti, on the outside, braked a fraction too late for Turn Seven and promptly skated into the escape road.

Andretti resumed in sixth place after his indiscretion, leaving Unser to come under pressure from Rahal. Sadly, the three-time champion's challenge was terminated on lap 78 when his Lola's transmission locked up solid. Emerson Fittipaldi then moved up into second place and was homing in on his Marlboro Penske-Mercedes teammate until his engine expired expensively.

Jimmy Vasser (Target/STP Reynard-Ford) and Jacques Villeneuve (Player's Ltd. Reynard-Ford) also ran among the top six before being hobbled, respectively, by engine and transmission troubles. The attrition continued as an uncharacteristically poor weekend for Robby Gordon's Valvoline/Cummins Reynard-Ford ended with an engine failure.

Andretti was able to regain second place on lap 86. But when he noticed the gap diminishing (from eight seconds to five) with just five laps to go – and despite the fact he was handicapped by a broken first gear – Andretti decided to go all-out for the win. Big mistake. Sure

the course before assuming the advantage into Turn One. Tracy, however, clearly rattled after losing two positions in as many laps, then tried to retaliate in Turn Three.

Unlike Unser, who had gained position on de Ferran by driving around the outside of Turn Two, Tracy merely followed the Brazilian through the left-hander, then made a banzai dive to the inside under braking. Predictably, Tracy's Kmart/Budweiser Lola nailed the rear of de Ferran's Pennzoil Reynard as the Brazilian turned innocently into the corner. An instant later, both cars were locked together against the tire wall. And out of the race.

'It was a very regrettable racing accident,' summarized the eloquent de Ferran with admirable restraint.

Photos: Michael C. Brown

Photos: Michael C. Brown

Bottom: Indy Car novice Christian Fittipaldi watches and learns as he chases his hugely experienced uncle around the demanding street circuit. Both ran strongly, but neither reached the finish.

enough, on lap 100, Andretti locked up his brakes once again on the approach to Turn Seven. This time he lost a lap before he was able to rejoin an angry ninth.

'I just drove too hard,' admitted Andretti. 'This one was really disappointing because I made a mistake at the end that was uncalled for. I should have just collected second-place points instead of going for the win. I didn't and I paid for it.'

Andretti's misjudgment should have elevated Christian Fittipaldi into second, the young Brazilian having driven a steady race in Derrick Walker's Marlboro/Chapeco Reynard-Ford. He even enjoyed a brief scrap with his illustrious uncle. Ultimately, however, he, too, was hobbled by transmission trouble, grinding to a halt just two laps from the finish.

Eddie Cheever also might have finished second, until his Copenhagen Lola-Ford was overtaken by both Fabi and Pruett on lap 101. Fabi, though, had made his pass

Happy to be back

Scott Pruett's fourth straight top-10 finish in Pat Patrick's Firestone Lola-Ford/Cosworth enabled him to leapfrog to the top of the PPG Cup points table.

'Once again the Firestone tires were superb,' said Pruett after equaling his career-best finish. 'We ran a lot of testing miles last year, getting ready for the new season, and it's obviously paid off. The Firestone engineers have really done a great job and it's wonderful to have a team that is 100 percent behind me.'

The 35-year-old Californian first made a name for himself in karting, then shone immediately upon making the transition to IMSA sedans in the middle 1980s. He went on to win championships in IMSA GTO and SCCA Trans-Am before investing his own money into an Indy Car drive with Dick Simon Racing in the 1988 Long Beach Grand Prix.

The gamble paid off when Pruett was invited to join Steve Horne's Budweiser

Truesports team the following year, although his progress was interrupted by an appalling accident during winter testing, when a complete brake failure pitched his car head-long into the wall. Pruett suffered a broken back among other severe injuries.

Incredibly, Pruett came back from that disaster, and in 1994 he was chosen by veteran Indy Car team owner Pat Patrick to conduct an exhaustive testing program on behalf of Bridgestone/Firestone. He also found time to win another Trans-Am title for Chevrolet before achieving his main objective: a full-time return to the Indy Car circuit.

'This is the first time I've really had a lot of fun in Indy Car racing,' says Pruett. 'When we were testing, it was often quite boring. There was nobody around. You had to imagine you were out there racing; and now we are out there racing. It's great to be back.'

under yellow flags, incurring a mandatory stop-and-go penalty.

Pruett took advantage of Cheever being forced off line and nipped past

moments later, outside the range of the localized caution. The Californian's Firestone Lola-Ford emerged with a second-place finish despite

losing time during a lengthy first pit stop. Alert crew member Butch Winkle had noticed a loose brake bleed nipple as he was changing the right-rear wheel, and quickly grabbed a wrench to fasten the offending component. Pruett fell to 21st but quickly worked his way through the field.

'I'm not sure what to say,' said an ecstatic Pruett. 'Finishing second and leading the championship, wow, I can hardly believe it! The team really did a fantastic job. The car just runs like a train. It never misses a beat.'

Cheever looked set for third place when Fabi pitted to serve his penalty, only for his fine run to terminate barely 100 yards from the finish line. He was out of fuel!

Fabi therefore regained third, while Cheever was classified next despite failing to complete the final lap. Fifth place was taken by Gugelmin, who charged hard after his earlier delay and passed Stefan Johansson's Alumax Penske-Mercedes just six laps from the end.

SNIPPETS

• Carlos Guerrero (right), a two-time Mexican Formula 2 champion and three-time Formula 3 title-winner, made an impressive debut in one of Dick Simon Racing's Lola-Fords. The 37-year-old qualified a respectable 16th on Friday, and although he fell three places on the final grid after experiencing fuel system problems, he bounced back to set second-quick time in the warmup – faster than his best qualifying effort. Guerrero rose as high as eighth before being hindered by a broken exhaust in the closing stages.

• Eliseo Salazar was forced to switch to his backup Cristal/Mobil 1/Copec Lola-Ford, a '94 car, following a crash in Turn Seven during practice on Saturday.

• Bobby Rahal tried to make light of the fact he was making the 200th start of his Indy Car career: 'I started as a child,' said the 42-year-old three-time PPG Cup champion with a broad smile.

• A seventh Brazilian joined the PPG Cup ranks in California. Marco Greco had intended to make his return at Phoenix with a second Galles Racing International Lola-Mercedes, although an off-course excursion in testing at Big Spring, Texas, meant the tub had to be sent to Indianapolis for repairs. Gary Armentrout and his crew worked wonders to rebuild the car in time for Long Beach, whereupon Greco drove a sensible race to finish just outside the points in 13th.

• Jacques Villeneuve and Team Green never really got a handle on their Player's Ltd. Reynard-Ford, despite trying a plethora of suspension and aerodynamic configurations during practice. 'We changed just about everything on the car last night except the engine manufacturer,' said team manager Kim Green on Saturday morning. 'We kept the driver too.'

• Payton-Coyne Racing enjoyed its best-ever result when Eric Bachelart and Alessandro Zampedri (below left) guided their respective Agfa and Mi-Jack Lola T94/00-Fords to seventh and eighth. 'It's easy to say I know both cars can finish in the top 10,' reflected Dale Coyne of his low-budget effort, 'but until you actually do it, everybody wonders.'

• The decision to install FIA curbing and move the cement walls back from the edge of the race track in Turns Two and Three met with universal driver approval. 'It takes a bit of precision out of it, because now you can jump all over the curbs, but it's much safer,' confirmed pole-winner Michael Andretti. 'You can see where you're going.'

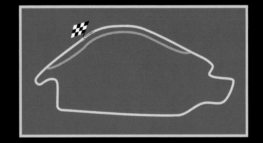

TOYOTA GRAND PRIX OF LONG BEACH

LONG BEACH STREET CIRCUIT, CALIFORNIA

APRIL 9, 105 LAPS – 166.950 MILES

Place	Driver (Nat.)	No.	Team Sponsors Car-Engine	Tires	Q Speed	Q Time	Q Pos.	Laps	Time/Status	Ave.	Pts.
1	Al Unser Jr. (USA)	1	Marlboro Team Penske Penske PC24-Mercedes	GY	108.463	52.774s	4	105	1h 49m 32.667s	91.442	21
2	Scott Pruett (USA)	20	Patrick Racing Firestone Lola T95/00-Ford	FS	107.705	53.145s	10	105	1h 49m 55.792s	91.122	16
3	Teo Fabi (I)	33	Forsythe Combustion Engineering/Indeck Reynard 95I-Ford	GY	108.243	52.881s	7	105	1h 50m 08.660s	90.944	14
4	Eddie Cheever (USA)	14	A.J. Foyt Copenhagen Racing Lola T95/00-Ford	GY	106.550	53.721s	18	104	Out of fuel		12
5	Mauricio Gugelmin (BR)	18	PacWest Racing Group Hollywood Reynard 95I-Ford	GY	108.455	52.778s	5	104	Running		10
6	Stefan Johansson (S)	16	Bettenhausen Alumax Aluminum Penske PC23-Mercedes	GY	105.506	54.253s	24	104	Running		8
7	Eric Bachelart (B)	19	Payton-Coyne The Agfa Car Lola T94/00-Ford	FS	105.908	54.047s	22	104	Running		6
8	Alessandro Zampedri (I)	34	Payton-Coyne The Mi-Jack Car Lola T94/00-Ford	FS	106.318	53.839s	20	104	Running		5
9	Michael Andretti (USA)	6	Newman-Haas Kmart/Texaco Havoline Lola T95/00-Ford	GY	109.066	52.482s	1	104	Running		5
10	Danny Sullivan (USA)	17	PacWest Racing Group VISA Reynard 95I-Ford	GY	106.702	53.645s	17	104	Running		3
11	*Carlos Guerrero (COL)	22	Simon Herdez/Bufalo/McCormick Lola T95/00-Ford	GY	106.325	53.835s	19	104	Running		2
12	*Andre Ribeiro (BR)	31	Tasman Motorsports LCI International Reynard 95I-Honda	FS	106.299	53.848s	21	104	Running		1
13	Marco Greco (BR)	55	Galles Brastemp Lola T95/00 Mercedes	GY	105.544	54.233s	23	104	Running		
14	*Christian Fittipaldi (BR)	15	Walker Marlboro/Chapeco Special Reynard 95I-Ford	GY	107.466	53.264s	12	103	Transmission		
15	*Franck Freon (F)	64	Project Indy No Touch/Van Dyne/Phos Reynard 94I-Ford	GY	104.616	54.714s	26	103	Running		
16	Raul Boesel (BR)	11	Rahal/Hogan Duracell Charger Lola T95/00-Mercedes	GY	107.402	53.295s	13	100	Running		
17	Dean Hall (USA)	99	Dick Simon Racing Subway Lola T95/00-Ford	GY	102.172	56.023s	28	99	Running		
18	Adrian Fernandez (MEX)	10	Galles Tecate/Quaker State Lola T95/00-Mercedes	GY	106.820	53.585s	16	99	Running		
19	Hiro Matsushita (J)	25	Arciero-Wells Panasonic/Duskin Reynard 94I-Ford	FS	102.379	55.910s	27	86	Running		
20	Emerson Fittipaldi (BR)	2	Marlboro Team Penske Penske PC24-Mercedes	GY	107.929	53.035s	9	85	Engine		
21	Bobby Rahal (USA)	9	Rahal/Hogan Miller Genuine Draft Lola T95/00-Mercedes	GY	108.253	52.876s	6	77	Transmission		
22	Robby Gordon (USA)	5	Walker Valvoline/Cummins Special Reynard 95I-Ford	GY	107.274	53.359s	14	57	Engine		
23	Jimmy Vasser (USA)	12	Ganassi Target/STP Reynard 95I-Ford	GY	107.996	63.002s	8	45	Engine		
24	*Eliseo Salazar (RCH)	7	Dick Simon Cristal/Mobil 1/Copec Lola T94/00-Ford	GY	104.790	54.623s	25	39	Electrical		
25	Jacques Villeneuve (CDN)	27	Team Green Player's Ltd. Reynard 95I-Ford	GY	107.512	53.241s	11	34	Transmission		
26	Bryan Herta (USA)	4	Ganassi Target/Scotch Video Reynard 95I-Ford	GY	107.159	53.416s	15	28	Accident		
27	*Gil de Ferran (BR)	8	Hall Racing Pennzoil Special Reynard 95I-Mercedes	GY	108.480	52.766s	3	16	Accident		
28	Paul Tracy (CDN)	3	Newman-Haas Kmart/Budweiser Lola T95/00-Ford	GY	108.861	52.581s	2	16	Accident		

* denotes Rookie driver

Caution flags: Lap 1, no-start; laps 16–23, accident/Tracy and de Ferran; laps 30–33, accident/Herta; laps 35–37, tow/Villeneuve; laps 79–82, tow/Rahal. **Total:** five for 20 laps.

Lap leaders: Michael Andretti, 1–16 (16 laps); Teo Fabi, 17–29 (13 laps); Al Unser Jr., 30–63 (34 laps); Bobby Rahal, 64 (1 lap); Andretti, 65 (1 lap); Unser, 66–105 (40 laps). **Totals:** Unser, 74 laps; Andretti, 17 laps; Fabi, 13 laps; Rahal, 1 lap.

Fastest race lap: Michael Andretti, 53.595s, 106.800 mph, on lap 60.

Championship positions: 1 Pruett, 46; **2** Gugelmin, 38; **3** Unser, 34; **4** Tracy, 32; **5** Villeneuve and Rahal, 30; **7** Andretti, 29; **8** Boesel, 21; **9** Gordon and Fabi, 20; **11** Cheever, 18; **12** Sullivan, 17; **13** E. Fittipaldi, 15; **14** C. Fittipaldi, 13; **15** Johansson, 8; **16** Danner and Bachelart, 6; **18** Vasser and Zampedri, 5; **20** Herta, 4; **21** Salazar and Fernandez, 3; **23** de Ferran, Matsushita, C. Guerrero and Hall, 2; **27** Ribeiro, 1.

EDS

NAZARETH

The topsy-turvy nature of this year's PPG Indy Car World Series continued throughout a thrilling Bosch Spark Plug Grand Prix at Nazareth Speedway. Seven drivers took turns at leading during the 200-lap contest, and in the closing stages Eddie Cheever appeared to have the upper hand in A.J. Foyt's Copenhagen Lola-Ford/Cosworth.

Cheever, who started only 21st, had worked his way steadily into contention. His crew knew its fuel strategy didn't leave much room for error, but two caution periods inside the final 30 laps served to ease their anxiety. Indeed, according to his telemetry information, Cheever should have had enough methanol on board to reach the finish line. Alas, the data was incorrect. The engine began to splutter as Cheever flashed past the pits with two laps remaining. Shortly afterward the black #14 car coasted to a halt. It was out of fuel.

Ironically, inferior fuel consumption had cost Emerson Fittipaldi an opportunity to win at Phoenix a month or so earlier. Now the Brazilian was able to take advantage of Cheever's misfortune as he swept through into the lead with his Marlboro Penske-Mercedes, then held off a determined challenge from Jacques Villeneuve's Player's Ltd. Reynard-Ford to become the fifth different winner in as many races.

'The last few laps was an incredible battle with Jacques,' said a jubilant Fittipaldi. 'I was trying to hold him off. It was an incredible race and I'm so happy to win.'

The Copenhagen Lola of Eddie Cheever closes on the slower car of Scott Pruett, with Danny Sullivan's VISA Reynard on the inside. Cheever was poised to give legendary team owner A.J. Foyt his first Indy Car victory in almost 14 years when he ran out of methanol with two laps remaining, allowing Emerson Fittipaldi *(inset)* to score his first win of the season.

QUALIFYING

Scott Pruett was full of confidence when he arrived in Pennsylvania. He was excited to be leading the PPG Cup points chase in his first season with Patrick Racing and especially optimistic of his chances for victory on Roger Penske's quirky three-cornered oval following a strong performance at Phoenix.

Sure enough, once the rain had subsided and practice was finally commenced at 5.20 p.m. on Friday, his Firestone Lola-Ford was soon up among the pace-setters. Pruett was the first driver to dip below the 20-second barrier and ended up fastest on the first day at 19.686 (an average speed of 182.873 mph).

Pruett continued to be consistently fast on Saturday morning, breaking into the 19s just about every time he ventured out onto the track. Unfortunately, however, as he attempted to simulate a qualifying run midway through the second session, Pruett made a mistake and crashed.

'Cold tires,' Pruett explained succinctly. 'Just pushing hard and trying to see how fast the tires would come up [to temperature]. My mistake.'

His crew scrambled to prepare the backup car and Pruett drove well to record a best of 19.633 in qualifying, but by then the stakes had been raised considerably. His time stood only 10th fastest in the closely matched field.

Another talented young Californian, Jimmy Vasser, rocked the establishment by posting a best of 19.356 on his two-lap run with Chip Ganassi's Target/STP Reynard-Ford. For almost an hour, the time stood proud of the field. But then came Robby Gordon, who had topped the practice charts earlier in the day with a sensational unofficial one-mile oval track record of 19.146 (188.029 mph) in Derrick Walker's similar Valvoline/Cummins Reynard-Ford.

Gordon couldn't quite equal that time in the heat of the afternoon, although he came awful close with two laps at 19.215 and 19.206. Incidentally, his final warmup lap at 19.212 also would have been good enough for the pole!

'The car was very well balanced,' confirmed Gordon after clinching the third pole of his career and his first on an oval. 'I could run flat-out through Turn Two and so the engine was on the rev-limiter before Turn Three.'

Vasser was nevertheless delighted to earn his first-ever front row starting position ahead of Villeneuve, whose Reynard ran out of fuel on its second lap. Next on the grid were Emerson Fittipaldi's Penske-Mercedes, local favorite Michael Andretti, who was pleased with the balance on Newman-Haas Racing's Kmart/Texaco Havoline Lola-Ford, and Brazilian rookie Andre Ribeiro, who secured a career-best sixth in Steve Horne's rapidly improving LCI International Reynard-Honda.

The top four qualifiers eclipsed Fittipaldi's old track record of 19.397, and all but three of the 26 starters were within one second of the pole-winner.

RACE

The traditional race morning warmup session saw Pruett back atop the timing sheets, with Gordon in 10th after experiencing his second right-rear wheel bearing failure of the weekend. There was no disguising the team's concern, especially as an identical problem had forced Gordon out of the race at Nazareth last year.

Nevertheless, the blue, white and red Valvoline/Cummins Reynard took off into the lead at the start of the race. Behind, Andretti delighted his hometown fans by accelerating around the outside of Fittipaldi and Villeneuve at the first corner. He then continued his patented first-lap charge by sweeping past Vasser for second place on the exit of the final turn.

Gordon, Andretti and Vasser were pursued by Villeneuve, Fittipaldi and Ribeiro at the completion of the first of 200 laps. Bobby Rahal's Miller Genuine Draft Lola-Mercedes ran seventh, chased by Paul Tracy's Kmart/Budweiser Lola-Ford, which had rocketed from 15th on the grid after being plagued by dire understeer throughout practice and qualifying.

Tracy continued his march forward, overtaking Rahal on lap two and soon chasing down both Ribeiro and Fittipaldi. Teammate Andretti, meanwhile, wasn't allowing Gordon to pull out much of a lead. In fact, by lap 17, the two pace-setters were embroiled in quite a battle, with Gordon clearly struggling to keep Andretti in his mirrors.

On lap 20, Andretti kept alive his streak of leading every PPG Cup race this year as he moved past Gordon in Turn Three. Two circuits later, Vasser and Villeneuve also demoted Gordon, soon to be followed by Tracy and Fittipaldi.

'My car started to get loose,' explained Gordon. 'I was thinking

Photos: Michael C. Brown

Rain delayed proceedings for much of Friday. Sheltered by a waterproof cover as he sits in the cockpit of Team Green's Player's Ltd. Reynard, Jacques Villeneuve waits for the action to begin.

Below far left: The intense competition out on the track continued on pit road. The Pennzoil Reynard of Gil de Ferran *(right)* races wheel to wheel with Christian Fittipaldi's Derrick Walker-entered car, while a third Brazilian, Mauricio Gugelmin, prepares to give chase.

Below left: Michael Andretti led once again but crashed out of the race after his right-front wheel came loose. Father Mario offers a sympathetic hearing.

perhaps it was another wheel bearing problem, so mentally I was screwed up and I lost confidence in the car.'

Gordon realized a pit stop to check out the cause of his handling imbalance would cost him at least one lap, so he chose to stay out on the track, driving carefully and hoping for a full-course caution. On lap 30, having fallen to eighth place, his prayers were answered.

An incident between Vasser and Tracy was the reason for the yellow. The pair had been involved in a close battle with Villeneuve and Fittipaldi when a slower car caused Vasser to slow momentarily in Turn Two. Tracy grasped his opportunity to make a pass, but Vasser, concentrating on the slower traffic ahead, was caught by surprise when Tracy drew alongside – on the outside – at the exit of the turn. Vasser inadvertently pinched the Canadian's car into the wall.

Damage to the Lola was extensive, although Vasser was able to continue after a very quick pit stop revealed no serious harm to his Reynard.

Predictably, the two drivers saw the incident from entirely different perspectives. In effect, it was an action replay of two separate incidents in 1994 involving Eddie Cheever/Mario Andretti and Adrian Fernandez/Jacques Villeneuve. Given the high speeds involved and the proximity of slower traffic, perhaps the fairest interpretation would be to classify the episode as a 'racing accident.'

Andretti continued to lead at the restart, chased by Villeneuve and Fittipaldi. Ribeiro and Rahal battled over fourth, with Rahal taking advantage of his vast experience to slip past the rookie as they accelerated back up to full speed.

'It was a lot of fun,' said Ribeiro. 'Bobby is very fast, very consistent, so I was learning a lot from him.'

Sure enough, Ribeiro regained the advantage some 35 laps later by moving back into fourth place.

Villeneuve, meanwhile, had usurped Andretti in the lead as the Nazareth resident began to struggle with his Lola's handling, especially in traffic. All of the leaders were obliged to make their first pit stops under green-flag conditions, with Villeneuve displaying exceptional economy as he stayed out until lap 93 before his initial 40 gallons of methanol were depleted.

Teo Fabi (Combustion Engineering/Indeck Reynard-Ford) and Stefan Johansson (Alumax Penske PC23-Mercedes), who had taken the opportunity to make pit stops during the early caution periods, took command of the race when Villeneuve finally made his first stop. The two Europeans were separated by a scant 0.103 seconds at the halfway stage in the race, with other early pit callers Christian Fittipaldi (Marlboro/Chapeco Reynard-Ford), Cheever and Gordon next in line.

The complexion of the race changed again on lap 105, when Mauricio Gugelmin spun his 15th-placed Hollywood Reynard on the exit of the final turn. Miraculously, the Brazilian managed to avoid contact, although he lost several laps before his stalled engine could be refired.

The resulting full-course caution triggered another round of pit stops. Fabi, Johansson, Cheever and Gordon grasped the opportunity for service, leaving rookie Christian Fittipaldi to assume the lead for the first time in his brief Indy Car career.

'I felt for the first time how it's like on an oval when your car is very good,' he reported, 'along with that sensation of leading the race. I hope to get it every time.'

Fittipaldi held off his uncle Emerson for a few laps at the restart before being obliged to make a stop himself. Walker Racing teammate Gordon also was called into the pits for a stop-and-go penalty after running over one of Cheever's air hoses during a scheduled stop a few laps earlier. The additional delay dropped Gordon off the lead lap.

Emerson Fittipaldi became the sixth different leader when he took over the point on lap 117. The veteran held the advantage for 35 laps before making his second pit stop and handing the baton to Villeneuve. A few laps later, Villeneuve's rapid progress was delayed by a group of slower cars, one of which caused him to stray off line in Turn One. For several laps the Canadian circulated at much reduced speed. It looked as though he was in trouble. Indeed, on lap 162, Cheever swept through into the lead after taking the high line in Turn Two.

Villeneuve, in fact, was merely struggling to dissipate the loose rubber that had been picked up on his tires when he was forced off the racing line. Once that task had been accomplished, he was able to resume the chase.

The yellow lights flashed on again on lap 173, when Andretti crashed in Turn Two as he accelerated out of

Photos: Michael C. Brown

There was a collective groan from the crowd when Eddie Cheever's Copenhagen Lola suddenly slowed just two laps shy of the checkered flag. Team owner A.J. Foyt (seen above, peering anxiously toward the pit entrance) was as exasperated as anyone, ripping off his headphones and hurling them against the pit wall.

The late caution periods had eased his crew's concern about fuel consumption. At long last, almost 14 years and a total 207 Indy Car races since Foyt had scored the last of his record 67 wins as a driver, the legendary Texan looked set for a return to Victory Lane. Sadly, it was not to be. The information supplied by the on-board computer system was incorrect.

'We either didn't get enough fuel into the car on one of the pit stops, or the computer wasn't calibrated right,' said crew chief Craig Baranouski.

'It was tough on the team,' added Ian Bisco, Vice President of Cosworth Engineering, which

supplies and maintains Foyt's Ford/Cosworth XB motors. 'The computer measures the amount of fuel actually used by the engine, but different injectors tend to flow at a different rate. Because of that, we tend to build in a "fudge factor," just to be on the safe side; but ultimately the system is only as good as the data that's put into it.'

Cheever was especially gracious afterward, answering questions patiently despite the agonizing frustration of losing what could (and should) have been his first major victory since driving for Tom Walkinshaw's Jaguar sports car team in 1988.

'This was just one more lost opportunity,' said Cheever. 'We really thought we had enough fuel to make it. It's disappointing but that's racing. The thing that bothers me more is when we're not competitive. Today we were competitive. The conditions were right for us and we didn't take advantage of them, but overall, the team did a great job today.'

the pits following a routine stop. Unfortunately, the right-front wheel had not been properly tightened.

'How many bad luck races can you have?' asked a disbelieving Andretti. 'Pit mistakes: That's life. I've made my mistakes this year, too. I'm not placing blame at all.'

Only four cars remained on the lead lap once the damaged Newman-Haas Lola had been retrieved. The restart came on lap 185, only for the yellows to blink on again almost immediately when rookie Gil de Ferran crashed in Turn Three after running strongly in seventh place with Jim Hall's Pennzoil Reynard-Mercedes.

The additional caution spelled relief for Cheever, who had pitted last on lap 104 and had been striving desperately to eke out his remaining reserves of fuel. The reduced pace, he firmly believed, would enable him to reach the finish without the need for a last-minute splash-and-go pit stop.

'My computer said I had enough fuel left on board,' related Cheever. 'I had absolutely no doubt in my mind. My only concern was that I was picking up dirt on my tires.'

The final restart came with six laps remaining. Cheever was confident he would be able to fend off the challenge from Fittipaldi. But on

lap 198, Cheever's engine coughed ominously.

'I thought it might be a vapor lock, so I kept going,' said Cheever. 'Then it stuttered again, so I knew I was in trouble.'

Fittipaldi and a close-following Villeneuve swept past the stricken Copenhagen car, which then ground to a halt on the very last lap.

The race, however, was still on, and Fittipaldi had his work cut out in keeping the determined Villeneuve at bay.

'Emerson had a strong car, so I knew it would be tough,' said Villeneuve. 'I was going to go for it, and with all the experience he has, he

was able to hold on, but it was actually a lot of fun.'

The margin between the two leaders was just 0.309 seconds at the finish line, with Johansson (below) claiming the final place on the victory rostrum after a fine drive in the Alumax car. Gordon unlapped himself in the closing stages to finish a strong fourth, with the unlucky Cheever classified fifth ahead of Rahal and Fabi. Pruett battled his way past Adrian Fernandez, Raul Boesel and Ribeiro in the fraught closing laps to maintain his lead in the PPG Cup standings, while Boesel just held on ahead of Ribeiro despite being slowed by a puncture.

SNIPPETS

• Michael Andretti, Paul Tracy, Bryan Herta and Jimmy Vasser all raced with the latest Series II Ford/Cosworth XB engine, although none was around at the finish. The Newman-Haas pair, Andretti and Tracy, were involved in separate incidents, while the two Target/Chip Ganassi Racing Reynards succumbed to overheating engines.

• With regular driver Eric Bachelart otherwise engaged in a prior commitment to the factory Peugeot touring car team in Belgium, Buddy Lazier *(above right)* showed a good turn of speed in Payton-Coyne Racing's #19 Agfa Film Lola T94/00-Ford. Lazier dipped beneath the 20-second barrier during practice, and although he qualified only 20th, one place shy of defending series champion Al Unser Jr., Lazier ran strongly in the race until making light contact with the wall following a contretemps with Eliseo Salazar.

• Andre Ribeiro enjoyed his strongest showing to date in Tasman's LCI Reynard-Honda. The rookie enjoyed lengthy battles with both Bobby Rahal and Emerson Fittipaldi, but lost two laps when he made his second scheduled pit stop moments before the yellow lights flashed on just 30 laps before the finish.

• Dean and Sandra Hall became the proud parents of a new baby boy, Max Dayton, who weighed in the previous Tuesday at a healthy 7lbs 12oz.

• Having been made aware of an American auto racing superstition equating the color green with bad luck, Sweden's Stefan Johansson decided to re-think the leaf motif he has always carried on his personalized helmet design. Johansson first of all disguised the green with a blue-liveried sticker at Long Beach, where he finished sixth. Suitably encouraged, he arranged for the entire

helmet *(below)* to be repainted prior to Nazareth, where his improved fortunes netted his first podium finish of the year.

• Emerson Fittipaldi displayed his usual joyful enthusiasm during the traditional post-race press conference, saying how pleased he was for Marlboro Team Penske, how hard his crew had worked on his behalf and how much he enjoyed the battle with Villeneuve in the closing stages. Later, however, the Brazilian became extremely emotional as he dedicated his victory to the memory of close friend Ayrton Senna, the three-time Formula 1 World Champion who had lost his life in a crash almost exactly one year earlier.

• Al Unser Jr. did not have a good weekend. The defending series champion qualified a lowly 19th in his Marlboro Penske-Mercedes, and although he rose as high as fourth in the race, a strategic mistake by Roger Penske caused Unser to lose a lap while making his second pit stop on lap 104.

PPG INDY CAR WORLD SERIES • ROUND 5

BOSCH SPARK PLUG GRAND PRIX

NAZARETH SPEEDWAY, NAZARETH, PENNSYLVANIA

APRIL 23, 200 LAPS – 200.000 MILES

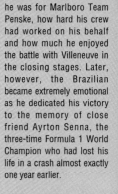

Place	Driver (Nat.)	No.	Team Sponsors Car-Engine	Tires	Q Speed	Q Time	Q Pos.	Laps	Time/Status	Ave.	Pts.
1	Emerson Fittipaldi (BR)	2	Marlboro Team Penske Penske PC24-Mercedes	GY	185.871	19.368s	4	200	1h 31m 23.410s	131.305	20
2	Jacques Villeneuve (CDN)	27	Team Green *Player's Ltd.* Reynard 95I-Ford	GY	185.910	19.364s	3	200	1h 31m 23.718s	131.298	17
3	Stefan Johansson (S)	16	Bettenhausen *Alumax Aluminum* Penske PC23-Mercedes	GY	182.862	19.687s	13	200	1h 31m 34.079s	131.050	14
4	Robby Gordon (USA)	5	Walker *Valvoline/Cummins Special* Reynard 95I-Ford	GY	187.441	19.206s	1	200	1h 31m 39.172s	130.929	13
5	Eddie Cheever (USA)	14	A.J. Foyt *Copenhagen Racing* Lola T95/00-Ford	GY	179.104	20.100s	21	199	Out of fuel		10
6	Bobby Rahal (USA)	9	Rahal/Hogan *Miller Genuine Draft* Lola T95/00-Mercedes	GY	184.163	19.548s	7	199	Running		8
7	Teo Fabi (I)	33	Forsythe *Combustion Engineering/Indeck* Reynard 95I-Ford	GY	180.881	19.903s	16	199	Running		6
8	Scott Pruett (USA)	20	Patrick Racing *Firestone* Lola T95/00-Ford	FS	183.368	19.633s	10	199	Running		5
9	Adrian Fernandez (MEX)	10	Galles *Tecate/Quaker State* Lola T95/00-Mercedes	GY	183.720	19.595s	9	199	Running		4
10	Raul Boesel (BR)	11	Rahal/Hogan *Duracell Charger* Lola T95/00-Mercedes	GY	183.862	19.580s	8	199	Running		3
11	*Andre Ribeiro (BR)	31	Tasman Motorsports *LCI International* Reynard 95I-Honda	FS	185.117	19.447s	6	199	Running		2
12	*Eliseo Salazar (RCH)	7	Dick Simon *Cristal/Mobil 1/Copec* Lola T95/00-Ford	GY	181.942	19.786s	14	198	Running		1
13	Al Unser Jr. (USA)	1	Marlboro Team Penske Penske PC24-Mercedes	GY	179.886	20.013s	19	198	Running		
14	Carlos Guerrero (MEX)	22	Simon *Herdez/Viva Mexico!* Lola T94/00-Ford	GY	176.301	20.420s	25	196	Running		
15	Alessandro Zampedri (I)	34	Payton-Coyne *The Mi-Jack Car* Lola T94/00-Ford	FS	178.315	20.189s	23	196	Running		
16	Dean Hall (USA)	99	Dick Simon Racing *Subway* Lola T95/00-Ford	GY	177.733	20.255s	24	194	Running		
17	Mauricio Gugelmin (BR)	18	PacWest Racing Group *Hollywood* Reynard 95I-Ford	GY	182.946	19.678s	12	186	Running		
18	Danny Sullivan (USA)	17	PacWest Racing Group *VISA* Reynard 95I-Ford	GY	178.717	20.144s	22	185	Running		
19	*Gil de Ferran (BR)	8	Hall Racing *Pennzoil Special* Reynard 95I-Mercedes	GY	180.581	19.936s	18	183	Accident		
20	*Christian Fittipaldi (BR)	15	Walker *Marlboro/Chapeco Special* Reynard 95I-Ford	GY	180.744	19.918s	17	179	Electrical		
21	Marco Greco (BR)	55	Galles *Brastemp* Lola T95/00-Mercedes	GY	173.054	20.803s	26	179	Running		
22	Michael Andretti (USA)	6	Newman-Haas *Kmart/Texaco Havoline* Lola T95/00-Ford	GY	185.315	19.426s	5	172	Accident		
23	Bryan Herta (USA)	4	Ganassi *Target/Scotch Video* Reynard 95I-Ford	GY	183.088	19.663s	11	155	Overheating		
24	Jimmy Vasser (USA)	12	Ganassi *Target/STP* Reynard 95I-Ford	GY	185.984	19.357s	2	57	Overheating		
25	Buddy Lazier (USA)	19	Payton-Coyne *The Agfa Car* Lola T94/00-Ford	FS	179.407	20.066s	20	38	Accident		
26	Paul Tracy (CDN)	3	Newman-Haas *Kmart/Budweiser* Lola T95/00-Ford	GY	181.241	19.863s	15	30	Accident		
NQ	Hiro Matsushita (J)	25	Arciero-Wells *Panasonic/Duskin* Reynard 94I-Ford	FS	172.050	20.924s	27	–	Did not qualify		

* denotes Rookie driver

Caution flags: Laps 29–34, accident/Tracy; laps 40–47, accident/Lazier; laps 104–112, spin/Gugelmin; laps 173–183, accident/Andretti; laps 185–193, accident/de Ferran. **Total:** five for 43 laps.

Lap leaders: Robby Gordon, 1–19 (19 laps); Michael Andretti, 20–56 (37 laps); Jacques Villeneuve, 57–93 (37 laps); Teo Fabi, 94–106 (13 laps); Christian Fittipaldi, 107–116 (10 laps); Emerson Fittipaldi, 117–152 (36 laps); Villeneuve, 153–160 (8 laps); Eddie Cheever, 161–198 (38 laps); E. Fittipaldi, 199–200 (2 laps). **Totals:** Villeneuve, 45 laps; E. Fittipaldi and Cheever, 38 laps; Andretti, 37 laps; Gordon, 19 laps; Fabi, 13 laps; C. Fittipaldi, 10 laps.

Fastest race lap: Emerson Fittipaldi, 20.294s, 177.388 mph, on lap 51.

Championship positions: **1** Pruett, 51; **2** Villeneuve, 47; **3** Rahal and Gugelmin, 38; **5** E. Fittipaldi, 35; **6** Unser, 34; **7** Gordon, 33; **8** Tracy, 32; **9** Andretti, 29; **10** Cheever, 28; **11** Fabi, 26; **12** Boesel, 24; **13** Johansson, 22; **14** Sullivan, 17; **15** C. Fittipaldi, 13; **16** Fernandez, 7; **17** Bachelart and Danner, 6; **19** Zampedri, 5; **20** Vasser, 5; **21** Herta and Salazar, 4; **23** Ribeiro, 3; **24** de Ferran, Matsushita, C. Guerrero and Hall, 2.

EDS

INDY 500

The Indianapolis 500 traditionally produces a potpourri of revelation, excitement, exultation and anguish. The 79th edition of the Memorial Weekend classic did not deviate from the norm.

The first bombshell came at the conclusion of an intense two weeks of practice and qualifying with the news that neither Al Unser Jr. nor Emerson Fittipaldi had made the cut. The two Marlboro Team Penske drivers, who had dominated the event in 1994, simply weren't fast enough this time around.

Then came a terrifying accident on the very first lap of the race, triggered by midget racer Stan Fox losing control of his Reynard in the middle of Turn One. When the dust had settled, six cars were out of contention and Fox was left fighting for his life after suffering a serious head injury.

A host of penalties also introduced a measure of confusion into an action-filled 200-lap race which boasted 23 lead changes among 10 different drivers.

Michael Andretti, Mauricio Gugelmin and Scott Goodyear all led convincingly at one stage or another, but at the end of the day it was Jacques Villeneuve who claimed the spoils of victory in Team Green's Player's Ltd. Reynard-Ford/Cosworth.

Villeneuve, who last year earned Rookie of the Year honors at Indianapolis, parlayed excellent strategy and a liberal slice of good fortune into his biggest ever payday despite being assessed a two-lap penalty early in the race.

'Luck certainly played a part,' admitted team owner Barry Green. 'At the same time, the team did a fantastic job and Jacques drove his heart out. I'm just so proud of him. He's the best driver I've worked with. This was a dream.'

1 – VILLENEUVE   **2 – C. FITTIPALDI**   **3 – RAHAL**

Bottom: The power of the Menard/Buick V6 helped Scott Brayton secure pole position for team owner John Menard *(left)*, but when a race of ever-shifting fortunes had run its course it was the boyish face of Jacques Villeneuve that would be joining the gallery of Indy 500 winners which adorns the magnificent Borg-Warner trophy *(left)*.

QUALIFYING

Prior to Indianapolis, Scott Brayton, Arie Luyendyk and Scott Goodyear had contested only one race between them this season, yet they proceeded to stun the PPG Cup regulars by sharing the front row of the grid. Brayton led the way by claiming the pole in John Menard's Quaker State Lola-Menard/Buick.

The amiable 36-year-old, who had been without a regular drive since parting company with Dick Simon at the end of the '93 season, was, in fact, the most experienced driver in the field with 13 previous Indy 500 starts to his credit.

In 1985, Brayton had seemed set to qualify on the pole until his Buick V6-powered March broke its transmission as it sped out of Turn Four on its fourth and final lap. A starting position in the middle of the front row brought scant consolation. Ten years later, driving a new Lola T95/00 powered by a vastly improved version of the same basic V6 stock-block engine, Brayton set the record straight.

'It's a dream come true,' said Brayton, who, due to the vagaries of the weather, had to wait almost 24 hours for his pole to be confirmed. 'I got my first go-kart when I was five and I remember thinking some day I would race at the Indy 500.'

Teammate Luyendyk, the 1990 Indianapolis 500 champion and 1993 pole-winner, couldn't quite match Brayton's pace in the blus-tery conditions and had to settle for the middle of the front row in John Menard's sister Glidden Paints Lola.

Goodyear, driving Steve Horne's LCI/Motorola/CNN Reynard-Honda, was the fastest of those running 'conventional' 2.65-liter four-cam engines at 45 inches of manifold boost pressure. (The 3.3-liter Menards are allowed 55 inches under the unique-for-Indy USAC regulations.) The Canadian's performance thrilled both the Honda engineers, who bounced back magnificently from the acute embarrassment of failing to qualify in 1994, and the strong Firestone contingent, who clinched a front row start on their return to Indianapolis following a 21-year absence.

'I haven't had much sleep the last couple of nights, because I knew we had a chance at taking the pole,' admitted Goodyear, who had to wait until Sunday before taking his qualifying run. 'It was hot today, which meant we had less grip, but I'm still really pleased. The whole Tasman team has worked really hard. They've done a great job and I'm just thrilled to be part of it.'

Michael Andretti's Kmart/Texaco Havoline Lola-Ford/Cosworth headed row two of the grid, and in many people's estimations he was a firm favorite for honors in the race. Villeneuve, who bounced back from a heavy crash just one day before the start of qualifying, and Gugelmin (Hollywood Reynard-Ford) also had

Photos: Michael C. Brown

Penske stars miss the show

The first indication that Marlboro Team Penske might face an uphill battle at Indianapolis came in April, when Al Unser Jr. and Emerson Fittipaldi – each of them two-time '500' winners – had difficulty getting up to speed during a Goodyear tire test session. Their troubles, however, were attributed to high winds and a trick aerodynamic setup, in the form of a low-mounted rear wing. Once the team adopted a conventional setup and the weather proved more conducive to fast laps, both drivers managed to circulate at almost 228 mph. No problem. Or so it seemed.

But when the track opened for official practice, it soon became apparent the Penske-Mercedes PC24s were no match for the rest of the field.

The team eschewed the opportunity to make a qualification attempt during the first weekend, whereupon Roger Penske set to work on several backup scenarios, including the purchase of two '94 Reynards and the retrieval of last year's winning PC23 from his museum in California.

Penske also received the offer of a loan of a '95 Lola-Mercedes from Rahal/Hogan Racing, since both Bobby Rahal and Raul Boesel had qualified solidly the first weekend.

Unser, however, did not feel comfortable in the Reynard and Fittipaldi could muster no more speed from the PC23. The Brazilian decided to concentrate on the Rahal/Hogan Lola, while Unser continued his quest to get

Nigel Bennett's PC24 up to speed. In vain. Finally, on the eve of the final weekend of qualifying, it was conceded that the car was possessed by an inherent aerodynamic handicap. So a second Lola was acquired from Rahal/Hogan.

At that stage it still seemed inconceivable that neither Penske driver would make the field. Both had managed to circulate their new Lolas in the 227 mph range, while the slowest qualifying speed was a little over 225. But Unser then used up two qualification attempts, first when he encountered too much understeer in Turn Two and then when his Mercedes engine blew.

Penske also made a fatal mistake by waving off Fittipaldi's first attempt which would have resulted in a four-lap average of 225.558. Ironically, the run would have been easily strong enough to make the show. But Penske wanted more of a margin to ensure absolutely no possibility of being bumped on the final day.

Fittipaldi could barely disguise his anger, although Penske reasoned that if Fittipaldi could do that time on Saturday, he could certainly repeat it on Sunday. Well, sadly, he couldn't. Nor could Unser. The Penske team was shut out.

'We didn't get the job done,' admitted Penske. 'We came here with two of the best drivers in the world and we didn't give them the tools to do the job. I take full responsibility.'

Photos: Michael C. Brown

proven consistently fast during practice, as had Robby Gordon, who lurked on the inside of row three with Derrick Walker's similar Valvoline/Cummins car.

The final day of qualifying brought the usual crescendo of excitement, heightened, of course, by the remarkable failure by Roger

Penske's team. In stark contrast, Dick Simon Racing dodged a bullet as Eliseo Salazar, Davy Jones and Lyn St. James (who finalized a deal late in the proceedings with the Whitlock Corporation to ensure her participation) all secured their positions in the field as the three slowest qualifiers.

Top: One of the rituals steadfastly observed by the organizers of the Indianapolis 500 is the presentation of a ring to each of the 33 drivers who have qualified for the race. Roberto Guerrero acknowledges the applause of the audience as he receives his memento.

Rookie Christian Fittipaldi *(above)* inherited second place after a gritty drive in Derrick Walker's Reynard.

Without a full-time ride in 1995, Scott Goodyear *(right)* paid dearly for a moment's impetuosity.

Thumbs up from Andre Ribeiro *(top right)*, who qualified the second Tasman Reynard-Honda a creditable 12th.

Far right: The bad luck that seems to dog Michael Andretti at Indy struck again.

Left: The competing cars are lost to view amid a seething mass of team members and well-wishers as final preparations are made on the grid prior to the start.

Below left: The race is on. Scott Goodyear swoops into Turn One ahead of the Lola-Menard/Buicks of pole-sitter Scott Brayton and teammate Arie Luyendyk with Mauricio Gugelmin, Michael Andretti and Jacques Villeneuve next up.

As the contest approached its climax Firestone seemed certain to crown its return to Indy with a remarkable victory. Things started to go wrong when Scott Pruett *(right)* crashed out of second place in his desperate efforts to keep pace with leader Scott Goodyear.

Michael C. Brown

RACE

The Indianapolis Motor Speedway was eerily quiet at 7 a.m. on race day. Usually the place is already teeming with fans making their way toward their seats in eager anticipation of what is appropriately billed as 'The Greatest Spectacle in Racing.' But on this occasion persistent overnight rain had served to dampen the spirits of the huge throng of party-goers that traditionally assembles in makeshift campsites all around the Speedway prior to the race.

Most of them took the opportunity to take a few hours' extra sleep (while others struggled to open another beer can or three), apparently secure in the knowledge that the '500' seemed unlikely to meet its traditional 11 a.m. start time.

The local weather forecasters didn't instill much optimism either, with talk of more rain showers and possible thunderstorms by mid-afternoon.

Thankfully, however, the precipitation ceased around breakfast-time and the dark clouds began to dissipate. Indeed by 10 a.m. the sun was meekly attempting to break through the hazy gray barrier. A brisk breeze also lent its assistance to the drying-out process.

Against the odds, the prerace ceremonies were concluded on schedule. Tom Binford, stepping down after 22 years as Chief Steward, made his final track inspection aboard the Chevrolet Corvette Official Pace Car at 10.35 a.m. A few minutes later Florence Henderson gave her usual glowing rendition of the National Anthem, and following the invocation, Jim Nabors chipped in with his highly individual theme 'Back Home Again in Indiana.'

The hallowed Speedway was by now packed to the rafters, ready for the Chairman Emeritus of the Indianapolis Motor Speedway, Mary Fendrich Hulman, to issue her famous command: 'Lady and Gentlemen, start your engines!'

To rapturous applause, the 33 engines burst into song and soon enough the field began to roll away from the grid in readiness for the start.

The two Team Menard cars of Brayton and Luyendyk couldn't shake Goodyear's Reynard-Honda in the initial burst of acceleration, and although Brayton led into the first turn, a judicious lift from the throttle permitted a pumped-up Goodyear to move into the lead around the outside line.

'It was a big thrill for me when he took the lead,' said a proud Tasman Motorsports team owner Steve Horne, 'because that was our team's first lap ever in the Indy 500 – and we led it, so that was OK!'

Luyendyk also blew around the outside of the pole-sitter in Turn One, to be followed by Michael Andretti. Behind, though, there was mayhem as Stan Fox's Delta Faucet/Bowling/Hemelgarn Racing Reynard-Ford snapped out of control on the low side of the groove. His car then turned sharp right, directly into the path of Eddie Cheever's Copenhagen Lola-Ford. Both cars slammed into the outside retaining wall with sickening ferocity.

Fox's car was torn apart by the impact, its driver's entire lower torso horribly exposed as the remnants of his Reynard spun crazily along the edge of the race track before finally coming to rest in Turn Two. Miraculously, the popular midget racer suffered no injuries to his legs or feet. But the ferocity of the crash left him unconscious with a closed head injury.

The emergency crews sprung into action, and after a brief visit to the infield medical center, Fox was transferred to Methodist Hospital. Within an hour, he was undergoing surgery to relieve the pressure on his brain due to a blood clot. The doctors later confirmed his survival was due in large part to the expertise of the attending physicians and the prompt attention he received.

No other drivers were hurt in the melee, although Cheever was done for the day. So, too, were Lyn St. James and Carlos Guerrero, whose cars sustained heavy damage. Gil de Ferran and Eric Bachelart limped back to the pits with broken suspension, although their hopes of rejoining the fray ultimately proved fruitless. Several other cars made unscheduled pit stops to change tires.

Robby Gordon, meanwhile, was thankful for the extended caution since it allowed Derrick Walker's crew time to diagnose the reason for a sticking throttle which had brought him into the pits on the final pace lap. After two more stops, Gordon was ready to join in the race, albeit one lap down to the leaders.

When the race was restarted, Luyendyk used the power of his Menard V6 to usurp Goodyear as they accelerated across the start/finish line to begin lap 10. A half-mile or so later, Andretti also moved past the Reynard-Honda and began to put the pressure on Luyendyk. The

leaders settled into a comfortable pace at around 216 mph, with Goodyear holding a watching brief in third place. Brayton, Gugelmin and Villeneuve gave the chase, but already they had begun to lag behind.

Luyendyk held a precarious advantage during the opening stages, whereupon Andretti made his move almost as soon as the leaders encountered some slower traffic for the first time.

The superior tractability of the Ford/Cosworth V8 engine had enabled Andretti to out-maneuver Luyendyk, and the other major disadvantage of the single-cam Menard V6 soon became apparent when Luyendyk became the first of the leaders to make a routine pit stop for fuel after just 28 laps. The Dutchman compounded his problems by stalling the engine as he attempted to leave his pit. The error left Luyendyk two laps behind the leader, Andretti, and effectively terminated his hopes of victory.

Teammate Brayton pitted next time around, also losing a lap, while Andretti stayed out in front for another four circuits before making his first pit stop. The rapid pace of the leaders enabled Goodyear to inherit a huge lead of almost half a lap before pitting himself on lap 35.

Villeneuve duly took over the point. Like most of the rest of the field, he was anxiously awaiting the opportunity to make his first pit stop. But then the caution lights flashed on after the discovery of a piece of debris in Turn One. In accordance with USAC regulations, the entrance to the pits was closed while the pace car driver attempted to position himself at the head of the field. Unfortunately, Villeneuve's crew failed to realize that its man was in fact leading the race, and amid mass confusion the Canadian inadvertently passed the pace car twice before the order was properly restored.

The pit entrance remained closed for several laps as the field continued to circulate at only a slightly reduced pace. The prolonged chaos almost spelled disaster for Pruett, who eventually coasted into his pit with the engine dead. He was out of fuel. Pruett fell from fifth place to 22nd.

Other drivers suffered similar consequences before the status quo was restored. Eventually, though, the race was resumed with Andretti at the front of the field, followed by Goodyear, Villeneuve and Andre Ribeiro, who had worked steadily up

into contention with the second Tasman Reynard-Honda. The Brazilian, incidentally, had overcome a crash during practice to place his name in the record books as the fastest ever rookie qualifier.

Villeneuve, meanwhile, was assessed a two-lap penalty for his role in the clutter, dropping him to 24th place and ostensibly out of contention.

Andretti then took control of the proceedings, extending an advantage of over 17 seconds before making his second pit stop. After many years of frustration at Indianapolis, everything finally seemed to be falling into place for the second-generation racer . . . until, on lap 77, he was edged off line in Turn Four as Gugelmin slowed down in preparation for a routine pit stop. Andretti's car slipped up into the marbles and then made solid contact with the wall. The agony continued. His suspension was broken. Andretti was out.

'Ultimately it was my mistake,' he admitted. 'I was coming up to pass Mauricio, and in the middle of Four he backed off to come into the pits. I realized it a little too late and I went high to go around him. When I did that it was like I hit ice and I went up into the wall.

'It's just a real shame because I think we had a real shot at winning. The car was perfect.'

Now it was Gugelmin's turn in the spotlight. The Formula 1 veteran had been consistently fast in the PacWest team's Hollywood Reynard-Ford; but this wasn't to be his day either. After leading the race for a total of 59 laps – more than any other driver – Gugelmin felt the previously perfect balance on his car go badly awry. He slipped back to sixth at the finish.

'I'm convinced something broke,' said the disappointed Brazilian. 'We were really under control until halfway and then it just got away from us.'

Jimmy Vasser was another who held legitimate hopes of victory. The gifted Californian had run solidly among the top 10 with Chip Ganassi's Target/STP Reynard-Ford, then took the lead inside the final 100 miles by virtue of adopting a unique approach to the intricacy of fuel strategy.

His team was optimistic he could reach the finish without the need for another pit stop. It turned out to be a moot point. Vasser was taken by surprise when Pruett dived for the lead on the inside line in Turn Three

Michael C. Brown

on lap 171, forcing him to deviate from his chosen line. An instant later he was headed toward the wall.

'When I came down into the corner, all of a sudden he was alongside me on the low line, with more speed, and he started moving up the track,' said Vasser. 'The bottom line is that he had the line, it was a clean pass, but it put me in a position that put me into the fence.'

Vasser's demise set the scene for an enthralling contest between Pruett and Goodyear. Both were running on Firestone tires. Pruett, of course, had fought back impressively after losing a lap earlier in the afternoon, while Goodyear had gradually tuned the handling of his car as the race progressed.

'We made a lot of little wing changes and stagger changes and tire pressure changes at each of our pit stops,' related Goodyear, 'and by the end of the race it was very good.'

Pruett was equally pleased with the balance on his Lola, although he was immediately passed by Goodyear on the ensuing restart. The pair then posted the fastest laps of the race – at better than 224 mph – as they quickly pulled clear of the pack at the rate of one second per lap.

Unfortunately, the duel ended in disaster on lap 185 when the increasingly strong wind caused Pruett's car to understeer up into the gray in Turn Two. Pruett tried to catch it but in vain. He hit the wall at the exit, then spun wildly down the track to the inside before slamming rear end first into the guard rail.

'I was going for it and I got a little high,' explained Pruett, who was fortunate to escape serious injury. 'I got in some dirty air and just hit the wall. I am heartbroken. Maybe I got a little greedy, but we did not come here to finish second.'

Pruett's superb charge was at an end, but Firestone still looked in great shape to record a sensational victory, since Goodyear (Scott, that is) remained firmly ensconced at the head of the field. No one seemed likely to challenge his supremacy.

But the drama wasn't over. With 10 laps to go, the pace car lights went out and Goodyear prepared to lead the field toward the final restart. He waited until the pace car was out of his sight, then gunned

the throttle as he entered Turn Three. Unfortunately, he hadn't waited long enough. As Goodyear blasted into Turn Four, he encountered the pace car still wending its way back to the pits.

'I knew Villeneuve was right with me, and as I went into Turn Three I realized that if I'd taken my foot off the gas, even just to breathe it, I was going to be passed,' reasoned Goodyear. 'All through the day it seemed like whoever was ahead at the restart would be second or third on the next lap; and it's very hard to pass when everybody's up to speed.'

Goodyear therefore sped on his way lest he should lose his advantage. Villeneuve, by contrast, having earlier earned a stiff penalty for passing the pace car, virtually stood on the brakes to ensure he didn't do so again. In the process, Villeneuve almost caused a multiple pile-up as several drivers close behind were forced into evasive action.

Goodyear duly took off into a clear lead, only to be informed he would be black-flagged for overtaking the pace car before it had left the race track.

'If I had passed three or four guys before the green light, then I'd understand the need for a stop-and-go, but in this situation, when you're the leader of the race, I think my penalty was a bit excessive,' claimed Goodyear.

The race officials disagreed, and when Goodyear steadfastly ignored the penalty flag, USAC retaliated by refusing to chart his subsequent progress.

'Obviously, in hindsight, I should have just hung back there before the restart,' continued Goodyear, who was classified an unrepresentative 14th, 'but when you're coming down to the last nine or 10 laps, the one thing on your mind is to make sure that you don't get passed into Turn One because you might never get it back again. You know you're not going to run into traffic and you probably won't see another yellow. You've just got to go for it.

'If I'd have driven into a corner too hard and gone into the wall I would have said, OK, I'm a dumb-ass and that's it. But this is just so disappointing.'

There were plenty of other hard-

luck stories, too. Paul Tracy, for example, lost a lap during the chaotic first yellow, then climbed as high as second before losing ground once more, this time due to a puncture. His Kmart/Budweiser Lola finally succumbed to a broken timing chain after Tracy had fought his way back to sixth. Raul Boesel also was unlucky – as ever, it seems, at Indy – when a broken oil fitting stranded his fourth-placed Duracell Lola-Mercedes inside the final 50 miles.

Team Menard also endured a bad day. Buddy Lazier, who qualified the team's third car easily, despite a minimum of track time, went out early with a fuel system failure, while both Brayton and Luyendyk were handicapped by a lack of boost which erased a significant portion of their power advantage. Substandard pop-off valves were suspected as the cause.

'We started out on Scottie's car at 54 inches of boost and ended up around 52,' said a frustrated John Menard. 'Arie's was about the same. He had 52.8.

'It's hard enough with 55 inches, and without that we just can't run with these guys.'

Brayton never really featured in the race, hindered also by a lack of fuel pressure as well as a lengthy pit stop which restricted him to a 17th-place finish. Luyendyk fared rather better, apart from his first pit stop, and the Dutchman passed Villeneuve right before the checkered flag to move back onto the lead lap and claim seventh at the finish.

The closing stages also featured a close battle for second place which eventually fell the way of rookie Christian Fittipaldi. The Brazilian's illustrious uncle Emerson, of course, wasn't even in the field after failing to qualify the previous weekend, but Christian upheld family honor with a magnificent performance in Derrick Walker's Marlboro/Chapeco Reynard-Ford. Christian's result earned him the coveted Rookie of the Year honors and was all the more meritorious for the fact his car's undertray had worked loose, causing a dangerous oversteer.

'The car was perfect through the first half of the race,' he said, 'but it was a nightmare for the last 90 laps or so. I thought I was going to hit the wall every lap I was out there.'

Veteran Bobby Rahal finished third in his Miller Genuine Draft Lola-Mercedes, despite a stop-and-go penalty (for exceeding the pit lane speed limit) during the closing stages of the race. Rahal disputed the call, to no avail, although, curiously, he was permitted to serve his sentence under caution instead of having to wait for the race to be restarted. The incident typified the confusion which prevailed throughout the day.

Eliseo Salazar drove spiritedly to fourth in Dick Simon's Cristal/Mobil 1/Copec Lola-Ford. Nevertheless, the Chilean rookie felt he might have had a shot at the victory had he not been forced to brake hard in Turn Four at the final restart.

Next was Fittipaldi's teammate, Gordon, who charged back superbly after his early delay. He, too, would surely have finished higher if not for an extra pit stop on lap 187 after erroneously believing he had a punctured tire.

'I just made a mistake,' admitted Gordon. 'When it gets late in the race, you start hearing weird things and feeling weird things. I thought I had a flat but I didn't.'

And so, finally, the day belonged to Villeneuve, who actually completed 202 laps following the imposition of his two-lap punishment.

'When we got that penalty, it knocked us on our backs,' said Barry Green. 'I mean, no one even wanted to talk on the radio – it was just quiet – so I rounded up the troops and I said, "Come on guys, we're not out of it yet. Let's work on it."'

Work on it they did. Villeneuve survived a couple of minor errors during his pit stops, fortunately without any serious consequences, and out on the race track he was flawless. The 24-year-old gained exceptional fuel mileage, which in turn enabled him to overcome his two-lap deficit by making his pit stops during a couple of perfectly timed cautions.

'I knew the team was ready to win the race and I knew I was ready,' said the triumphant Villeneuve, who took over the lead in the PPG Cup standings for good measure. 'When we were behind Goodyear, I thought the first Canadian to win the race was going to be him, but it turned out to be us.

'This is the best feeling I've had in motor racing so far. Indy is the race to win. To win this race is as big as winning a championship. It's a great feeling.'

SNIPPETS

Photos: Michael C. Brown

• John Menard's team set the pace almost from the moment the Indianapolis Motor Speedway opened for official practice on Saturday, May 6. Arie Luyendyk *(above)* recorded a startling lap at 233.281 mph on the very first day, then proceeded to trade for the honor of fastest speed with teammate Scott Brayton throughout the first week. One or the other of the team's Lola-Menards was fastest on each and every day, with Luyendyk finally claiming a new unofficial track record of 234.913. Brayton turned the tables by securing the pole, although unsuitable weather conditions ensured that, against expectations, he was unable to break Roberto Guerrero's outright four-lap record of 232.482.

• Bryan Herta hit the wall hard in one of Chip Ganassi's Target Reynard-Fords during the second week of practice. Herta suffered a concussion but returned to start the race from the 33rd position in his backup machine.

• The United States Auto Club introduced one of the most popular regulations of all time – at least so far as the individual team members were concerned – by issuing a decree that the Gasoline Alley garage area would be locked shut promptly at 8 p.m. each day.

• Raul Boesel tried but failed to get his Duracell Lola-Mercedes up to speed on Pole Day, while on his second qualifying attempt he was looking secure at better than 226 mph until slowing dramatically on his fourth and final lap. The car, incredibly, was out of fuel! 'I knew we had enough speed in the car, and fortunately we had enough time to take another run,' said a relieved Boesel. 'It was difficult just sitting there and waiting, hoping we would have time to go again. It was a relief when we made it. It was one of those days you really don't want to repeat.'

• Mirroring the problems experienced by Marlboro Team Penske, Stefan

Johans-son strug-gled throughout the first week with Tony Bettenhausen's Alumax Penske PC23. Bettenhausen, however, quickly hatched an alternate plan by leasing a year-old Reynard-Ford from Arciero/Wells Racing. Johansson encountered several more difficulties before finally – and with supreme irony – bumping Emerson Fittipaldi from the field with nine minutes remaining on the final day of qualifying.

with a four-lap average of 227.818, comfortably eclipsing the best efforts of established stars Rahal and Boesel who took to the track shortly afterward.

• Prior to the race, thankfully, there were few incidents during more than two weeks of practice and qualifying. Villeneuve and Ribeiro both emerged unscathed from high-speed wrecks, while rookie Davey Hamilton suf-

• Impecunious team owner Greg Beck confirmed his deal with Hideshi Matsuda *(above)* only a few days before the track opened for official practice, then hastily bought and prepared the '94 Lola-Ford with which Scott Pruett had conducted the bulk of his testing miles last year for Patrick Racing. Matsuda struggled to make up for lost time after missing the first five days of official practice, then mirrored his feat of one year ago by recording easily his four quickest laps of the month during his second qualifying attempt. In fact, Matsuda claimed the award as the fastest second-day qualifier

fered a broken right ankle after the right-rear wheel broke on his Reynard-Ford in Turn Four. Ron Hemelgarn's team built up a replacement car for the West Coast Super-Modified star, who looked set to make the field with a courageous effort on the final day, only for the undertray to break and almost cause him to crash again.

• French rookie driver Franck Freon *(top)* made a valiant attempt to qualify a three-year-old Lola-Menard/Buick entered by Steve Erickson's Autosport Racing Team. Freon posted his four best laps during his qualifying

attempt on the final Saturday, and indeed his average of 224.432 mph, which, incredibly, would have stood as sixth fastest overall in 1994, was bumped only inside the final hour.

• The average qualifying speed for the 33-car field was a new record 226.912 mph (an increase of 3.642 mph over the 1994 standard). As a further measure of the level of competition, 27 of the 33 starters were covered by a mere 2.508 mph – or a fraction over one percent.

• Undeterred by USAC's decision to restrict boost for purpose-built, single-cam, 209-cubic-inch engines to 48 inches (from 55) following the Ilmor/Mercedes romp in 1994, the father-and-son team of Peter and Michael Greenfield returned with their own engine for a second attempt at making the race. Sadly, the enterprising and tightly budgeted team's slim hopes of qualifying were dashed when Michael understeered into the Turn One wall on the second Friday. Nevertheless, the engine *(below)* had shown distinct promise, running strongly and without any major dramas. Peter Greenfield claimed it produced around 800 hp, even with the boost reduction, and reckoned the greatest handicap was with their 1993 Lola's underbody aerodynamics, which had been necessarily compromised in order to fit the engine into the car.

Safety under scrutiny

Immediately following Stan Fox's crash, Adrian Reynard and his chief designer, Malcolm Oastler, commenced a detailed investigation aimed at discovering how and why the chassis broke open like an eggshell.

Oastler pored over the wreckage in Hemelgarn Racing's garage while the race was still in progress. He determined that the integrity of the composite chassis had been severely compromised in the initial contact with Eddie Cheever's car, as evidenced by marks found on the side of the cockpit surround, and that it had been substantially weakened prior to the immense impact against the Turn One wall.

Reynard concluded that the new rules being implemented by Championship Auto Racing Teams/IndyCar in time for the 1996 PPG Indy Car World Series, calling for more extensive use of puncture-proof materials such as Kevlar, which is used in the production of bullet-proof vests, should significantly improve the structural rigidity of the chassis and its ability to sustain an explosive secondary impact, such as was experienced by Fox.

In addition, Reynard recommended the introduction of several additional safety measures, including a broadening of the roll-over hoop to a dimension two inches wider than the helmets currently being worn by the drivers.

'I'm definitely going to incorporate that into our car for next year,' declared Reynard, 'and I've written a letter to our teams and the other chassis manufacturers, as well as to CART and USAC, imploring them to make these alterations mandatory.'

Allsport U.K.

PPG INDY CAR WORLD SERIES • ROUND 6
79TH INDIANAPOLIS 500

INDIANAPOLIS MOTOR SPEEDWAY, INDIANAPOLIS, INDIANA

MAY 28, 200 LAPS – 500.000 MILES

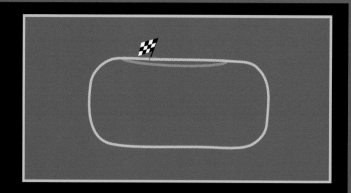

Place	Driver (Nat.)	No.	Team Sponsors Car-Engine	Tires	Q Speed	Q Time	Q Pos.	Laps	Time/Status	Ave.	Pts.
1	Jacques Villeneuve (CDN)	27	Team Green *Player's Ltd.* Reynard 95I-Ford	GY	228.397	2m 37.620s	5	200	3h 15m 17.561s	153.616	20
2	*Christian Fittipaldi (BR)	15	Walker *Marlboro/Chapeco Special* Reynard 95I-Ford	GY	226.375	2m 39.028s	27	200	3h 15m 20.042s		16
3	Bobby Rahal (USA)	9	Rahal/Hogan *Miller Genuine Draft* Lola T95/00-Mercedes	GY	227.081	2m 38.534s	21	200	3h 15m 20.527s		14
4	*Eliseo Salazar (RCH)	7	Simon *Cristal/Mobil 1/Copec* Lola T95/00-Ford	GY	225.023	2m 39.984s	24	200	3h 15m 22.329s		12
5	Robby Gordon (USA)	5	Walker *Valvoline/Cummins Special* Reynard 95I-Ford	GY	227.531	2m 38.220s	7	200	3h 15m 32.466s		10
6	Mauricio Gugelmin (BR)	18	PacWest Racing Group *Hollywood* Reynard 95I-Ford	GY	227.923	2m 37.948s	6	200	3h 15m 34.638s		9
7	Arie Luyendyk (NL)	40	Team Menard *Glidden/Quaker State* Lola T95/00-Menard	GY	231.031	2m 35.823s	2	200	3h 15m 59.520s		6
8	Teo Fabi (I)	33	Forsythe Racing *ABB/Indeck* Reynard 95I-Ford	GY	225.911	2m 39.355s	15	199	Running		5
9	Danny Sullivan (USA)	17	PacWest Racing Group *VISA* Reynard 95I-Ford	GY	225.496	2m 39.648s	18	199	Running		4
10	Hiro Matsushita (J)	25	Arciero-Wells *Panasonic/Duskin/YKK* Reynard 95I-Ford	FS	226.867	2m 38.683s	10	199	Running		3
11	*Alessandro Zampedri (I)	34	Payton-Coyne *The Mi-Jack Car* Lola T94/00-Ford	FS	225.753	2m 39.466s	17	198	Running		2
12	Roberto Guerrero (USA)	21	Pagan *Upper Deck/General Components* Reynard 94I-Mercedes	GY	226.402	2m 39.009s	13	198	Running		1
13	Bryan Herta (USA)	4	Ganassi *Target/Scotch Video* Reynard 95I-Ford	GY	225.551	2m 39.609s	33	198	Running		
14	Scott Goodyear (CDN)	24	Tasman Motorsports *LCI/Motorola/CNN* Reynard 95I-Honda	FS	230.759	2m 36.007s	3	195	Running**		
15	Hideshi Matsuda (J)	54	Beck Motorsports *Taisan/Zunne Group* Lola T94/00-Ford	FS	227.818	2m 38.021s	20	194	Running		
16	Stefan Johansson (S)	16	Bettenhausen *Alumax Aluminum* Reynard 94I-Ford	GY	225.547	2m 39.612s	31	192	Running		
17	Scott Brayton (USA)	60	Team Menard *Quaker State/Glidden* Lola T95/00-Menard	GY	231.604	2m 35.438s	1	190	Running		1
18	*Andre Ribeiro (BR)	31	Tasman Motorsports *LCI International* Reynard 95I-Honda	FS	226.495	2m 38.944s	12	187	Running		
19	Scott Pruett (USA)	20	Patrick Racing *Firestone/Pennzoil* Lola T95/00-Ford	FS	227.403	2m 38.309s	8	184	Accident		
20	Raul Boesel (BR)	11	Rahal/Hogan *Duracell Charger* Lola T95/00-Mercedes	GY	226.028	2m 39.272s	22	184	Oil line		
21	Adrian Fernandez (MEX)	10	Galles *Tecate/Quaker State* Lola T95/00-Mercedes	GY	227.803	2m 38.031s	25	176	Engine		
22	Jimmy Vasser (USA)	12	Ganassi *Target/STP* Reynard 95I-Ford	GY	227.350	2m 38.346s	9	170	Accident		
23	Davy Jones (USA)	77	Simon *Jonathan Byrd/Bryant Heating* Lola T95/00-Ford	GY	225.135	2m 39.904s	32	161	Accident		
24	Paul Tracy (CDN)	3	Newman-Haas *Kmart/Budweiser* Lola T95/00-Ford	GY	225.795	2m 39.437s	16	136	Engine		
25	Michael Andretti (USA)	6	Newman-Haas *Kmart/Texaco Havoline* Lola T95/00-Ford	GY	229.294	2m 37.004s	4	77	Accident		
26	Scott Sharp (USA)	41	A.J. Foyt *Copenhagen Racing* Lola T95/00-Ford	GY	225.711	2m 39.496s	30	74	Accident		
27	Buddy Lazier (USA)	80	Team Menard *Glidden/Quaker State* Lola T95/00-Menard	GY	226.017	2m 39.280s	23	45	Fuel system		
28	Eric Bachelart (B)	19	Payton-Coyne *The Agfa Car* Lola T94/00-Ford	FS	226.875	2m 38.678s	26	6	Handling		
29	*Gil de Ferran (BR)	8	Hall Racing *Pennzoil Special* Reynard 95I-Mercedes	GY	225.437	2m 39.690s	19	1	Accident		
30	Stan Fox (USA)	91	Hemelgarn *Delta Faucet/Bowling* Reynard 95I-Ford	FS	226.588	2m 38.879s	11	0	Accident		
31	Eddie Cheever (USA)	14	A.J. Foyt *Copenhagen Racing* Lola T95/00-Ford	GY	226.314	2m 39.071s	14	0	Accident		
32	Lyn St. James (USA)	99	Simon *Whitlock Auto Supply* Lola T95/00-Ford	GY	225.346	2m 39.825s	28	0	Accident		
33	*Carlos Guerrero (MEX)	22	Simon *Herdez/Viva Mexico!* Lola T95/00-Ford	GY	225.831	2m 39.411s	29	0	Accident		
NQ	Emerson Fittipaldi (BR)	9T	Marlboro Team Penske Lola T95/00-Mercedes	GY	224.907	2m 40.066s	34	–	Did not qualify		
NQ	*Franck Freon (F)	92	Autosport Racing Team *Earl's* Lola T92/00-Menard	FS	224.432	2m 40.405s	35	–	Did not qualify		
NQ	Al Unser Jr. (USA)	11T	Marlboro Team Penske Lola T95/00-Mercedes	GY	224.101	2m 40.642s	36	–	Did not qualify		
NQ	Marco Greco (BR)	55	Galles *Brastemp* Lola T95/00-Mercedes	GY		waved off attempt		–	Did not qualify		
NQ	*Davey Hamilton (USA)	95	Hemelgarn *Delta Faucet/Alfa Laval* Reynard 94I-Ford	FS		waved off attempt		–	Did not qualify		
NQ	*Jeff Ward (USA)	44	Arizona Motor Sports *Executive Air* Lola T94/00-Ford	FS		waved off attempt		–	Did not qualify		
NQ	Johnny Parsons (USA)	64	Project Indy *James Dean/Van Dyne* Reynard 94I-Ford	GY		waved off attempt		–	Did not qualify		
NQA	Al Unser Jr. (USA)	1	Marlboro Team Penske Penske PC24-Mercedes	GY	–			–	Did not attempt to qualify		
NQA	Emerson Fittipaldi (BR)	2	Marlboro Team Penske Penske PC24-Mercedes	GY	–			–	Did not attempt to qualify		
NQA	Mike Groff (USA)	4T	Ganassi *Target/Scotch Video* Reynard 95I-Ford	GY	–			–	Did not attempt to qualify		
NQA	Dean Hall (USA)	99	Dick Simon Racing *Subway* Lola T95/00-Ford	GY	–			–	Did not attempt to qualify		
NQA	Jim Crawford (GB)	96	Adcox *Rain-X/Indiana Buick Dealers* Lola T92/00-Buick	FS	–			–	Did not attempt to qualify		
NQA	*Michael Greenfield (USA)	42	Greenfield Industries Lola T93/00-Greenfield	FS	–			–	Did not attempt to qualify		
NQA	Dick Simon (USA)	77	Simon *Jonathan Byrd/Bryant Heating* Lola T95/00-Ford	GY	–			–	Did not attempt to qualify		

* denotes Rookie driver; ** stopped scoring after lap 195

Caution flags: Laps 1–9, accident/Fox, Cheever, St. James and C. Guerrero; laps 37–44, debris; laps 80–86, accident/Sharp; laps 89–95, spin/Johansson; laps 123–126, tow in/Ribeiro; laps 138–141, tow in/Tracy; laps 163–169, accident/Jones; laps 171–176, accident/Vasser; laps 185–190, accident/Pruett. **Total:** nine for 58 laps.

Lap leaders: Scott Goodyear, 1–9 (9 laps); Arie Luyendyk, 10–16 (7 laps); Michael Andretti, 17–32 (16 laps); Goodyear, 33–35 (3 laps); Jacques Villeneuve, 36–38 (3 laps); Andretti, 39–66 (28 laps); Goodyear, 67 (1 lap); Mauricio Gugelmin, 68–76 (9 laps); Andretti, 77 (1 lap); Goodyear, 78–81 (4 laps); Gugelmin, 82–116 (35 laps); Goodyear, 117–120 (4 laps); Bobby Rahal, 121 (1 lap); Raul Boesel, 122–123 (2 laps); Gugelmin, 124–138 (15 laps); Goodyear, 139 (1 lap); Jimmy Vasser, 140–155 (16 laps); Villeneuve, 156–162 (7 laps); Scott Pruett, 163–165 (3 laps); Robby Gordon, 166 (1 lap); Vasser, 167–170 (4 laps); Pruett, 171–175 (5 laps); Goodyear, 176–195 (20 laps); Villeneuve, 196–200 (5 laps). **Totals:** Gugelmin, 59 laps; Andretti, 45 laps; Goodyear, 42 laps; Vasser, 20 laps; Villeneuve, 15 laps; Pruett, 8 laps; Luyendyk, 7 laps; Boesel, 2 laps; Rahal, 1 lap; Gordon, 1 lap.

Fastest race lap: Scott Goodyear, 40.177s, 224.009 mph, on lap 179.

Championship positions: 1 Villeneuve, 67; **2** Rahal, 52; **3** Pruett, 51; **4** Gugelmin, 47; **5** Gordon, 43; **6** E. Fittipaldi, 35; **7** Unser, 34; **8** Tracy, 32; **9** Fabi, 31; **10** Andretti and C. Fittipaldi, 29; **12** Cheever, 28; **13** Boesel, 24; **14** Johansson, 22; **15** Sullivan, 21; **16** Salazar, 16; **17** Zampedri and Fernandez, 7; **19** Danner, Bachelart and Luyendyk, 6; **22** Vasser and Matsushita, 5; **24** Herta, 4; **25** Ribeiro, 3; **26** de Ferran, C. Guerrero and Hall, 2; **29** R. Guerrero and Brayton, 1.

1 – TRACY   **2 – UNSER**   **3 – ANDRETTI**

MILWAUKEE

Paul Tracy had endured a difficult time since claiming a worthy triumph at Surfers Paradise in March. The Canadian had been consistently outpaced – at least in qualifying – by Newman-Haas teammate Michael Andretti and had failed to reap a single PPG Cup point from the subsequent three races. Along the way he had faded from the overall points lead to a distant eighth, 35 markers adrift of countryman Jacques Villeneuve.

Crucially, however, Tracy never lost faith in his own ability. And when the opportunity presented itself, Tracy bounced back to prominence by guiding his Kmart/Budweiser Lola Ford/Cosworth to an accomplished victory on the Milwaukee Mile.

The Miller Genuine Draft 200 featured an exhilarating duel between Tracy and his former Penske teammate, Al Unser Jr, who finished less than one second behind after 200 laps of intense competition. Indeed, the pair exchanged positions several times in the closing stages before Tracy was able to cement his 10th win in just 54 Indy Car starts and his second in seven outings with the Newman-Haas team. Tracy's teammate, Michael Andretti, finished one lap down in third place.

'This is especially satisfying after our disappointment at Indy,' said Tracy. 'I thought I was in contention until we had a problem and Michael was surely in a position to win the race. Instead, we left there kind of with our tail between our legs, so it was good that we both ran strong this weekend. We couldn't be happier.'

ael C. Brown

The many faces of Paul Tracy. The victorious Canadian celebrates on the podium with second-place finisher

Teo Fabi took pole position in Jerry Forsythe's Indeck/Combustion Engineering Reynard-Ford and led the race until tire wear slowed his pace.

Michael Andretti *(right)* relishes the unique challenge posed by the bumpy Milwaukee track surface but handling problems restricted him to third place.

QUALIFYING

The historic track set within the Wisconsin State Fair Park represents an entirely different challenge when compared to the other one-mile ovals on the Indy Car schedule. Most noticeably, its corners are barely banked at all. Also, the venerable layout has been subjected to many harsh winters, which have inevitably taken their toll on the track itself.

Perhaps as a result of the chatterboard surface, the Milwaukee Mile traditionally throws up a surprise or two. This year it was the turn of Teo Fabi to claim some headlines, as the diminutive Italian showed spectacular form throughout the weekend in Jerry Forsythe's Combustion Engineering/Indeck Reynard-Ford.

A persistent drizzle allowed only a bare minimum of track time on Friday, and once that had cleared, making way for perfect conditions Saturday morning, Fabi set the pace from the moment the green flag was waved. Against the odds, too, having drawn last position in the qualifying line, Fabi produced two storming laps to provide a sensational climax to the one-at-a-time session. Either lap would have been good enough for the pole.

'We've been competitive this year but finally we have a result to prove it,' said Fabi. 'I'm happy for myself, of course, and also the team, because this is our first year together and I think there is still some improvement to come.'

Prior to Fabi's last-minute showstopper, Emerson Fittipaldi and Marlboro Penske-Mercedes teammate Al Unser Jr. had looked set to clinch the front row, marking a triumphant return following their embarrassing failure at Indianapolis.

'I was with all the crew waiting for Fabi to run and my mind went back to Indianapolis when we were watching Stefan [Johansson] bump us from the race,' said Fittipaldi. 'It

is a much better feeling to be bumped from the pole than to be bumped from the race. This time we are at the opposite end of the field. It's a much better feeling. I'm very pleased.'

Unser was similarly gratified – and relieved – to be back on the pace, although it seemed odd for the Penske team to be situated at the beginning of the pit lane, rather than their habitual location adjacent to the exit. The positions, you see, are allocated according to qualifying positions in the previous race . . . and since the Penskes didn't make the field at Indy, they were low men on the totem pole.

Andretti lined up fourth on the grid, content with the balance on his Kmart/Texaco Havoline Lola-Ford/Cosworth, followed by rookie Andre Ribeiro, who once again displayed the potency of Steve Horne's LCI International Reynard-Honda. Robby Gordon also maintained his strong oval track form, sixth in Derrick Walker's Valvoline/Cummins Reynard-Ford. Tracy would start seventh.

The top 10 drivers were all within a half-second of Fabi's pole-winning time of 22.160 seconds (162.456 mph), with the fastest 20 separated by a mere 0.792 seconds.

RACE

The closely matched field and a continuation of near-perfect weather conditions enticed a record crowd of 47,700 to the celebrated one-mile oval. They were not to be disappointed.

Fabi led the 26-car field toward the starter's stand at a brisk pace which ensured he was able to maintain his pole advantage into the first corner. Fittipaldi tucked in behind, while Gordon stormed around the high line in Turns One and Two to emerge in fourth as the cars sped down the back straightaway. Gordon's charge continued as he

usurped Andretti around the outside line in Turn Three, then out-fumbled Fittipaldi next time around to move up into second.

Fabi, meanwhile, had taken off into a clear lead, and such was his superiority that he began lapping some of the slower cars as early as lap six.

'The car was just perfect at the start,' said Fabi. 'In fact, I was trying to look after the tires, but obviously not well enough, because they soon began to lose grip.'

By lap 15, the race had taken on an entirely different complexion. Fabi still led, but by a much reduced margin over Unser, who had worked his way past Fittipaldi, Andretti and Gordon in quick succession. Andretti now lay third, followed by Tracy, Fittipaldi and Gordon, whose car had developed a dangerous oversteer due to an inadvertent tap from Andretti.

'It lifted the back of the car and knocked the toe out,' claimed Gordon. 'I started falling back after that. The car started sliding going into the corners. It doesn't take much of a hit to change the balance on these cars. They're pretty fragile.'

Unser moved up onto Fabi's tail by lap 20, and seven laps later he swept past into the lead on the exit of Turn Two.

At that stage it looked as though Unser might drive off into the distance, as he had done in 1994 when he and teammate Fittipaldi finished two laps clear of the entire field. A third Penske, driven, of course, by Tracy, finished third on that illustrious occasion.

But Tracy wasn't beaten yet. Sure enough, on lap 37, he passed Fabi for second place. He was then able to stabilize the deficit to Unser at around six seconds.

Unser continued to set a comfortable pace out in front of the field, and only Tracy was able to offer a serious challenge. Andretti slipped

past Fabi on lap 41, but he was losing ground to the two leaders due to a persistent understeer.

'Right from the beginning, people were just blowing by me on the outside,' lamented Andretti. 'I couldn't run the high line. That was really killing me in traffic because I couldn't pass anybody on the outside.'

His comments were echoed by Fabi, who was also struggling in traffic.

'I was OK when I was running on my own,' he related, 'but in traffic the car seemed to lose a lot of grip and a lot of downforce, so I lost a lot of time trying to overtake slower cars.'

Fittipaldi followed in fifth despite a worsening oversteer complaint, and he duly became the first of the leaders to make a pit stop on lap 52.

Fabi took the opportunity for service on lap 61, while Unser relinquished the lead when he came in three laps later. Unser had intended to stay out longer, but his hand was forced by a telemetry/computer system failure which meant neither he nor his crew had an accurate reading on his Mercedes-Benz engine's fuel consumption.

'We just had to go on plain old dead-reckoning,' explained race engineer Grant Newbury. 'The old calculators were working overtime. It was only when he came in for the pit stop that we were able to determine exactly how much fuel he had used.'

Tracy led for 11 laps before making his first stop for fuel and handing the point briefly to Andretti, who was the last of the leaders to take on service. Andretti thereby maintained his streak of leading every race so far this year.

Unfortunately, Andretti then stalled his engine as he went to leave the pits. His quick-thinking crew soon had the Ford/Cosworth fired up again, and Andretti smoked his way back into the fray, but by then he was back in fourth behind Fabi. Both were one lap down to the leaders, with Unser having resumed ahead of Tracy.

The gap between the Penske and the Lola remained steady until the half-distance point. Then, little by little, Tracy began to erode Unser's advantage. By lap 116 they were virtually nose to tail. The crowd loved it, especially as the pair were constantly having to deal with lapped traffic.

One more round of pit stops loomed, and almost on cue Eliseo Salazar spun Dick Simon's Cristal/Mobil 1/Copec Lola-Ford in Turn Four – amazingly without making any firm contact – in order to

Contrasting views

The teams, the drivers and the fans all look forward to the PPG Cup series' annual pilgrimage to the famed Milwaukee Mile, which has hosted auto racing events since 1903. The atmosphere is always convivial and it provides a stark contrast to the high-pressure environment of Indianapolis, which traditionally precedes the visit to Wisconsin.

Nevertheless, the uneven track surface continues to provide a hot topic of conversation. It creates a formidable challenge not only for the drivers, who have to cope with a constant battering inside the cars, but also the team engineers, who strive to ensure consistent performance from their increasingly sophisticated steeds. Interestingly, however, opinion is divided as to whether or not the track should be repaved.

Some drivers, including Eddie Cheever, have no doubts: 'This place has the same surface as it did when Jim Clark raced here in the '60s,' he says. 'It's a joke. The cars go airborne every time on the exit of Turn Four. It's so bumpy you can't run the car low to get the aerodynamic benefit, which means you have to lean on the tires more and then they wear through like marshmallows.'

Cheever unwittingly proved his point by crashing heavily on the exit of Turn Four during final practice on Saturday afternoon. He was therefore obliged to run A.J. Foyt's '94 Lola chassis for the race, since Foyt's spare '95 car had been extensively damaged at Indianapolis.

But Cheever's views are not shared by everyone. Michael Andretti, for example, a four-time winner at Milwaukee, is not necessarily in favor of removing the bumps: 'They give the place its character,' he claims. 'It's a great track. Personally, I don't mind the bumps because they automatically slow the cars down – during the race we're always two to three seconds a lap slower than in qualifying. And because the place is so wide, it makes for really great racing.'

The enthusiastic fans certainly will attest to that. Andretti's concern, however, centers upon the inevitability that a smoother surface will lead to a substantial increase in speed, which in turn will provide fewer passing opportunities and, quite possibly, more accidents.

Nevertheless, taking into account the new aerodynamic restrictions which will be introduced for the 1996 season with the intention of slowing the cars significantly, Andretti's car owner, Carl Haas, who also acts as the promoter for the Milwaukee Mile, has decided the time is ripe. Accordingly, when the Indy cars next grace the historic fairgrounds track, they will do so on a brand-new surface to be laid over the winter at an estimated cost of $1.2 million.

Rookie Gil de Ferran *(right)* curbed his natural aggression and was rewarded with an encouraging eighth-place finish in the Pennzoil Reynard.

A routine pit stop for the colorful Panasonic/Duskin/YKK Reynard-Ford of Hiro Matsushita. The depth of the Indy Car field has never been greater.

Michael C. Brown

bring out the race's only full-course caution on lap 124. At last, the frantic pace was relaxed for a few moments.

Instead the emphasis switched onto pit lane, where Tracy's crew serviced its man slightly faster than Unser's. The two cars accelerated out virtually in unison, but the nose of Tracy's Lola was ahead as they crossed the blend line which is used to determine positions at the end of the pit lane. Advantage Newman-Haas.

Almost simultaneously, back in the Penske pit, Fittipaldi had come in too hot, lost control over the bumps under braking and spun around backward into the pit wall. It was an ignominious end to his day.

Tracy and Unser resumed their duel for the lead after the brief caution period, and as if to add to the excitement, Gordon ran immediately ahead of them on the road. The Californian was running strongly, even though he was now fighting to stay just two laps down on the leaders

after losing more time due to a mix-up with teammate Christian Fittipaldi during his first pit stop. For several laps, Gordon was able to remain a few lengths clear of the Tracy–Unser battle.

'He was just quick enough to keep out of range,' said Tracy. 'He was hanging in there until he got into turbulence [caused by slower cars] and then he got loose, so I was able to creep up on him; but it was frustrating, because I could see Al creeping up on me.'

Sure enough, on lap 144, Unser regained the lead after finding better traction coming off Turn Four. Unser proceeded to pull out an advantage of a couple of seconds over the course of the next 15 laps or so; but Tracy was prepared to bide his time.

'I had watched his car earlier and although he was a little bit faster than me in the middle of the stint, my car stayed good all through while his started to develop an oversteer,'

noted Tracy. 'I radioed in to my crew and I said not to worry. I concentrated on trying to conserve fuel a little bit, and then when we got into traffic, I tried to keep the pressure on because I knew his car would go loose at the end.'

By lap 175, the two leaders were once again joined together. Four laps later, as they swept past a couple of slower cars, Tracy regained the point amid traffic on the exit of Turn Four.

Tracy encountered one scare when another lapped car caused him to run high out of the groove in Turns One and Two with 15 laps to go. The incident allowed Unser to close to within a car length, but Tracy recovered from that near-miss and was able to reel off the remaining laps without undue difficulty.

'I think it's one of the best races I've ever seen Paul drive,' said car owner Carl Haas. 'He hung in there. It looked dismal in the late stages when Al got around him, but Paul

started closing it up and it turned out just right. I'm very proud of him.'

Unser was reasonably content with second place, especially considering the handicap of a painful tendinitis in his right shoulder. Andretti persevered to third ahead of Fabi, who was unfortunate to fall two laps off the pace when he made his second pit stop moments before the race's only caution. Otherwise the Italian would surely have earned a place on the podium.

Gordon hung onto fifth following a thrilling battle with PPG Cup points leader Jacques Villeneuve in the closing stages. The pair exchanged positions twice inside the final 20 laps, before Gordon emerged on top by just 0.331 seconds.

'It was good clean racing,' said Gordon. 'We knew we had to beat him because he's the PPG points leader. It's a 17-race championship and we just need to start racking up the points.'

Michael C. Brown

SNIPPETS

Photos: Michael C. Brown

• 'I think we made the show this week, boys,' quipped a buoyant Al Unser Jr. during the post-qualifying press conference after posting the third fastest time. 'I really want to thank my team for doing a heck of a job after we didn't get into the Indianapolis 500, because it's really easy to get down. It's a great feeling because the cars came off the trailer really quick and they were set up really good. The attention to detail was fantastic, just like it always is with Penske Racing.'

• Back-in-form Italian Teo Fabi was equally delighted after clinching the 10th pole of his Indy Car career – and the first since Denver in 1990 with the ill-fated March-Porsche.

• Lyn St. James' early race car, crash at Indy had St. James rendered her 1995 Lola *hors* *(below)* was oblig-*de combat*, so she began the ed to take over teammate weekend with Dick Simon Carlos Guerrero's spare '94 Racing's Lola T94/00, chas-car. Despite that, she drove sis 01, which Raul Boesel to a 20th-place finish. qualified on the pole at Mil-waukee in 1994. Then, after • Jacques Villeneuve raced another wall-banging with a new Reynard chassis, episode on Saturday morn-carrying the number plate ing caused extensive rear-95I-004A, to replace the car end damage to her intended written off in his crash dur-ing practice at Indianapolis.

• Emerson Fittipaldi was suitably embarrassed after his spectacular spin into the pits and out of the race, but there were some mitigating circumstances. First, his Penske had picked up a good deal of debris on its right-rear tire immediately prior to making the pit stop. Second, he was unaccustomed to pitting at the beginning of the pit lane, which obliged him to make a sharp left-hand turn prior to entering his pit. 'It was kind of a hard pit to come into,' admitted his race engineer, Tom Brown, who then displayed his keen sense of reality by adding: 'But it hadn't moved. It had been there all weekend.'

• IndyCar introduced a brand-new pop-off valve (the means of regulating the tur-bocharged engines' inlet manifold boost pressure at the specified 45 inches of mercury absolute) in Milwaukee. The latest valve *(above)*, which had been subjected to rigorous testing with input from a variety of sources, including all three current engine manufacturers, immediately proved to be much more reliable and consistent than the previous valve, which had been in use since 1980.

PPG INDY CAR WORLD SERIES • ROUND 7

MILLER GENUINE DRAFT 200

MILWAUKEE MILE,
WISCONSIN STATE FAIR PARK, WEST ALLIS, WISCONSIN

JUNE 4, 200 LAPS – 200.000 MILES

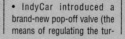

Place	Driver (Nat.)	No.	Team Sponsors Car-Engine	Tires	Q Speed	Q Time	Q Pos.	Laps	Time/Status	Ave.	Pts.
1	Paul Tracy (CDN)	3	Newman-Haas *Kmart/Budweiser* Lola T95/00-Ford	GY	159.913	22.512s	7	200	1h 27m 23.853s	137.304	20
2	Al Unser Jr. (USA)	1	Marlboro Team Penske Penske PC24-Mercedes	GY	161.191	22.334s	3	200	1h 27m 24.699s	137.281	17
3	Michael Andretti (USA)	6	Newman-Haas *Kmart/Texaco Havoline* Lola T95/00-Ford	GY	161.018	22.358s	4	199	Running		14
4	Teo Fabi (I)	33	Forsythe *Combustion Engineering/Indeck* Reynard 95I-Ford	GY	162.456	22.160s	1	198	Running		13
5	Robby Gordon (USA)	5	Walker *Valvoline/Cummins Special* Reynard 95I-Ford	GY	160.493	22.431s	6	197	Running		10
6	Jacques Villeneuve (CDN)	27	Team Green *Player's Ltd.* Reynard 95I-Ford	GY	158.706	22.683s	11	197	Running		8
7	*Christian Fittipaldi (BR)	15	Walker *Marlboro/Chapeco Special* Reynard 95I-Ford	GY	158.288	22.743s	13	196	Running		6
8	*Gil de Ferran (BR)	8	Hall Racing *Pennzoil Special* Reynard 95I-Mercedes	GY	157.159	22.907s	18	195	Running		5
9	Jimmy Vasser (USA)	12	Ganassi *Target/STP* Reynard 95I-Ford	GY	158.236	22.751s	14	195	Running		4
10	Adrian Fernandez (MEX)	10	Galles *Tecate/Quaker State* Lola T95/00-Mercedes	GY	159.229	22.609s	9	195	Running		3
11	Raul Boesel (BR)	11	Rahal/Hogan *Duracell Charger* Lola T95/00-Mercedes	GY	159.623	22.553s	8	194	Running		2
12	Scott Pruett (USA)	20	Patrick Racing *Firestone/Pennzoil* Lola T95/00-Ford	FS	158.412	22.726s	12	194	Running		1
13	Bobby Rahal (USA)	9	Rahal/Hogan *Miller Genuine Draft* Lola T95/00-Mercedes	GY	158.103	22.770s	16	193	Running		
14	Mauricio Gugelmin (BR)	18	PacWest Racing Group *Hollywood* Reynard 95I-Ford	GY	158.951	22.649s	10	193	Running		
15	*Carlos Guerrero (MEX)	22	Simon *Herdez/Viva Mexico!* Lola T95/00-Ford	GY	156.847	22.952s	20	191	Running		
16	*Eliseo Salazar (RCH)	7	Dick Simon *Cristal/Mobil 1/Copec* Lola T95/00-Ford	GY	156.966	22.935s	19	191	Running		
17	Danny Sullivan (USA)	17	PacWest Racing Group *VISA* Reynard 95I-Ford	GY	155.402	23.166s	21	188	Running		
18	Buddy Lazier (USA)	19	Payton-Coyne *The Agfa Car* Lola T94/00-Ford	FS	151.789	23.717s	24	188	Running		
19	Hiro Matsushita (J)	25	Arciero-Wells *Panasonic/Duskin/YKK* Reynard 95I-Ford	FS	154.534	23.296s	22	184	Running		
20	Lyn St. James (USA)	99	Simon *Whitlock Auto Supply* Lola T94/00-Ford	GY	no speed	no time	26	184	Running		
21	Stefan Johansson (S)	16	Bettenhausen *Alumax Aluminum* Penske PC22-Mercedes	GY	158.135	22.765s	15	177	Running		
22	Alessandro Zampedri (I)	34	Payton-Coyne *The Mi-Jack Car* Lola T94/00-Ford	FS	149.410	24.095s	25	173	Running		
23	Emerson Fittipaldi (BR)	2	Marlboro Team Penske Penske PC24-Mercedes	GY	161.201	22.332s	2	122	Accident		
24	Bryan Herta (USA)	4	Ganassi *Target/Scotch Video* Reynard 94I-Ford	GY	152.434	23.617s	23	42	Handling		
25	*Andre Ribeiro (BR)	31	Tasman Motorsports *LCI International* Reynard 95I-Honda	FS	160.692	22.403s	5	35	Suspension damage		
26	Eddie Cheever (USA)	14	A.J. Foyt *Copenhagen Racing* Lola T94/00-Ford	GY	157.813	22.1812	17	32	Handling		

denotes Rookie driver

Caution flags: Lap 1, yellow start; laps 123–127, spin/Salazar. **Total:** two for 6 laps.

Lap leaders: Teo Fabi, 1–27 (27 laps); Al Unser Jr., 28–64 (37 laps); Paul Tracy, 65–75 (11 laps); Michael Andretti, 76 (1 lap); Unser, 77–124 (48 laps); Tracy, 125–143 (19 laps); Unser, 144–178 (35 laps); Tracy, 179–200 (22 laps). **Totals:** Unser, 120 laps; Tracy, 52 laps; Fabi, 27 laps; Andretti, 1 lap.

Fastest race lap: Teo Fabi, 23.601s, 152.537 mph, on lap 4.

Championship positions: 1 Villeneuve, 75; **2** Gordon, 53; **3** Tracy, Rahal and Pruett, 52; **6** Unser, 51; **7** Gugelmin, 47; **8** Fabi, 44; **9** Andretti, 43; **10** E. Fittipaldi and C. Fittipaldi, 35; **12** Cheever, 28; **13** Boesel, 26; **14** Johansson, 22; **15** Sullivan, 21; **16** Salazar, 16; **17** Fernandez, 10; **18** Vasser, 9; **19** Zampedri and de Ferran, 7; **21** Danner, Bachelart and Luyendyk, 6; **24** Matsushita, 5; **25** Herta, 4; **26** Ribeiro, 3; **27** C. Guerrero and Hall, 2; **29** R. Guerrero and Brayton, 1.

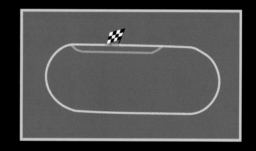

EDS

DETROIT

Robby Gordon made full use of his pole position to take the lead at the start with Al Unser Jr. (1) and Paul Tracy disputing second place, followed by Teo Fabi, Michael Andretti, Scott Pruett, Bobby Rahal, Adrian Fernandez, Jacques Villeneuve, Danny Sullivan, Stefan Johansson, Mauricio Gugelmin and Jimmy Vasser.

ITT AUTOMOTIVE MOVES DETROIT

ITT AUTOMOTIVE

The picturesque temporary road course set within Belle Isle Park provides an interesting test of the drivers' skills, yet its tortuous layout allows precious few opportunities for overtaking. A premium, therefore, is placed on qualifying and track position.

Starting at the front of the field assures a clear track for the race leader, so outright speed is important, while on race day, assuming the pole-sitter can make a clean start, the emphasis switches more toward the elimination of any errors.

Pit strategy also is likely to play a critical role in determining the outcome. And especially the timing of those pit stops.

Robby Gordon and his Walker Racing team played the game to perfection in this year's ITT Automotive Detroit Grand Prix. The 26-year-old Californian recognized the importance of starting at the front of the pack in Derrick Walker's Valvoline/Cummins Reynard-Ford/Cosworth, and even though he fell back to fifth place after encountering tire trouble in the early stages, an inspired pit call, a slice of good fortune and judicious fuel management enabled Gordon to regain the advantage shortly after the halfway mark in the 77-lap race. Gordon took care of the rest of the business, refusing to be distracted by a train of cars in his mirrors and holding on to earn an accomplished victory.

Jimmy Vasser employed a similar strategy en route to his best finish to date for the Target-backed Chip Ganassi Racing team, while Scott Pruett earned the other podium position after another strong drive in Pat Patrick's Firestone Lola-Ford.

QUALIFYING

Newman-Haas Racing was seeking its seventh consecutive pole in Motor City. Michael Andretti had claimed the honor the first four times the race was held, including three times on the downtown course, while Nigel Mansell continued the sequence by qualifying fastest on each of his two visits to Belle Isle.

Andretti, now reunited with the team following a two-year sabbatical, responded by setting quick time in the opening Friday session. He then decided to concentrate on Goodyear's 'option' tire, which was slightly harder than the 'recommended' compound, and despite that he felt he had a good shot at the pole until tangling with Gordon just a few minutes from the end of the final session Saturday afternoon.

'He was trying to get out of my way,' said Andretti, 'so I can't be too mad. He didn't know which way to go. As I was alongside him he lost control. I almost got away with it but I just clipped him with my rear wheel.

'It's very disappointing because the car had more grip than it had all weekend.'

The incident ensured that Gordon's time from Friday remained good enough for the pole, although it was a close-run thing, as Al Unser Jr. posted a substantial improvement and came within a couple of tenths of Gordon's best.

'Everyone was creeping up on my time during the session,' said Gordon. 'I started to get worried that someone would take the pole from me. It's a big relief qualifying is over.'

Unser recorded the fastest time in the second session yet he had to be content with a place on the outside of row one with his Marlboro Penske-Mercedes.

'We just kept working with the car and we helped the car,' said Unser. 'I didn't want to risk crashing the car just to get a couple tenths. We're definitely ready to go racin'.'

Teo Fabi followed up his pole-winning performance in Milwaukee with another strong effort aboard his Combustion Engineering/Indeck Reynard-Ford, which shared row two of the grid with Paul Tracy's Kmart/Budweiser Lola-Ford. Next up following an exciting final session were Pruett, who successfully gambled on negating his Friday time when he switched to the softer Firestone option tire, and Andretti. Adrian Fernandez also drove well to earn his best starting position of the season to date in Rick Galles' Tecate/Quaker State Lola-Mercedes.

RACE

Raul Boesel has not enjoyed much in the way of good fortune since switching to Rahal/Hogan Racing over the winter. In Detroit he didn't even get to see the green flag due to a blown engine. Bryan Herta didn't fare much better, a broken wastegate exhaust pipe causing the rear end of his Target/Scotch Video Reynard to catch fire on the opening lap. His race, too, was over almost before it had started.

The demise of Boesel's Duracell Lola brought out the caution flags midway around the opening lap. Already there had been several notable changes from the original grid order. Gordon maintained his advantage, but now he was followed by Tracy, who executed an audacious pass around the outside of both Fabi and Unser at the first turn. Andretti followed his teammate past Fabi, relegating the disgruntled Italian to fifth ahead of Pruett and Bobby Rahal, who displaced Fernandez.

The restart was altogether more orderly. Gordon once again took off into the lead, although he wasn't able to shake off the advances of the pursuing pack. By lap seven, the first eight cars remained in very tight formation.

The next significant change came on lap eight, when Unser used his Penske's excellent traction characteristics on the exit of Turn 12, then dived to the inside of Tracy under braking for Turn 13. It was a beautifully executed pass, a mirror image of the manner in which he relieved Mansell of the lead in 1994.

Unser repeated the maneuver on the very next lap. This time Gordon was his victim. In their wake, Andretti followed suit with an identical pass on Tracy.

Unser quickly pulled clear of Gordon, who was already struggling as his tires began to lose grip. Next time around the pole-sitter was passed by both Andretti and Tracy, who proceeded to close on Unser with incredible rapidity. Clearly, the Newman-Haas team had made an astute choice in deciding to run the more durable Goodyear tires.

'We were definitely in trouble on our first set of tires,' admitted Gordon. 'I had run those tires in qualifying, and being a soft tire, they were worn out after a total of about 24 laps. I just hoped for a caution so I could change to the harder compound.'

Gordon's wish came true on lap 14. Unser, who also had been fighting for grip, seized the opportunity to make a pit stop, as did most of the field. Surprisingly, Andretti and Tracy also pitted, so Unser, now on the harder tires, resumed in front. The Newman-Haas pair had lost their advantage.

Unser soon took control of the race, edging clear of Tracy, who had usurped Andretti by virtue of a slightly faster pit stop. Farther back, Rahal's hopes of a strong finish were dashed by an incident in the pit lane. The fracas was precipitated by Fabi inadvertently running into the back of Mauricio Gugelmin's Hollywood Reynard, which then caromed into the side of Rahal's Miller Genuine Draft Lola-Mercedes, puncturing its radiator.

The decisive moment of the race came on lap 37, following an accident in Turn 14 involving Christian Danner and Carlos Guerrero. The three leaders – Unser, Tracy and Andretti – chose to remain on the track.

'There was no point in pitting,' explained Roger Penske, who as usual was calling the strategy on Unser's car. 'We weren't within the fuel window. If there hadn't been another yellow, we would have had to pit again.'

The Newman-Haas team continued its simple policy of following Unser's lead. Thus, when Unser chose not to make a pit stop, neither did Tracy or Andretti.

Derrick Walker, by contrast, was prepared to roll the dice. He called Gordon into the pits for fuel and fresh tires, despite knowing that only another extended caution period would enable Gordon to finish the race without an additional pit stop for a splash of fuel.

Veteran team manager Jim McGee followed the same strategy with his man, Pruett, as did Tom Anderson with Vasser.

Four laps later, with the field still circulating behind the pace car, Penske decided to pursue the same strategy. Andretti and the rest followed like lambs – all, that is, except Tracy, who was so close behind Unser that he wasn't able to react fast enough when the race leader turned abruptly into the pit lane. Tracy, understandably, blamed his crew for not informing him of Unser's impending pit stop. The error was compounded when Tracy pitted on the next lap, so the additional delay left the irate Canadian at the tail of the pack. All hope of victory had long since passed by.

'No one informed me we were within the fuel window,' he protested. 'If I'd have known, I'd have been watching out [for Unser to make a pit stop].'

Two huge street sweepers cleared the race track of debris while the drama was unfolding in pit lane, and by the time the green flags flew again at the end of lap 43, the previous front-running regime also had been swept away. Gordon had now regained the lead, followed briefly by Andre Ribeiro, who had moved up impressively with the Tasman team's LCI Reynard-Honda, only to retire soon afterward due to a broken gearbox. Vasser was therefore elevated to second ahead of Pruett, who had made another brief pit stop, taking on a splash of fuel, on lap 41.

A half-dozen laps later, out came the caution flags once more. They were greeted by a collective sigh of relief from the drivers and team members of the leading contenders,

129

Overtaking is extremely difficult on the tortuous parkland circuit but there was no shortage of close action. *Top left:* The Tecate/Quaker State Lola of Adrian Fernandez holds off Teo Fabi's Combustion Engineering/Indeck Reynard.

Center left: Danny Sullivan took the final point on offer with the VISA Reynard but Parker Johnstone failed to finish on his first outing of the season with Comptech Racing's Motorola Cellular Reynard-Honda.

Left: Paul Tracy leads teammate Michael Andretti. Anxious to counter the threat posed by Al Unser Jr., Newman-Haas decided to shadow the Penske team's pit strategy – and lost all chance of victory as a result.

Jimmy Vasser *(above)* resisted unrelenting pressure from Scott Pruett and Michael Andretti in the closing stages to take second place, the best result of his Indy Car career to date. The first four finishers were covered by little more than a second.

The close confines of the Detroit circuit make collisions almost inevitable. The smudge of rubber on the nose of Gil de Ferran's Pennzoil Reynard *(right)* tells its own story.

A question of timing . . .

Michael C. Brown

Robby Gordon's winning drive, during which he displayed caution in the early stages and later held off a group of anxious pursuers, provided further proof of his growing maturity. During practice and qualifying, however, he survived three separate scrapes with the wall.

The first incident came in practice on Friday morning: 'The car went loose in the second part of Turn Two,' explained Gordon, who had been fastest up until that point. 'I backed off the throttle and the car went straight into the wall. It was the first time the car got loose on that part of the track. I was just along for the ride.'

Undaunted, and with the car repaired, Gordon went on to earn the provisional pole later in the afternoon.

The following day, having ventured out onto the track in the waning moments of qualifying, just as Andretti was attempting to bump him from the pole, Gordon once again lost control of his car, which was on fresh tires, in Turn Three. Andretti was unable to avoid clipping the errant Reynard. Fortunately, neither car suffered any serious damage, although the incident certainly cost Andretti any chance of taking the pole.

Gordon's third contretemps came during the race morning warmup, when a momentarily stuck throttle caused him to run into the tire wall in Turn Three. His car once again escaped serious damage. Indeed it was repaired prior to the end of the session.

'These things happen,' he said. 'That's where my crew is 100 percent behind me. If I crash the car, they'll do whatever they have to do to fix it for me. If you have to have accidents, you want to have them in practice, not the race.'

Sure enough, Gordon succeeded in banishing all thought of the incidents to the back of his mind. On Sunday he matched consistency with resilience to move within four points of distant ninth-place finisher Jacques Villeneuve in the battle for this year's PPG Indy Car World Series title.

'It was a tough weekend,' concluded an elated Gordon. 'We fought every step of the way. That's what makes this win so rewarding.'

especially Gordon and the Walker crew. Fuel consumption remained an issue, but with the team's electronics guru Ron Ruzewski keeping a close eye on the telemetry information and Gordon himself making judicious use of the mixture control inside the car, they realized they should have no difficulty in reaching the finish.

'The main key was not to run too hard,' explained Gordon, who took off from the final restart narrowly ahead of a snarling pack comprising Vasser, Pruett, Andretti and Unser. 'The first couple of laps I opened up a bit of a lead and Derrick came on the radio and said, "Hey, don't go too hard."

'My team won this race for me. Derrick made all the right calls and we won by fuel strategy and quick pit stops.'

Vasser, who started a distant 14th after encountering a group of slower cars when his tires were at their best in qualifying, also drove magnificently to record the highest finish of his burgeoning Indy Car career.

'The team called the shots perfectly,' noted Vasser. 'At the end, I knew

Robby had been struggling with his tires and I was hoping he'd struggle some more. But it was very tough to pass. I was more or less hoping for something to happen, and at the same time making sure nothing went wrong with my car.'

Ditto Pruett, whose third-place finish elevated him to third in the PPG Cup standings.

'The tires were fabulous,' said Pruett of his Firestones. 'In fact, I think we had a little edge. We just weren't in a position to do anything about it. It was the same situation we had in Miami. If you have the opportunity, you try to make a pass, but with the caliber of drivers we have at the front of the field, they just don't make mistakes.'

Andretti, in turn, echoed Pruett's comments after finishing a close fourth – a mere 1.055 seconds behind the race winner.

'They were really holding me up but I just couldn't pass,' said Andretti. 'I tried everything but it's impossible to pass.

'Our strategy was right on the

Bottom: **Emerson Fittipaldi lifts a wheel on a patch of newly laid concrete on his way to a disappointing 10th place for Marlboro Team Penske.**

tires. The yellows screwed up the race for us. We were going to do whatever [Unser] Junior did. He didn't pit [on lap 37], so we didn't pit. That's just our luck: The one time Roger makes the wrong call and we follow him!'

Nevertheless, Andretti wasn't looking for excuses: 'The car was good all weekend. The race just didn't go our way. Shoulda, woulda, coulda – didn't!'

Unser was similarly upbeat, having also held a legitimate hope of victory. Indeed he would surely have finished ahead of Andretti had he not been beaten out of the pits during the second round of pit stops.

'I think we had the quickest car out there,' he claimed. 'We gave it away on that last stop. You just can't see those yellows coming and that's the way it was.'

This day the luck wasn't with Andretti or Unser. Gordon was the beneficiary, but he, too, had driven a flawless race. His second victory of the season was no more than he deserved.

Michael C. Brown

SNIPPETS

Photos: Michael C. Brown

• Parker Johnstone (above) made his first PPG Cup start of the season with Comptech Racing's Motorola Cellular Reynard-Honda. Veteran race engineer Trevor Harris also made a welcome return to the series. Johnstone struggled to find a good balance on his car but was running a solid 12th before tangling with Eliseo Salazar.

• Most notable among the improvements made to the parkland circuit since the previous year was a complete repaving and widening of the back straightaway, a.k.a. The Strand. 'They definitely helped the race track,' said Al Unser Jr., 'but there's still nowhere to pass.' If present plans reach fruition, however, all that could change before the Indy cars return to Belle Isle in 1996 . . .

• Newman-Haas Racing caused a stir on Sunday morning when its spare chassis was dispatched to the Ford proving ground in nearby Dearborn. Michael Andretti and Paul Tracy had experienced excessive graining of their Goodyear tires during the final warmup, so veteran driver Mario Andretti was employed to scrub in some fresh rubber for the afternoon's race. Rival team owner Pat Patrick lodged a protest against the ploy, although the IndyCar officials adjudged it to be legal since Mario was not officially entered in Detroit. The session was, however, charged as one of the team's maximum 16 permitted test days.

• Jimmy Vasser's fine drive included a fraught battle in the early stages with Gil de Ferran and Christian Fittipaldi. 'I had a very eventful race,' summarized Vasser (right). 'I got smacked from behind by one rambunctious Brazilian

[de Ferran], then I got blocked by another [Fittipaldi], who was weaving from side to side down the straightaways. It was absolutely ridiculous. Then one Brazilian got by me and proceeded to take the other Brazilian out. I thought they deserved each other at that stage. I was snickering to myself when they both went into the tires.'

• Robby Gordon became the first driver this season to claim the maximum 22 PPG Cup points for winning from the pole and leading most laps. The feat earned him a windfall of $105,000 under the Marlboro Pole Award bonus scheme.

• Carlos Guerrero was forced to switch to his backup '94 Lola after causing extensive damage to his '95 machine on Friday afternoon. The Mexican then completed an awful weekend by colliding with a fourth gearless Christian Danner on race day.

• Alan Mertens (above), technical director of the PacWest team, took on an additional role as Danny Sullivan's race engineer following the sudden resignation of Will Phillips.

PPG INDY CAR WORLD SERIES • ROUND 8

ITT AUTOMOTIVE DETROIT GRAND PRIX

THE RACEWAY ON BELLE ISLE PARK, DETROIT, MICHIGAN

JUNE 11, 77 LAPS – 161.700 MILES

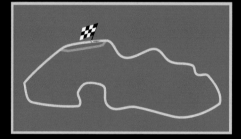

Place	Driver (Nat.)	No.	Team Sponsors Car-Engine	Tires	Q Speed	Q Time	Q Pos.	Laps	Time/Status	Ave.	Pts.
1	Robby Gordon (USA)	5	Walker *Valvoline/Cummins Special* Reynard 95I-Ford	GY	108.318	1m 09.795s	1	77	1h 56m 11.607s	83.499	22
2	Jimmy Vasser (USA)	12	Ganassi *Target/STP* Reynard 95I-Ford	GY	106.723	1m 10.838s	14	77	1h 56m 11.952s	83.495	16
3	Scott Pruett (USA)	20	Patrick Racing *Firestone/Pennzoil* Lola T95/00-Ford	FS	107.405	1m 10.388s	5	77	1h 56m 12.387s	83.489	14
4	Michael Andretti (USA)	6	Newman-Haas *Kmart/Texaco Havoline* Lola T95/00-Ford	GY	107.318	1m 10.445s	6	77	1h 56m 12.662s	83.486	12
5	Al Unser Jr. (USA)	1	Marlboro Team Penske Penske PC24-Mercedes	GY	108.034	1m 09.978s	2	77	1h 56m 15.633s	83.450	10
6	Adrian Fernandez (MEX)	10	Galles *Tecate/Quaker State* Lola T95/00-Mercedes	GY	107.306	1m 10.453s	7	77	1h 56m 18.866s	83.412	8
7	Teo Fabi (I)	33	Forsythe *Combustion Engineering/Indeck* Reynard 95I-Ford	GY	108.014	1m 09.991s	3	77	1h 56m 24.599s	83.343	6
8	Paul Tracy (CDN)	3	Newman-Haas *Kmart/Budweiser* Lola T95/00-Ford	GY	107.816	1m 10.119s	4	77	1h 56m 24.894s	83.340	5
9	Jacques Villeneuve (CDN)	27	Team Green *Player's Ltd.* Reynard 95I-Ford	GY	106.962	1m 10.679s	9	77	1h 56m 52.252s	83.015	4
10	Emerson Fittipaldi (BR)	2	Marlboro Team Penske Penske PC24-Mercedes	GY	106.184	1m 11.197s	17	77	1h 56m 52.974s	83.006	3
11	Stefan Johansson (S)	16	Bettenhausen *Alumax Aluminum* Penske PC23-Mercedes	GY	106.806	1m 10.783s	12	77	1h 56m 53.071s	83.005	2
12	Danny Sullivan (USA)	17	PacWest Racing Group *VISA* Reynard 95I-Ford	GY	106.945	1m 10.690s	10	77	1h 56m 55.803s	82.973	1
13	Marco Greco (BR)	55	Galles *Brastemp/Int. Sports* Lola T95/00-Mercedes	GY	105.005	1m 11.996s	21	77	1h 57m 18.609s	82.704	
14	Hiro Matsushita (J)	25	Arciero-Wells *Panasonic/Duskin/YKK* Reynard 95I-Ford	FS	100.240	1m 15.419s	26	75	Running		
15	Mauricio Gugelmin (BR)	18	PacWest Racing Group *Hollywood* Reynard 95I-Ford	GY	106.885	1m 10.730s	11	74	Running		
16	*Gil de Ferran (BR)	8	Hall Racing *Pennzoil Special* Reynard 95I-Mercedes	GY	106.311	1m 11.112s	16	73	Running		
17	*Christian Fittipaldi (BR)	15	Walker *Marlboro/Chapeco Special* Reynard 95I-Ford	GY	106.757	1m 10.815s	13	72	Running		
18	*Andre Ribeiro (BR)	31	Tasman Motorsports *LCI International* Reynard 95I-Honda	FS	105.796	1m 11.459s	19	52	Transmission		
19	Parker Johnstone (USA)	49	Comptech *Motorola Cellular* Reynard 95I-Honda	FS	100.210	1m 15.441s	27	49	Accident		
20	*Eliseo Salazar (RCH)	7	Dick Simon *Cristal/Mobil 1/Copec* Lola T95/00-Ford	GY	103.656	1m 12.934s	24	47	Accident		
21	*Carlos Guerrero (MEX)	22	Simon *Herdez/Viva Mexico!* Lola T94/00-Ford	GY	99.820	1m 15.736s	28	36	Accident		
22	Christian Danner (D)	64	Project Indy *No-Touch/Van Dyne* Reynard 94I-Ford	GY	104.683	1m 12.218s	23	35	Accident		
23	Eric Bachelart (B)	19	Payton-Coyne *The Agfa Car* Lola T94/00-Ford	FS	103.487	1m 13.053s	25	33	Transmission		
24	Bobby Rahal (USA)	9	Rahal/Hogan *Miller Genuine Draft* Lola T95/00-Mercedes	GY	107.026	1m 10.637s	8	16	Holed radiator		
25	Eddie Cheever (USA)	14	A.J. Foyt *Copenhagen Racing* Lola T95/00-Ford	GY	105.443	1m 11.697s	20	13	Accident		
26	Alessandro Zampedri (I)	34	Payton-Coyne *The Mi-Jack Car* Lola T94/00-Ford	FS	104.789	1m 12.145s	22	13	Accident		
27	Bryan Herta (USA)	4	Ganassi *Target/Scotch Video* Reynard 95I-Ford	GY	106.033	1m 11.298s	18	1	Fire		
NS	Raul Boesel (BR)	11	Rahal/Hogan *Duracell Charger* Lola T95/00-Mercedes	GY	106.717	1m 10.842s	15	–	Did not start/engine		

* denotes Rookie driver

Caution flags: Lap 1, stall/Boesel; laps 13–16, accident/Bachelart; laps 31–33, accident/C. Fittipaldi; laps 36–42, accident/Guerrero and Danner; laps 49–55, accident/Johnstone and Salazar. **Total:** five for 22 laps.

Lap leaders: Robby Gordon, 1–8 (8 laps); Al Unser Jr., 9–40 (32 laps); Paul Tracy, 41–42 (2 laps); Gordon, 43–77 (35 laps). **Totals:** Gordon, 43 laps; Unser, 32 laps; Tracy, 2 laps.

Fastest race lap: Michael Andretti, 1m 12.339s, 104.509 mph, on lap 11.

Championship positions: 1 Villeneuve, 79; **2** Gordon, 75; **3** Pruett, 66; **4** Unser, 61; **5** Tracy, 57; **6** Andretti, 55; **7** Rahal, 52; **8** Fabi, 50; **9** Gugelmin, 47; **10** E. Fittipaldi, 38; **11** C. Fittipaldi, 35; **12** Cheever, 28; **13** Boesel, 26; **14** Vasser, 25; **15** Johansson, 24; **16** Sullivan, 22; **17** Fernandez, 18; **18** Salazar, 16; **19** Zampedri and de Ferran, 7; **21** Danner, Bachelart and Luyendyk, 6; **24** Matsushita, 5; **25** Herta, 4; **26** Ribeiro, 3; **27** C. Guerrero and Hall, 2; **29** R. Guerrero and Brayton, 1.

EDS

PORTLAND

So far as the vast majority of the record crowd of 81,000 was concerned, Al Unser Jr. had scored a clear victory in the Budweiser/G.I. Joe's 200, presented by Texaco/Havoline. The result apparently catapulted the defending PPG Cup series champion into the lead of the 1995 title-chase.

But then came the mandatory post-race technical inspection. Within a few minutes, a rumor began to circulate to the effect that something was amiss with the race-winning Marlboro Penske-Mercedes. One by one, the cars of the other top finishers were examined and released. But not the Penske. Finally, after almost three hours of deliberation, IndyCar Vice President of Competition Kirk Russell solemnly announced that the winning car did not comply with the so-called 'two-inch rule.' The penalty would be exclusion from the results.

Jimmy Vasser was instead declared the winner. It was perhaps no more than he deserved following a heads-up drive in Chip Ganassi's Target/STP Reynard-Ford/Cosworth. But the story didn't end there. Marlboro Team Penske lodged a protest against the stewards' ruling. When that was denied, a formal appeal was submitted. The results were held in abeyance while a panel of three judges was appointed and both sides prepared their cases to be presented before an Appeals Court. Ultimately, in September, following a three-day hearing, the matter was decided in Penske's favor. And Unser's victory was restored.

Jacques Villeneuve made a storming start from pole position to grab an early lead *(left)* but the Penske-Mercedes of Al Unser Jr. went on to dominate the race.

Jimmy Vasser *(below)* was proclaimed the winner on Sunday evening – but prematurely, as it turned out.

Villeneuve backed up his comments by being fastest in qualifying on both days with Team Green's Player's Ltd./Klein Tools Reynard-Ford. Just to be sure of his first-ever pole in an Indy car, the 26-year-old improved his own new track record three times during the final half-hour session.

'We made little improvements [to the car] every session and it was very well balanced today,' he said. 'With the Indy Car series as competitive as it is, you need a lap near to perfect to be on the pole. I think that was the nearest to a perfect lap I have ever done.

'Of course, pole is not as important as the race, but it means you have put together the best lap, so it's always a great feeling to be the fastest car out there.'

Target/Chip Ganassi Racing made a welcome return to true competitiveness, with Vasser claiming the outside front row grid placing and teammate Bryan Herta setting the second fastest time of the weekend during Saturday morning practice. In fact, Herta and Villeneuve were the only members of the sub-one minute club, although Herta didn't improve as much as he expected on new tires and wound up a slightly disappointed eighth.

Unser found a significant improvement on the second day, jumping from ninth on the provisional grid to third ahead of Mauricio Gugelmin, who wasn't happy with the handling of his Hollywood/PacWest Reynard.

'It's hard to put a lap together,' said the Brazilian. 'If I go deep into the corners, it goes loose on the exit. I managed to do a good lap but it's not the answer.'

Countrymen Christian Fittipaldi (Marlboro/Chapeco Reynard-Ford) and Gil de Ferran (Pennzoil Reynard-Mercedes) occupied row three, both showing good form on their first visit to Portland, followed by Paul Tracy, who was far from content despite being fastest of the Lola contingent.

'Fundamentally, we've just got something wrong suspension-wise,' confided Tracy. 'The car's getting a little better but we're just struggling with understeer and we can't put our finger on it.'

RACE

Portland International Raceway was at its very best on race morning. The track was bathed in sunshine, with the snow-capped Mount Hood providing a majestic vista to the east. Already a huge crowd was beginning to gather. It was a glorious spectacle.

An entertaining PPG-Firestone Indy Lights contest provided a suitable curtain-raiser and the spacious spectator viewing areas, including a couple of exciting new vantage points in Turn One and on the back straightaway, were crammed almost to capacity well before the Indy cars began assembling on the main straightaway prior to the scheduled start at 1 p.m.

Villeneuve was determined to make full use of his advantage of starting from the pole, and sure enough he accelerated hard and early. Official starter Jim Swintal confessed afterward that he considered waving off the start, but given the proximity of the very tight Festival Curves, which often provide first-corner dramatics due to the

QUALIFYING

The visit to Oregon represented the first opportunity of the season for the Indy Car drivers to display their talents on a permanent road course. It was a task most of the front-runners relished.

'It's easier to get up to speed on a road course,' declared PPG Cup points leader Jacques Villeneuve. 'You can hustle a car more. A street circuit, like Detroit, is always very dirty on the first day; a track like this is already good.

'On a street course you work your way around the track like a go-kart – there's no room for mistakes because of the walls – but at road courses you can work on the setup of the car much easier.'

Right: Stefan Johansson lost a couple of places when his Alumax Penske ran out of fuel within sight of the flag.

It was another disappointing race for Gil de Ferran *(far right)* but Bobby Rahal *(center right)* was on the rostrum again with the Miller Genuine Draft Lola.

Marco Greco *(below right)* scored his first points of the season with Dick Simon's Lola-Ford, while fellow countryman Raul Boesel *(bottom)* brought the Duracell Lola-Mercedes home fifth.

In the thick of the action as ever, Michael Andretti *(bottom right)* finished an incident-filled afternoon in fourth place.

Photos: Michael C. Brown

sometimes overwhelming temptation for drivers to leave their braking too late, he decided to err on the side of safety and wave the green. The race was on.

Unser was tucked in close behind Villeneuve and immediately passed Vasser, whose rear wheels broke loose momentarily as he jumped on the throttle. Tracy, meanwhile, made a sensational start from the fourth row, jumping all the way up to third as he outbraked Vasser in the middle of the Festival turns.

Villeneuve completed the opening lap with a handy one-second cushion over Unser and Tracy, with Vasser holding down fourth ahead of Gugelmin, Christian Fittipaldi, de Ferran, Herta and Rahal. Andretti rounded out the top 10.

The leader extended his advantage by as much as a second per lap over the opening three tours, but then, just as swiftly, Unser began to reduce the deficit. By lap seven the two leaders were running in close formation, and clearly Unser had his sights set on the lead. Tracy couldn't (or wouldn't) match that pace in the early stages, but he in turn began to edge clear of Vasser, while Gugelmin, in fifth, struggled to keep a long train of anxious pursuers behind his PacWest Reynard.

By the 20-lap mark it had become obvious Unser was in possession of the fastest car. The PPG Cup champion dodged and weaved as he tried to find a way past Villeneuve, but the Canadian withstood the challenge bravely. Until lap 25, that is, when Unser forced him to adopt a defensive line under braking for the Festival Curves. At the last moment, Unser jinked wide to the outside, and when Villeneuve slid wide after leaving his braking just a fraction too late and momentarily locking his front wheels, Unser nipped smartly through on the inside. It was a classical example of the master teaching the youngster a lesson.

'I wish I could say I set him up,' recalled Unser with a gleam in his eye, offering his young rival the benefit of any doubt. 'I got a good run on him out of the last corner [Turn Nine] and he definitely knows how to make his car extremely wide! He took his car very deep in there [at the Festival] and I tried to get right over on a wide line so he didn't know where I was. I was hoping it would distract him and it did. For whatever reason, he went in too deep and I was able to get by.

'It reminded me of a couple of

Michael C. Brown

years ago, when [Nigel] Mansell made the same mistake Jacques did.'

Unser, rightly, found the maneuver intensely satisfying. And once into the lead he quickly made good his escape, pulling out a gap of more than nine seconds before making his first scheduled pit stop on lap 33. Villeneuve regained the point for three laps before he, too, stopped for service. Unser then took control of the proceedings and was never seriously challenged. He eventually won by a margin of 28.561 seconds.

The real race was going on way behind the #1 Marlboro Penske. Villeneuve resumed in second after his pit stop, but soon Tracy began to challenge. On lap 54, just before the pace car was summoned following an incident at the Festival Curves, Tracy took advantage of a momentary hesitation by Villeneuve amidst traffic by diving through on the inside in Turn One.

Unfortunately, neither Canadian survived until the finish. Villeneuve was forced out on lap 70, when a rear shock absorber mounting failed under braking for the Festival Curves, while Tracy, who woke up in the morning feeling lousy and was diagnosed as suffering from tonsillitis, succumbed to a similarly obscure mechanical problem when his clutch – these days generally regarded as one of the most reliable of components – exploded just seven laps from the end.

Their misfortunes should have played into the hands of Christian Fittipaldi, who had driven strongly

and sensibly in Derrick Walker's Marlboro/Chapeco Reynard . . . until spinning off the road in Turn Three while running all alone in third place on lap 83. Worse, he allowed the engine to stall.

'It's a shame because we were done with the pit stops and very little could still happen to ruin a good finish,' said a crestfallen Fittipaldi. 'I'm really mad at myself because I know that one mistake is always too many in motor racing.'

At least he was able to admit his error. This day the otherwise impressive young rookie deserved much more than his eventual 11th-place finish.

Herta also held aspirations of a solid finish, having run strongly in the early stages. He gained two positions during his first pit stop, then moved up to fifth when Vasser, his Target/Chip Ganassi teammate, braked too late into the Festival Curves while trying to lap a struggling Scott Pruett on lap 47. Sadly, Herta's hopes evaporated at the same place just four laps later, when Andretti misjudged his braking and punted Herta squarely in the rear, just as he was turning into the corner. The impact was enough to force Herta out of the race.

Andretti rejoined behind Vasser (again) and de Ferran, then clambered back to third place, behind teammate Tracy, before being forced into the pits to change a delaminated rear tire (incurred following another clash with Vasser) less than 10 laps before the finish.

The various dramas enabled Vasser to regain second place on lap 96, and in the final stages he had to work hard to keep at bay a charging Bobby Rahal, who had driven with his usual blend of speed and guile in the Miller Genuine Draft Lola-Mercedes.

'I was gaining on Jimmy at the end but I couldn't afford to make a run at him because I would lose so much on the track if I missed the pass,' concluded the three-time champion, whose Rahal/Hogan crew had been forced to install a new engine in his car following the race morning warmup.

'That was a little worrisome,' he confessed, 'because you always like to run in a new engine – to make sure there are no leaks – but the crew did a great job. The car ran well. We made changes with each pit stop and the car responded.'

Stefan Johansson rose as high as fourth after a fine run from a disappointing 12th on the grid in the Alumax Penske PC23-Mercedes, only to run out of fuel on the exit of the final corner. A close-following Andretti had absolutely no chance of avoiding the Swede's suddenly slowing car and punted it squarely in the rear.

'That was really a fun race,' said Johansson, who fell to sixth in the final classification. 'It was hard because there was always someone close behind and someone in front to catch.'

Andretti's dramatic day ended with fourth-place points, while Raul Boesel completed a good day for Rahal/Hogan by finishing fifth in the Duracell Lola-Mercedes.

Vasser stakes his claim

Al Unser Jr.'s emotional roller-coaster continued in Portland. The defending series champion drove exquisitely to what appeared to be a clear victory, only for his joy to be succeeded by utter dejection following notification that his Penske did not comply with the 'two-inch rule.'

The regulation has been in effect for more than a dozen years, introduced as a means of reducing performance after the 'skirted' cars were outlawed. It demands a minimum clearance of two inches between the lowest point on the car's underbody – usually a skid-plate mounted beneath the fuel tank (a.k.a. 'the reference plane') – and the bottom of the sidepod.

In fact, Unser's car, which had benefited from a brand-new underbody, had been running noticeably lower than its rivals all weekend, regularly emitting a plume of fine dust particles from its Jabroc (an expensive, high-density wood material) skid-plates. In accordance with usual IndyCar procedure, the officials notified the Penske team to that effect.

'We always inform the crew of a bottoming

Unser wins, then loses, then wins again

condition because that can exacerbate the problem [and grind away the skid-plate],' said IndyCar Vice President of Competition Kirk Russell.

Penske chose to ignore the warnings, and 10 laps from the end of the race, one of the skid-plates became detached from the bottom of the car. The team argued that because

the plate had been lost – due, it was claimed, to Unser running over a high curb – then the measurement was invalid. The officials didn't buy that one.

'The integrity of the rule is important because the teams prepare their race cars based on the integrity of the rules,' said Russell. 'We inspect the cars regularly and it's seldom that we find a car that is out of specification.

'The Penske car has three areas that act as a reference plane. One piece was torn off but the two remaining pieces were severely worn and the measurement did not meet the specification.'

Accordingly, Unser's car was excluded from the official results, although Roger Penske declared his team's innocence. A lengthy protest and appeal process ensued during the following three months, and it wasn't until September that the matter was finally resolved during a three-day Appeals Court hearing.

The judges deliberated for two more days before revealing their decision, which was in favor of Penske Racing. Unser's victory and PPG Cup points were restored.

chael C. Brown

SNIPPETS

• For the first time this season, the Firestone Firehawk tires were no match for the Goodyear Eagles. Lead driver Scott Pruett was intensely frustrated after qualifying only 17th and finishing 13th. 'From the first day we decided to re-enter Indy racing, we knew this season would be one of learning,' said Bridgestone/Firestone Motorsports Manager Al Speyer *(below)*. 'It has taken until the ninth event for us to encounter somewhat of a problem. We realized there would be situations of this nature.'

Photos: Michael C. Brown

• 'We are on holiday,' claimed Renault Sport technical director Bernard Dudot when asked to explain why he and his immediate boss, Christian Contzen, were visiting the Indy Car race at PIR. The pair spent most of the weekend in the company of Jacques Villeneuve, who was subsequently invited to test a Formula 1 Williams-Renault at Silverstone, England . . .

• Sector times taken through the twisting series of turns at the western end of the circuit revealed Stefan Johansson's Alumax Penske-Mercedes to be fastest on a regular basis, although a broken rear wing during the final qualifying session prevented the Swede from repeating his best lap time from the morning practice.

• Robby Gordon did not have a good weekend. He was consistently outpaced by Walker Racing teammate Christian Fittipaldi and fell to 16th on the grid after a locating bracket for the gear shift lever broke in qualifying. Gordon *(above)* made two poor pit stops but salvaged useful PPG Cup points by finishing eighth.

• Gil de Ferran posted another strong performance in Jim Hall's Pennzoil Reynard-Mercedes. The impressive Brazilian was running fourth until being eliminated by a broken throttle mechanism three laps from the finish.

• Danny Sullivan and the VISA/PacWest team encountered a major scare when a miscommunication on their second pit stop led to Sullivan accelerating a mite too early and tearing the refueling hose from the pit-side fuel tank. Leaking methanol erupted into flames within a few seconds, but sterling work by several crews, including A.J. Foyt's, enabled everyone to escape injury.

• Following the long-established lead taken by major league baseball, IndyCar President Andrew Craig *(right)* announced in Portland that the PPG Cup series would host a 'spring training' routine of testing at the new Homestead Motorsports Park in Florida prior to the start of the 1996 season.

'We think it's a great way to kick-start the season with a major promotion for Indy Car racing,' said Craig. 'It will provide a great opportunity for the fans to get up close and personal with the teams and the drivers, and it will allow the media to get some stories during what is traditionally a fairly quiet time of the year.'

PPG INDY CAR WORLD SERIES • ROUND 9
BUDWEISER/G.I. JOE'S 200 PRESENTED BY TEXACO/HAVOLINE

PORTLAND INTERNATIONAL RACEWAY, PORTLAND, OREGON

JUNE 25, 102 LAPS – 198.900 MILES

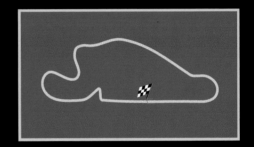

Place	Driver (Nat.)	No.	Team Sponsors Car-Engine	Tires	Q Speed	Q Time	Q Pos.	Laps	Time/Status	Ave.	Pts.
†1	Al Unser Jr. (USA)	1	Marlboro Team Penske Penske PC24-Mercedes	GY	116.875	1m 00.064s	3	102	1h 54m 49.410s	103.933	†
2	Jimmy Vasser (USA)	12	Ganassi *Target/STP* Reynard 95I-Ford	GY	116.969	1m 00.016s	2	102	1h 55m 17.971s	103.504	20
3	Bobby Rahal (USA)	9	Rahal/Hogan *Miller Genuine Draft* Lola T95/00-Mercedes	GY	116.127	1m 00.451s	9	102	1h 55m 19.229s	103.486	16
4	Michael Andretti (USA)	6	Newman-Haas *Kmart/Texaco Havoline* Lola T95/00-Ford	GY	116.029	1m 00.502s	10	102	1h 55m 30.433s	103.318	14
5	Raul Boesel (BR)	11	Rahal/Hogan *Duracell Charger* Lola T95/00-Mercedes	GY	115.908	1m 00.565s	11	102	1h 55m 32.071s	103.294	12
6	Stefan Johansson (S)	16	Bettenhausen *Alumax Aluminum* Penske PC23-Mercedes	GY	115.901	1m 00.569s	12	101	Out of fuel		10
7	Mauricio Gugelmin (BR)	18	PacWest Racing Group *Hollywood* Reynard 95I-Ford	GY	116.754	1m 00.126s	4	101	Running		8
8	Robby Gordon (USA)	5	Walker *Valvoline/Cummins Special* Reynard 95I-Ford	GY	115.444	1m 00.809s	16	101	Running		6
9	Adrian Fernandez (MEX)	10	Galles *Tecate/Quaker State* Lola T95/00-Mercedes	GY	115.514	1m 00.772s	14	101	Running		5
10	*Gil de Ferran (BR)	8	Hall Racing *Pennzoil Special* Reynard 95I-Mercedes	GY	116.678	1m 00.166s	6	100	Running		4
11	Marco Greco (BR)	99	Simon *Brastemp/Int. Sports* Lola T95/00-Ford	GY	113.537	1m 01.830s	22	100	Running		3
12	*Christian Fittipaldi (BR)	15	Walker *Marlboro/Chapeco Special* Reynard 95I-Ford	GY	116.751	1m 00.128s	5	100	Running		2
13	Scott Pruett (USA)	20	Patrick Racing *Firestone/Pennzoil* Lola T95/00-Ford	FS	115.143	1m 00.968s	17	99	Running		1
14	*Andre Ribeiro (BR)	31	Tasman Motorsports *LCI International* Reynard 95I-Honda	FS	114.090	1m 01.531s	20	99	Running		
15	*Eliseo Salazar (RCH)	7	Dick Simon *Cristal/Mobil 1/Copec* Lola T95/00-Ford	GY	113.448	1m 01.878s	23	99	Running		
16	Alessandro Zampedri (I)	34	Payton-Coyne *The Mi-Jack Car* Lola T94/00-Ford	FS	111.768	1m 02.809s	25	97	Running		
17	Hiro Matsushita (J)	25	Arciero-Wells *Panasonic/Duskin/YKK* Reynard 95I-Ford	FS	112.270	1m 02.528s	24	96	Running		
18	Paul Tracy (CDN)	3	Newman-Haas *Kmart/Budweiser* Lola T95/00-Ford	GY	116.567	1m 00.223s	7	95	Clutch		
19	Eric Bachelart (B)	19	Payton-Coyne *The Agfa Car* Lola T94/00-Ford	FS	110.662	1m 13.436s	26	95	Running		
20	Jacques Villeneuve (CDN)	27	Team Green *Player's Ltd.* Reynard 95I-Ford	GY	117.614	59.687s	1	70	Suspension		2
21	Emerson Fittipaldi (BR)	2	Marlboro Team Penske Penske PC24-Mercedes	GY	115.460	1m 00.800s	15	69	Engine		
22	Danny Sullivan (USA)	17	PacWest Racing Group *VISA* Reynard 95I-Ford	GY	115.038	1m 01.023s	18	63	Pit fire		
23	Teo Fabi (I)	33	Forsythe *Combustion Engineering/Indeck* Reynard 95I-Ford	GY	115.849	1m 00.596s	13	62	Accident		
24	*Carlos Guerrero (MEX)	22	Simon *Herdez/Viva Mexico!* Lola T95/00-Ford	GY	113.645	1m 01.771s	21	62	Accident		
25	Eddie Cheever (USA)	14	A.J. Foyt *Copenhagen Racing* Lola T95/00-Ford	GY	114.671	1m 01.218s	19	60	Overheating		
26	Bryan Herta (USA)	4	Ganassi *Target/Scotch Video* Reynard 95I-Ford	GY	116.534	1m 00.240s	8	49	Accident		

* denotes Rookie driver

Caution flags: Laps 50–52, accident/Herta and Andretti; laps 63–68, accident/Fabi and Guerrero. **Total:** two for nine laps.

Lap leaders: Jacques Villeneuve, 1–24 (24 laps); Al Unser Jr., 25–32 (8 laps); Villeneuve, 33–34 (2 laps); Unser, 35–102 (68 laps). **Totals:** Unser, 76 laps; Villeneuve, 26 laps.

Fastest race lap: Al Unser Jr., 1m 01.466s, 114.209 mph, on lap 7.

Championship positions: 1 Villeneuve and Gordon, 81; 3 Andretti, 69; 4 Rahal, 68; 5 Pruett, 67; 6 Unser, 61; 7 Tracy, 57; 8 Gugelmin, 55; 9 Fabi, 50; 10 Vasser, 45; 11 E. Fittipaldi and Boesel, 38; 13 C. Fittipaldi, 37; 14 Johansson, 34; 15 Cheever, 28; 16 Fernandez, 23; 17 Sullivan, 22; 18 Salazar, 16; 19 de Ferran, 11; 20 Zampedri, 7; 21 Danner, Bachelart and Luyendyk, 6; 24 Matsushita, 5; 25 Herta, 4; 26 Greco and Ribeiro, 3; 28 C. Guerrero and Hall, 2; 30 R. Guerrero and Brayton, 1.

† Al Unser Jr. initially disqualified but reinstated as winner after appeal hearing in September. Championship positions and points totals provisional pending outcome of appeal.

EDS

ROAD AMERICA

Jacques Villeneuve has developed a real affinity for Road America. He is now two-for-two on the challenging and ultra-fast Wisconsin road course.

As was the case in 1994, when he earned his maiden Indy Car victory, Villeneuve, working in cahoots with veteran race engineer Tony Cicale, opted for a low-downforce setup on Team Green's Player's Ltd. Reynard-Ford/Cosworth. Once again it paid dividends on the long straightaways which dominate the four-mile layout.

'We managed to get the car working in the corners, despite running little downforce,' said Villeneuve, 'so we had a very strong car.'

Villeneuve's Barry Green-led crew contributed greatly to his victory by calling the pit strategy perfectly. By contrast, the hopes of Brazilians Gil de Ferran and Christian Fittipaldi were effectively dashed during the second round of pit stops. Countryman Raul Boesel also was set to challenge until his Duracell Lola-Mercedes succumbed to transmission failure.

Paul Tracy overcame intense pain from a broken left foot to finish a strong second for Newman-Haas Racing, while another fine drive by Jimmy Vasser enabled him to become the first driver to earn three consecutive podium appearances during this intensely competitive season. Andre Ribeiro's LCI Reynard-Honda shadowed Vasser across the finish line to ensure a career-best result both for himself and the emerging Tasman Motorsports team.

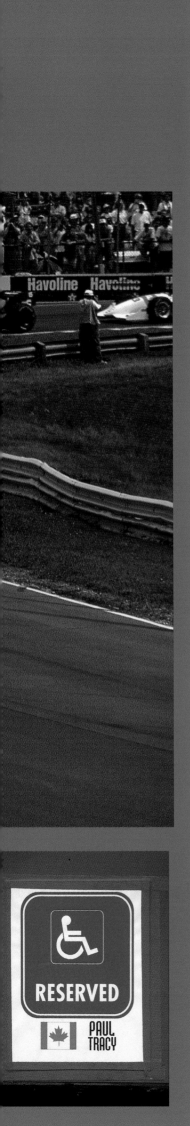

Capitalizing on his second pole position in succession, Jacques Villeneuve sets about consolidating his advantage over the Pennzoil Reynard of Gil de Ferran, with Raul Boesel, Michael Andretti, Al Unser Jr., Scott Pruett, Paul Tracy, Bobby Rahal and Christian Fittipaldi leading the pursuit.

QUALIFYING

A recent repaving of the race track ensured a dramatic increase in speeds compared to the previous year. Several teams, including Newman-Haas, PacWest, Forsythe and Patrick Racing, had taken the opportunity to test on the new surface, although, ironically, their conclusions were upset by some subsequent patching in many of the corners following the SCCA June Sprints race weekend.

'The track's really slippery compared to when we tested here,' reported Michael Andretti. 'They took away a lot of grip. It's about two seconds per lap slower than it was.'

Gradually, however, as the race cars laid down some rubber on the new track sealing compound, the lap times began to tumble. The final session of qualifying proved significantly faster than on Friday, and the closing few minutes provided some sensational action as no fewer than 24 drivers dipped below Paul Tracy's old lap record of 1m 45.416s.

Andretti was the first to show his hand, rising to the top of the charts with a lap at 1m 41.673s in his Kmart/Texaco Havoline Lola-Ford. De Ferran then took over the premier position, stopping the clocks at 1m 41.294s on his final flying lap with Jim Hall's Pennzoil Reynard-Mercedes. Even that wasn't good enough. A half-mile or so farther back on the race track, Villeneuve was determined to improve upon his third position.

'I knew I was P-3, and on the last lap you go a little bit over the edge,' said Villeneuve with an impish grin. 'Sometimes you crash and sometimes it comes off. This time it worked!'

So Villeneuve was able to secure the pole. De Ferran had to settle for a position on the outside of the front row.

'That was fun,' he admitted. 'I enjoyed it. I saw the time on my dash and I said, "No way anyone's gonna beat that!" But it was not to be. My guys came on the radio and said Jacques had beaten me. He did well.'

Andretti was a little disappointed to end up third. 'I think there was a little more time in there,' he said.

'It was just a question of timing. It was incredible how much grip the track picked up toward the end, and we just weren't quite able to take advantage of it.'

Boesel moved up strongly to secure his best grid position since the season opener in Miami, while

Al Unser Jr. was fifth fastest for Marlboro Team Penske, hindered by a tad too much understeer. Another notable effort was posted by Scott Pruett, despite slipping to seventh in Pat Patrick's Lola-Ford after setting fastest time on the first day.

'Actually I'm surprised,' declared Pruett. 'We're consistent, just not quite fast enough. Everyone else is running strong; it's a very competitive field.'

Andre Ribeiro overcame major gearbox problems on Friday and a clutch failure Saturday morning to qualify 12th on his very first visit to Road America in the Tasman team's backup LCI Reynard-Honda. The similarly equipped Parker Johnstone posted his best performance to date, 13th in Comptech Racing's Motorola Cellular machine.

RACE

The small vacation town of Elkhart Lake, set amid Wisconsin's picturesque Kettle Moraine region, offers a scene of peaceful tranquility for most of the year. A mile or so to the south, the famed Road America race track provides a curious juxtaposition, especially when the Indy cars come to town. This year a combination of the circuit's 40th anniversary and the wide-open nature of the PPG Cup title-chase was sufficient to draw the largest single-day crowd in the state's professional sports history.

Trust me, with 75,000 enthusiastic race fans eagerly anticipating a 200-mile race on one of the finest (and fastest) road courses in the world, peace and tranquility are not words that spring readily to mind.

The excitement reached fever pitch as Villeneuve prepared to lead the 28-strong field up toward the green flag. The pole-sitter slowed the pace to a crawl through the final corner, Turn 14, then unleashed 800 of Cosworth's finest horses as he accelerated to almost 200 mph on the drag race up the hill and past the pits toward Turn One.

Villeneuve was able to maintain his advantage over de Ferran, while Boesel got the better of Andretti in the initial spurt. Andretti tried to redress the situation under braking for Turn One, and then again at Turn Five, but to no avail. Boesel remained in third.

Unser was next, fifth at the end of the first lap, just ahead of Pruett and Tracy, who had made one of his patented early charges after another

disappointing final period of qualifying had left his Kmart/Budweiser Lola a distant 11th on the grid.

Tracy moved past Pruett on lap two, then gained two more positions when, just ahead of him, Andretti and Unser were involved in a frightening accident on the high-speed acceleration test leading away from Turn Three.

'I guess he had a run on me and I didn't know he was there in my blind spot,' said Andretti, who was fortunate to emerge unscathed after his car spun around several times without ever making heavy contact with the barriers. 'It was just racing luck. It's such close racing.'

Unser, however, viewed the incident from a slightly different perspective: 'I went up alongside him and he moved over on me,' he claimed after limping to the next corner and then pulling off with a broken left-front suspension. 'I'm upset with Michael because he knows better. When I saw him starting to move back and forth I would have backed out of it, but there was nothing I could do because I was too committed.'

The remainder of the field circulated behind the pace car for two laps while the debris was cleared. Villeneuve then resumed in control of the proceedings, as he would be for the rest of the afternoon.

The French-Canadian's only real drama came during the warmup on race morning, when a glitch within the full-throttle shift mechanism prevented him from completing more than a couple of laps. But his Player's Reynard ran perfectly when it mattered.

'The car was slipping a bit in the corners,' he said, 'especially on full tanks, but it was fast.'

De Ferran gave valiant chase in second place. An inoperative clutch wasn't causing a problem out on the track, but de Ferran realized it would severely hamper his progress during the pit stops. Accordingly, team manager Gerald Davis decided to call de Ferran into the pits one lap earlier than originally planned. That way, he reasoned, there would be no other cars in the way when the crew went to push-start the Pennzoil Reynard.

Fuel strategy is always critical on the four-mile track, and while most of the teams chose to stop after 17 laps, Villeneuve, Tracy and Bryan Herta, in Chip Ganassi's Target/Scotch Video Reynard-Ford, all gained an advantage by staying out for one extra circuit on hot tires.

141

Main picture: The magnificent Road America circuit allowed Gil de Ferran to display his unquestioned talent but there was no change in his luck.

Insets, left to right: An aggressive pass by teammate Bobby Rahal left Raul Boesel scrambling across the sand trap at Turn Six; Paul Tracy overcame intense pain from his broken left foot to take a brave second place for Newman-Haas; rookie Andre Ribeiro confirmed the potential of the Honda engine with fourth place in the LCI Reynard; Jimmy Vasser turned in another impressive drive at the wheel of the Target/STP Reynard.
Photos: Michael C. Brown

Michael C. Brown

The feel-good factor

Jacques Villeneuve's third win of the season moved him into a commanding lead in the PPG Cup standings. His status was further assisted by the fact Robby Gordon, with whom he was tied for the lead following the race at Portland, endured a dismal weekend in Wisconsin, retiring early with transmission failure after a couple of excursions into the scenery.

Villeneuve arrived in the dairy state in a confident state of mind. In 1994, of course, he emerged triumphant following a battle with Paul Tracy, while this time around his self-assurance had received an additional boost after claiming his first Indy Car pole in Portland.

'Road America is a lot of fun to drive,' he asserted, 'especially when you have a good car. It's a long track, with long straight lines, and so you can run very low downforce. We had a good setup here last year and we learned a few more things at Portland, so we were able to run very strong.

'It was a lot of work but the whole of Team Green did a tremendous job. We have a very good chemistry within the team. It's one thing to have a fast car but it has to feel good too. So it's really important to work well with your crew.

'It's more important to have the chemistry with the team than to have the best equipment.'

At this stage in the season, it seemed Villeneuve had the best of both worlds.

Villeneuve resumed with an increased lead over Boesel (who had moved past de Ferran), only for his margin to be erased by another full-course caution caused when Eddie Cheever tangled with Eric Bachelart and was punted into the sand trap at Turn 12.

Christian Fittipaldi had moved up from ninth to fourth in his Marlboro/Chapeco Reynard, ahead of Herta and Tracy, who was hindered by his broken foot and, as he feared, had stalled his engine after stopping for service.

Tracy blew past Herta under braking for Turn Five at the restart, and after Herta had been forced wide on the exit, he then paid the price of trying to hold off a determined Bobby Rahal (Miller Genuine Draft Lola-Mercedes) up the hill to Turn Six. Herta was hung out to dry on the outside line and promptly skated off into the sand trap.

After another brief caution, Tracy continued his charge by muscling his way past Boesel into Turn Five, only to lose the place again next time around when he ran wide on the exit of Turn One. A close-following Teo Fabi also took the opportunity to nip past when Tracy slid sideways in Turn Three, due to dirty tires. But the Canadian fought right back with a magnificent outside-line pass at Turn Five. This was great stuff!

The caution flags flew once more on lap 30, due to an incident between PacWest teammates Mauricio Gugelmin and Danny Sullivan. After a quick review of the race leader's fuel consumption, Barry Green called in Villeneuve for his second pit stop.

The strategy caught some teams by surprise, since 19 laps is widely regarded as the maximum an Indy car will achieve on a 40-gallon tankful of methanol. Boesel, Tracy, Jimmy Vasser (Target/STP Reynard-Ford), Fabi, Rahal, Adrian Fernandez (Tecate/Quaker State Lola-Mercedes), Pruett – who was delayed by a puncture early in the race – and Eric Bachelart (Agfa Lola T94/00-Ford) all

chose to pit at the 30-lap mark, thereby gaining a jump on everyone else, even though they also stopped under caution a lap or two later.

De Ferran, having missed the chance to pit with Villeneuve, inherited the lead for a few laps during the caution. Team manager Davis and race engineer Bill Pappas contemplated the notion of attempting to pull away from the field at the restart, taking advantage of a light fuel load before making their final pit stop, but were overruled by team owner Jim Hall. De Ferran therefore fell all the way to 15th when he pitted on the final lap of yellow. All hope of a podium finish had long since disappeared when a gearbox problem caused him to slide off the road shortly before the finish.

The restart on lap 35 saw Villeneuve once again assert himself at the front. In the leader's wake, Tracy dived down the inside of Boesel into Turn Five, and in a virtual mirror image of the incident involving Herta earlier in the race, Rahal again took advantage, tucking inside his teammate as they sped up toward Turn Six. In his defence, Boesel was distracted by a gearshift problem, and after extricating himself from the sand, he retired shortly afterward with a broken transmission.

The race was interrupted by two more brief full-course cautions, first when Alessandro Zampedri's Mi-Jack Lola T94/00-Ford ran off the road in Turn 12 while disputing 10th place with teammate Bachelart and

then when de Ferran required extrication from the same sand trap. The intrusions nullified any concerns about fuel consumption, and even though Tracy pushed hard to the finish he was unable to prevent Villeneuve from taking the checkered flag. Under the circumstances, Tracy was delighted with second.

'My foot's very, very sore,' said Tracy. 'It actually feels like my heart. It's just pounding: boom, boom!

'I had some problems on my first stop – it felt like someone jabbing a knife in my foot – so all in all I think it was a great result for the team. We made our positions back on the track, and that's what racing's all about.'

Excellent strategy and an error-free drive allowed Vasser to claim third, just ahead of Ribeiro and Rahal, who crossed the line less than two-tenths of a second apart. Fernandez and Pruett also were in close contention.

A mistimed pit stop and a stalled engine negated Christian Fittipaldi's good work early in the race and restricted him to eighth ahead of Fabi, who had run fourth until making an off-course excursion with five laps to go. Stefan Johansson, who, like de Ferran, made his final pit stop too late, rounded out the top 10 in his Alumax Penske PC23.

Bachelart survived an eventful afternoon to finish 11th for Payton-Coyne Racing, while Johnstone claimed the final PPG Cup point – and the first of his career – after a steady drive in Comptech's Reynard-Honda.

Michael C. Brown

SNIPPETS

• Hubert Stromberger *(below)* made a low-key Indy Car debut at the wheel of Andreas Leberle's Project Indy Reynard 94I-Ford. The 32-year-old Austrian's previous experience had been limited primarily to the European Formula Opel series, in which he had scored a couple of significant victories during the previous two years. Stromberger qualified toward the tail of the field and survived one spin to finish in 16th.

• In addition to collecting the $10,000 Marlboro Pole Award, Jacques Villeneuve pocketed a $30,000 bonus for winning from the pole.

• Robby Gordon's miserable weekend included narrowly avoiding a deer during first practice on Friday. 'It was huge,' exclaimed Gordon. 'It scared me to death. I'm not sure whose eyes were bigger, mine or the deer's.'

• Emerson Fittipaldi *(right)* looked more competitive at Road America than at any of the last three races, although the results didn't properly reflect that information, since he was restricted to 21st on the grid by a blown engine in the significantly faster final period of qualifying. He then lost a lap due to a bungled pit stop. 'It's amazing,' said a frustrated Fittipaldi. 'It seems that things that never happened in the last 10 years have all happened in the last three races. All we can do is move on to Toronto and hope for some better luck there.'

• Paul Tracy suffered a broken left foot when he crashed his go-kart during a race near his new home in

• Lola engineer Mike Wright, who worked with A.J. Foyt's team through the early part of the season, offered some valuable assistance to Payton-Coyne driver Eric Bachelart after the Belgian driver had struggled to find a good balance on his '94 Lola on Friday. Ironically, during the race, Bachelart was involved in a pair of incidents with Foyt's driver, Eddie Cheever.

Phoenix, Ariz., the previous weekend. Dr. Terry Trammell, IndyCar's Director of Medical Services, inserted a metal plate and five screws to assist the healing process and outfitted Tracy with a carbon fiber insole for his left shoe. Just to add to his misery, Tracy's home was subjected to a burglary the same week.

• Christian Fittipaldi suffered a monumental engine failure on Saturday morning which left Derrick Walker's Marlboro/Chapeco Reynard engulfed in smoke and (briefly) flames. Surprisingly, the car suffered relatively little damage, although Fittipaldi switched to his backup car for the balance of the weekend.

Photos: Michael C. Brown

PPG INDY CAR WORLD SERIES • ROUND 10
TEXACO/HAVOLINE 200

ROAD AMERICA, ELKHART LAKE, WISCONSIN

JULY 9, 50 LAPS – 200.000 MILES

Place	Driver (Nat.)	No.	Team Sponsors Car-Engine	Tires	Q Speed	Q Time	Q Pos.	Laps	Time/Status	Ave.	Pts.
1	Jacques Villeneuve (CDN)	27	Team Green *Player's Ltd.* Reynard 95I-Ford	GY	142.206	1m 41.261s	1	50	1h 55m 29.659s	103.901	22
2	Paul Tracy (CDN)	3	Newman-Haas *Kmart/Budweiser* Lola T95/00-Ford	GY	140.471	1m 42.512s	11	50	1h 55m 30.625s	103.887	16
3	Jimmy Vasser (USA)	12	Ganassi *Target/STP* Reynard 95I-Ford	GY	139.425	1m 43.281s	14	50	1h 55m 32.038s	103.866	14
4	*Andre Ribeiro (BR)	31	Tasman Motorsports *LCI International* Reynard 95I-Honda	FS	140.359	1m 42.594s	12	50	1h 55m 32.956s	103.852	12
5	Bobby Rahal (USA)	9	Rahal/Hogan *Miller Genuine Draft* Lola T95/00-Mercedes	GY	141.053	1m 42.090s	6	50	1h 55m 33.151s	103.849	10
6	Adrian Fernandez (MEX)	10	Galles *Tecate/Quaker State* Lola T95/00-Mercedes	GY	139.295	1m 43.378s	15	50	1h 55m 34.951s	103.822	8
7	Scott Pruett (USA)	20	Patrick Racing *Firestone/Pennzoil* Lola T95/00-Ford	FS	140.796	1m 42.276s	7	50	1h 55m 35.416s	103.815	6
8	*Christian Fittipaldi (BR)	15	Walker *Marlboro/Chapeco Special* Reynard 95I-Ford	GY	140.703	1m 42.343s	9	50	1h 55m 41.858s	103.719	5
9	Teo Fabi (I)	33	Forsythe *Combustion Engineering/Indeck* Reynard 95I-Ford	GY	140.707	1m 42.340s	8	50	1h 55m 43.059s	103.701	4
10	Stefan Johansson (S)	16	Bettenhausen *Alumax Aluminum* Penske PC23-Mercedes	GY	139.037	1m 43.570s	17	50	1h 55m 45.207s	103.669	3
11	Eric Bachelart (B)	19	Payton-Coyne *The Agfa Car* Lola T94/00-Ford	FS	136.228	1m 45.705s	25	50	1h 55m 50.783s	103.585	2
12	Parker Johnstone (USA)	49	Comptech *Motorola Cellular* Reynard 95I-Honda	FS	139.504	1m 43.223s	13	50	1h 55m 50.902s	103.584	1
13	Hiro Matsushita (J)	25	Arciero-Wells *Panasonic/Duskin/YKK* Reynard 95I-Ford	FS	136.144	1m 45.770s	26	50	1h 55m 52.413s	103.561	
14	Bryan Herta (USA)	4	Ganassi *Target/Scotch Video* Reynard 95I-Ford	GY	140.633	1m 42.394s	10	49	Running		
15	Emerson Fittipaldi (BR)	2	Marlboro Team Penske Penske PC24-Mercedes	GY	138.656	1m 43.854s	21	49	Running		
16	*Hubert Stromberger (A)	64	Project Indy *No-Touch/Van Dyne/Marcelo* Reynard 94I-Ford	GY	132.412	1m 48.752s	27	49	Running		
17	Eddie Cheever (USA)	14	A.J. Foyt *Copenhagen Racing* Lola T95/00-Ford	GY	137.859	1m 44.454s	22	48	Running		
18	*Eliseo Salazar (RCH)	7	Dick Simon *Cristal/Mobil 1/Copec* Lola T95/00-Ford	GY	138.728	1m 43.800s	20	48	Running		
19	*Carlos Guerrero (MEX)	22	Simon *Herdez/Viva Mexico!* Lola T95/00-Ford	GY	127.331	1m 53.091s	28	48	Running		
20	Alessandro Zampedri (I)	34	Payton-Coyne *The Mi-Jack Car* Lola T94/00-Ford	FS	137.717	1m 44.562s	23	48	Running		
21	*Gil de Ferran (BR)	8	Hall Racing *Pennzoil Special* Reynard 95I-Mercedes	GY	142.161	1m 41.294s	2	45	Accident		
22	Raul Boesel (BR)	11	Rahal/Hogan *Duracell Charger* Lola T95/00-Mercedes	GY	141.314	1m 41.901s	4	41	Transmission		
23	Marco Greco (BR)	99	Simon *Brastemp/Int. Sports* Lola T95/00-Ford	GY	136.776	1m 45.281s	24	38	Running		
24	Mauricio Gugelmin (BR)	18	PacWest Racing Group *Hollywood* Reynard 95I-Ford	GY	139.017	1m 43.585s	18	29	Accident		
25	Danny Sullivan (USA)	17	PacWest Racing Group *VISA* Reynard 95I-Ford	GY	138.845	1m 43.713s	19	29	Accident		
26	Robby Gordon (USA)	5	Walker *Valvoline/Cummins Special* Reynard 95I-Ford	GY	139.182	1m 43.461s	16	17	Transmission		
27	Michael Andretti (USA)	6	Newman-Haas *Kmart/Texaco Havoline* Lola T95/00-Ford	GY	141.631	1m 41.673s	3	2	Accident		
28	Al Unser Jr. (USA)	1	Marlboro Team Penske Penske PC24-Mercedes	GY	141.282	1m 41.924s	5	2	Accident		

* denotes Rookie driver

Caution flags: Laps 3–4, accident/Unser and Andretti; laps 19–20, tow/Cheever; lap 22, tow/Herta; laps 29–33, accident/Gugelmin and Sullivan; lap 37, tow/Zampedri; laps 45–47, tow/de Ferran. **Total:** six for 14 laps.

Lap leaders: Jacques Villeneuve, 1–29 (29 laps); Gil de Ferran, 30–33 (4 laps); Villeneuve, 34–50 (17 laps). **Totals:** Villeneuve, 46 laps; de Ferran, 4 laps.

Fastest race lap: Jacques Villeneuve, 1m 45.684s, 136.255 mph, on lap 29.

Championship positions: 1 Villeneuve, 103; **2** Gordon, 81; **3** Rahal, 78; **4** Tracy and Pruett, 73; **6** Andretti, 69; **7** Unser, 61; **8** Vasser, 59; **9** Gugelmin, 55; **10** Fabi, 54; **11** C. Fittipaldi, 42; **12** E. Fittipaldi and Boesel, 38; **14** Johansson, 37; **15** Fernandez, 31; **16** Cheever, 28; **17** Sullivan, 22; **18** Salazar, 16; **19** Ribeiro, 15; **20** de Ferran, 11; **21** Bachelart, 8; **22** Zampedri, 7; **23** Danner and Luyendyk, 6; **25** Matsushita, 5; **26** Herta, 4; **27** Greco, 3; **28** C. Guerrero and Hall, 2; **30** R. Guerrero, Johnstone and Brayton, 1.
Championship positions and points totals provisional pending outcome of appeal by Penske following race at Portland.

EDS

TORONTO

1 – ANDRETTI	
2 – RAHAL	
3 – VILLENEUVE	

Toronto's Exhibition Place temporary circuit has long been a happy hunting ground for Michael Andretti. He has now emerged triumphant in five out of the 10 Molson Indy events held in the cosmopolitan city on the edge of Lake Ontario.

Andretti's latest victory came exactly 12 months on from his last Indy Car success, and on the same track. It represented the third win of the season for Newman-Haas Racing and finally ended a sequence of misfortunes that had plagued the 1991 PPG Cup champion's #6 Kmart/Texaco Havoline Lola-Ford/Cosworth.

This time, in fact, Lady Luck smiled Andretti's way. He had been content to run a little way behind the leaders during the early stages of the 98-lap contest, and because Jacques Villeneuve (Player's Ltd. Reynard-Ford) and Jimmy Vasser (Target/STP Reynard-Ford) had j-u-s-t passed the pit entrance when the caution flags flew for the first time on lap 19, Andretti was able to steal an advantage when Newman-Haas team manager Lee White frantically called his man in for service.

'Lee was really on the ball. Being able to make that pit stop gave us track position, and that's what won the race for us,' declared Andretti. 'I really want to thank Lee.'

Bobby Rahal kept the pressure on Andretti by finishing a close second in his Miller Genuine Draft Lola-Mercedes, despite concerns about an overheating engine. Pole-winner Villeneuve maintained his charge toward the PPG Indy Car World Series title with a mature drive to third.

A unique challenge

Toronto's Exhibition Place street circuit is notoriously bumpy and dangerous in parts, yet for the drivers it represents a demanding test of skill and commitment.

The track boasts a wide variety of corners within its 1.78 miles as well as extremes of speed ranging from the long straightaway on Lake Shore Boulevard, where the cars reach a terminal velocity of around 180 mph, to the ensuing tight hairpin in Turn Three, which is negotiated at a sedate 35 mph or so. Turns 10 and 11, a pair of sweeping corners immediately preceding the start/finish line, provide perhaps the greatest challenge, especially with some fearsome bumps which the bravest drivers attempt to negotiate at full throttle – at close to 170 mph in qualifying trim!

The Indy cars provide a spectacular sight as they buck their way through those turns in full view of the pits and the packed grandstands, although in 1994 the aspect of danger was highlighted during practice when Bryan Herta lost control of A.J. Foyt's Lola and crashed heavily on the exit of Turn 11. Herta sustained severe injuries including a broken leg and pelvis.

Thankfully, there were no repeats of that accident this time around. Nevertheless, due to on-going major reconstruction within the Exhibition Place facility, that section of track will be replaced by a new sequence of corners, as well as a revised pit lane, in time for the 1996 Molson Indy Toronto. The news attracted mixed reactions from the drivers.

'No question, they are the toughest corners we race on all year,' said Michael Andretti. 'They're dangerous but you really respect them. They are drivers' corners. I'm gonna miss them when we come back next year.'

Second-place finisher Bobby Rahal also said he will be sorry to see the changes: 'The corners are rough, the car jumps all over the place, and yeah, you'd love them to be smoother, but as a racing driver, those are the sort of corners you live for because they really demand some attention.'

Michael C. Brown

QUALIFYING

The battle for supremacy between rival chassis manufacturers Reynard and Lola continued unabated in Toronto. Interestingly, and not for the first time this season, the Lolas appeared to have the upper hand during morning practice on each day, whereas in afternoon qualifying, in slightly warmer temperatures, it was the Reynards that emerged on top.

'That's been the story all year for us,' noted Paul Tracy, who was third fastest in the morning with Newman-Haas Racing's Kmart/Budweiser Lola-Ford/Cosworth, then slipped to a disappointing 10th on the final grid. 'The car's great when the track is cool, but as soon as the track heats up, the car starts to pick up an understeer.'

Rahal, who set the pace on Saturday morning with what would stand as the fastest lap of the weekend, 57.646s, was similarly afflicted in qualifying, clearing the way for the Reynards to annex the premier grid positions.

Sure enough, for the third race in a row, Villeneuve emerged with the pole.

'The car is very good in the high-speed corners and we didn't lose any speed in the slow-speed corners,' he declared. 'That's very important on this race track because it's got a bit of everything. You really need a good all-around car.'

Villeneuve, as usual, paid tribute to his Team Green crew for providing him with the tools to do the job. He, too, deserved credit for his daredevil style. His speed through the dangerously bumpy Turn 11 in front of the pits was awesome to behold. Indeed, the EDS official timing and scoring system revealed that he crossed the start/finish line, immediately on the exit of the corner, at an amazing 169 mph.

Vasser sprung from sixth on the provisional grid to claim the other front row position, while Teo Fabi ensured three Reynard-Fords at the front of the pack with a strong effort in Jerry Forsythe's Combustion Engineering/Indeck car.

Scott Pruett was fastest of the Lola contingent, celebrating the arrival of Nike as a major associate sponsor for Pat Patrick's team by securing the outside of the second row in his Firestone Lola-Ford. Pruett was close to the ultimate pace all weekend, although in the final

ed' for eight minutes after causing a red flag stoppage when he spun (without damage) and stalled in Turn One.

'The car was good, I just didn't get it done,' he reflected with refreshing candor. 'The temperature was getting warmer and we didn't get a chance to fine-tune the car for when we went out on the best set of tires.'

Fellow Lola drivers Rahal and Andretti were within almost the same tick of the watch as Pruett on the closely packed grid, which saw the top 10 qualifiers separated by a scant half-second.

RACE

Villeneuve led the 27-car field toward the waiting green flag in a remarkably precise two-by-two order and was greeted by a roar of approval from the huge (and hugely partisan) crowd as he headed Vasser & Co. into Turn One in front of the imposing Princes Gate arch. The start was clean, although an electrical problem caused Fabi's engine to cut out momentarily. The hiccup allowed Pruett to move up to third, followed around the outside line by Andretti. Rahal found himself boxed in behind the Italian, so was passed by both Andretti and Tracy, who

Tracy also sped past Fabi on the drag race along Lake Shore Boulevard, then tucked in behind teammate Andretti under braking for Turn Three. Farther back in the pack, Bryan Herta's miserable season continued as he was inadvertently side-swiped by Stefan Johansson under braking for the hairpin turn. Exit the #4 Target/Scotch Video car with its front suspension awry.

The order quickly settled down after the initial shuffling of positions, with Villeneuve maintaining a slender lead over Vasser and Pruett. Andretti and Tracy were next ahead of Fabi, whose mirrors were filled by the sight of Rahal, Al Unser Jr. (Marlboro Penske-Mercedes) and Gil de Ferran (Pennzoil Reynard-Mercedes).

The first significant change came on lap 17, when Pruett performed a quick spin in Turn Eight. It transpired the pirouette had been caused by water spilled from a broken union on his Ford/Cosworth engine, which in turn brought about Pruett's demise a few laps later due to an overheated XB powerplant.

Next time around, Unser also fell from contention following an uncharacteristically bold attempt to outbrake Rahal in Turn Three: 'I just tried to run in a hole that wasn't there and ran into the back of

Unser's car sustained a broken left-front suspension and came to rest on the exit of the blind turn, precipitating the first full-course caution of the afternoon.

The crossed yellow flags were displayed on lap 18 just as Villeneuve and Vasser were nearing completion of lap 18. Andretti, meanwhile, running a few seconds in arrears of the race leaders after being delayed slightly by Pruett's spin, was able to heed Lee White's frantic radio call to make a pit stop.

Swift service by Tim Bumps and the Newman-Haas crew enabled Andretti to rejoin without even losing a place, since almost everyone else also grasped the opportunity to take on fuel and fresh tires.

Villeneuve and Vasser continued in front when the green flag waved at the start of lap 24. Toward the back of the pack, however, there was chaos as a large group of cars became entangled even before the green flag was waved. The Dick Simon and Payton-Coyne teams were eliminated entirely in the melee. It was little short of a miracle that all the drivers emerged unscathed, especially as Carlos Guerrero's car had vaulted clear over the top of Alessandro Zampedri's.

As the yellow flags waved again

Above, top to bottom: Jacques Villeneuve tightened his grip on the PPG Cup with another rostrum finish; a stop-and-go penalty restricted Christian Fittipaldi to ninth place; Teo Fabi was fourth after another strong showing; Eddie Cheever survived a clash with the race winner.

Right: Displaying characteristic precision, Bobby Rahal eases away from the
Hollywood Boxnard of Mauricio Gugelmin

Raul Boesel *(right)* sweeps past the stately Princes Gate arch, the Toronto circuit's most distinctive landmark, on his way to a hard-earned sixth place.

Below: Clutching trophies that reflect another aspect of Canadian culture, Bobby Rahal, Michael Andretti and local favorite Jacques Villeneuve celebrate on the rostrum.

to negotiate a path through the carnage, Villeneuve and Vasser took the opportunity to charge on toward their pits for much-needed service. Such was the delay in mid-pack that the erstwhile leaders were able to rejoin in fifth and sixth. Ahead lay only Andretti, who had inherited the lead, Mauricio Gugelmin, who had yet to make a stop in his Hollywood/PacWest Reynard, plus Tracy and Rahal.

After a lengthy clean-up process, Andretti made full use of his track position by taking off into a clear lead. Gugelmin's advantage of running a light fuel load was offset by his less-than-fresh tires, and it was immediately apparent that he was holding up the group of cars in his wake.

Tracy, in particular, decided he couldn't afford to wait. The Canadian duly drew alongside Gugelmin on the approach to the Turn Three hairpin. Gugelmin, however, ensured that Tracy would have to take the longer route around the outside, and when Tracy attempted to turn into the corner he made light contact with the Brazilian's left-front tire – just enough to send his Kmart/Budweiser Lola into a lazy spin. Tracy's impatience cost him dearly. He had to wait until the entire field had passed by before he was able to turn around and head off again in the right direction. By then he had fallen all the way to 17th.

Rahal, by contrast, chose a more conservative approach. Sure, he could see Andretti pulling away by at least a half-second per lap, but he reasoned that with more than half the race still to run, there would be

plenty of time for him to make up the deficit. Wise man.

By lap 43, Andretti had extended his lead to more than eight seconds over Gugelmin, who had a huge train of cars in his mirrors. When the Brazilian finally peeled into the pits next time around, the prudence of Rahal's waiting game became apparent as he set off in pursuit of the race leader. Inside five laps Rahal had halved the deficit to Andretti. Already he was six seconds clear of Villeneuve, who was struggling to hold off the attentions of Vasser, Fabi and de Ferran.

'The car was good for the first 10 or 15 laps,' explained Villeneuve. 'After that the tires went away a little bit and it was tough. Michael and Bobby were definitely a bit quicker than us today.'

The running order remained unchanged following the second round of pit stops. Andretti continued to lead, albeit with a steadily diminishing margin over Rahal. Villeneuve slipped an increasing distance behind in third.

Villeneuve did manage to edge away from Vasser after the pit stops, only for the Californian to gradually close in again as the race reached toward its climax. Unfortunately, Vasser wasn't able to capitalize on his speed, retiring inside the final dozen laps with a broken exhaust header. Fabi moved in to challenge Villeneuve, without ever managing to find a way past, while de Ferran's hopes of a good finish were thwarted by a broken clutch.

Gordon (Valvoline/Cummins Reynard-Ford) charged hard in the clos-

ing stages, finishing on the tail of the Villeneuve–Fabi battle. Boesel also was close behind after a strong run from 16th in his Duracell Lola-Mercedes. Adrian Fernandez drove solidly to seventh in Rick Galles' similar Tecate/Quaker State car, followed by the recovered Tracy. The two Fittipaldis rounded out the top 10, Christian just ahead of uncle Emerson despite losing valuable ground due to a stop-and-go penalty for a blend-line violation after making his second scheduled pit stop.

The major interest, however, was centered on the sharp end of the field. By lap 71, Rahal had whittled down the deficit to Andretti to virtually nothing. But then came the entirely different prospect of finding a way past.

'Michael is a fair competitor,' declared Rahal. 'He won't weave down the track. He won't chop you. There was a time or two I thought about forcing the issue but I think we'd both have ended up sitting on the wall. It wasn't worth the risk.'

Rahal set the fastest lap of the race as he relentlessly chased down Andretti. On lap 76 his pressure almost paid off when Andretti came close to being taken out of the race while attempting to lap Eddie

Cheever. Sullivan, who had lost several laps after running out of fuel, had just passed Cheever under braking for Turn Three. Andretti tried to follow him through, only for Cheever to carve across his nose. The pair made wheel-to-wheel contact, but fortunately no lasting damage was done.

Rahal wasn't able to take advantage of the leader's momentary slip. Indeed he had troubles of his own.

'The water temperature went off the clock with about 15 laps to go,' related Rahal. 'The crew told me I had to back off to get some air into the radiators. I didn't want to let Michael cruise to the end, but every time I tried to close up, the temperature alarm would come back on. I guess we were lucky to finish second.'

Andretti was grateful for the respite: 'Bobby was strong. He really kept the pressure on. It was really fun. I knew I couldn't make a mistake and I just had to drive as hard as I could.

'This win is huge for us. It's been a really tough year. We've certainly had better race cars than this one but we haven't been able to win races. Today we had an average car and we won. It's strange. When it's your day, it's your day.'

Michael C. Brown

SNIPPETS

Photos: Michael C. Brown

• Andre Ribeiro *(above)* followed his career-best finish at Road America by moving Tasman's LCI Reynard-Honda to the top of the timing charts Saturday morning, only to blunt his effort by glancing off the wall at the exit of Turn One. The incident thwarted his hopes of a strong starting position, since a hairline crack in a rear suspension component did not manifest itself until final qualifying. Ribeiro finished 13th after a spin while attempting to pass Gordon, although once again he displayed promise by setting third fastest lap of the race.

• Robby Gordon was unable to repeat his pole-winning performance of 1994. Indeed he qualified only seventh after [...] struggling to find a balance on his Valvoline/Cummins Reynard, especially under braking. Gordon's progress in the race was hindered by a loose condition, as well as his team's pit location, in the middle of the curving pit lane, which he felt cost him several seconds.

• The motto 'Just do it' adorned the side of Scott Pruett's Patrick Racing Lola-Ford, although in keeping with Nike's stylish advertising campaign, which also provides substantial support for tennis star Andre Agassi and basketball legend Michael Jordan, the Nike name was not in evidence.

• Carlos Guerrero's Steve Gough-led crew endured [...] another busy week following a fire during practice at Road America which inflicted substantial damage to one side of the Mexican's Herdez/Viva Mexico! car and obliged him to use the backup '94 Lola for the balance of the weekend. Guerrero not only reverted to his regular chassis at Toronto, but following consummation of a deal that will see him remain with Dick Simon Racing in 1996, he also had the luxury of a second '95 car as a backup.

• Jacques Villeneuve's pace came as a pleasant surprise to Team Green, which last year languished in mid-pack throughout the Toronto weekend. 'We thought we were going to struggle here again,' admitted crew chief Kyle Moyer. 'We thought if we'd get out of here with a top five, we'd have been pleased.' Villeneuve exceeded expectations by qualifying on the pole, finishing third and extending his PPG Cup points lead.

• A commitment to test his German Touring Car Championship Alfa Romeo precluded Christian Danner from taking the wheel of his Project Indy Reynard. Veteran Jeff Wood responded with alacrity to a last-minute invitation to drive the car, only for his first-ever experience of a sequential-shift gearbox to result in an over-revved engine. With no additional funding to cover the costs of a Ford/Cosworth rebuild, a disappointed Wood stepped down on Saturday, whereupon journeyman Buddy Lazier *(below)* was called upon to complete the balance of the weekend.

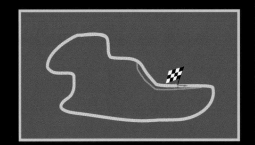

MOLSON INDY TORONTO

EXHIBITION PLACE CIRCUIT,
TORONTO, ONTARIO, CANADA

JULY 16, 98 LAPS – 174.440 MILES

Place	Driver (Nat.)	No.	Team Sponsors Car-Engine	Tires	Q Speed	Q Time	Q Pos.	Laps	Time/Status	Ave.	Pts.
1	**Michael Andretti (USA)**	6	Newman-Haas *Kmart/Texaco Havoline* Lola T95/00-Ford	GY	109.936	58.289s	6	98	1h 50m 25.202s	94.787	21
2	**Bobby Rahal (USA)**	9	Rahal/Hogan *Miller Genuine Draft* Lola T95/00-Mercedes	GY	109.967	58.272s	5	98	1h 50m 25.627s	94.781	16
3	**Jacques Villeneuve (CDN)**	27	Team Green *Player's Ltd.* Reynard 95I-Ford	GY	110.396	58.046s	1	98	1h 50m 58.015s	94.320	15
4	**Teo Fabi (I)**	33	Forsythe *Combustion Engineering/Indeck* Reynard 95I-Ford	GY	110.029	58.239s	3	98	1h 50m 58.543s	94.313	12
5	**Robby Gordon (USA)**	5	Walker *Valvoline/Cummins Special* Reynard 95I-Ford	GY	109.648	58.441s	7	98	1h 50m 59.893s	94.293	10
6	**Raul Boesel (BR)**	11	Rahal/Hogan *Duracell Charger* Lola T95/00-Mercedes	GY	108.756	58.921s	16	98	1h 51m 03.646s	94.240	8
7	**Adrian Fernandez (MEX)**	10	Galles *Tecate/Quaker State* Lola T95/00-Mercedes	GY	108.885	58.851s	15	98	1h 51m 07.838s	94.181	6
8	**Paul Tracy (CDN)**	3	Newman-Haas *Kmart/Budweiser* Lola T95/00-Ford	GY	109.462	58.541s	10	98	1h 51m 19.005s	94.024	5
9	***Christian Fittipaldi (BR)**	15	Walker *Marlboro/Chapeco Special* Reynard 95I-Ford	GY	109.227	58.667s	12	98	1h 51m 22.049s	93.981	4
10	**Emerson Fittipaldi (BR)**	2	Marlboro Team Penske Penske PC24-Mercedes	GY	108.688	58.958s	17	98	1h 51m 22.698s	93.972	3
11	**Eddie Cheever (USA)**	14	A.J. Foyt *Copenhagen Racing* Lola T95/00-Ford	GY	108.470	59.076s	20	97	Running		2
12	**Mauricio Gugelmin (BR)**	18	PacWest Racing Group *Hollywood* Reynard 95I-Ford	GY	109.066	58.754s	14	96	Running		1
13	*Andre Ribeiro (BR)	31	Tasman Motorsports *LCI International* Reynard 95I-Honda	FS	109.566	58.485s	9	96	Running		
14	Stefan Johansson (S)	16	Bettenhausen *Alumax Aluminum* Penske PC23-Mercedes	GY	108.676	58.964s	18	94	Running		
15	Buddy Lazier (USA)	64	Project Indy *No-Touch/Van Dyne/Marcelo* Reynard 94I-Ford	GY	103.480	1m 01.925s	27	93	Running		
16	*Gil de Ferran (BR)	8	Hall Racing *Pennzoil Special* Reynard 95I-Mercedes	GY	109.390	58.579s	11	89	Clutch		
17	Jimmy Vasser (USA)	12	Ganassi *Target/STP* Reynard 95I-Ford	GY	110.215	58.141s	2	85	Exhaust		
18	Danny Sullivan (USA)	17	PacWest Racing Group *VISA* Reynard 95I-Ford	GY	109.099	58.736s	13	83	Engine		
19	Hiro Matsushita (J)	25	Arciero-Wells *Panasonic/Duskin/YKK* Reynard 95I-Ford	FS	105.963	1m 00.474s	26	66	Cooling system		
20	Marco Greco (BR)	55	Galles *Brastemp/Int. Sports* Lola T95/00-Mercedes	GY	106.435	1m 00.206s	25	45	Transmission		
21	*Eliseo Salazar (RCH)	7	Dick Simon *Cristal/Mobil 1/Copec* Lola T95/00-Ford	GY	107.390	59.670s	22	23	Accident		
22	Eric Bachelart (B)	19	Payton-Coyne *The Agfa Car* Lola T94/00-Ford	FS	106.511	1m 00.163s	24	22	Accident		
23	Alessandro Zampedri (I)	34	Payton-Coyne *The Mi-Jack Car* Lola T94/00-Ford	FS	107.766	59.462s	21	22	Accident		
24	*Carlos Guerrero (MEX)	22	Simon *Herdez/Viva Mexico!* Lola T95/00-Ford	GY	107.312	59.714s	23	22	Accident		
25	Scott Pruett (USA)	20	Patrick Racing *Firestone/Nike* Lola T95/00-Ford	FS	109.982	58.264s	4	19	Cooling system		
26	Al Unser Jr. (USA)	1	Marlboro Team Penske Penske PC24-Mercedes	GY	109.638	58.447s	8	17	Accident		
27	Bryan Herta (USA)	4	Ganassi *Target/Scotch Video* Reynard 95I-Ford	GY	108.590	59.011s	19	0	Accident		
NS	Jeff Wood (USA)	64	Project Indy *No-Touch/Van Dyne/Marcelo* Reynard 94I-Ford	GY	99.163	1m 04.621s	–	–	Withdrawn		

* denotes Rookie driver

Caution flags: Laps 17–22, accident/Unser; laps 23–30, accident/Salazar, Bachelart, Guerrero and Zampedri. **Total:** two for 14 laps.

Lap leaders: Jacques Villeneuve, 1–23 (23 laps); Michael Andretti, 24–62 (39 laps); Villeneuve, 63 (1 lap); Andretti, 64–98 (35 laps). **Totals:** Andretti, 74 laps; Villeneuve, 24 laps.

Fastest race lap: Bobby Rahal, 58.830s, 108.924 mph, on lap 60.

Championship positions: 1 Villeneuve, 118; **2** Rahal, 94; **3** Gordon, 91; **4** Andretti, 90; **5** Tracy, 78; **6** Pruett, 73; **7** Fabi, 66; **8** Unser, 61; **9** Vasser, 59; **10** Gugelmin, 56; **11** C. Fittipaldi and Boesel, 46; **13** E. Fittipaldi, 41; **14** Johansson and Fernandez, 37; **16** Cheever, 30; **17** Sullivan, 22; **18** Salazar, 16; **19** Ribeiro, 15; **20** de Ferran, 11; **21** Bachelart, 8; **22** Zampedri, 7; **23** Danner and Luyendyk, 6; **25** Matsushita, 5; **26** Herta, 4; **27** Greco, 3; **28** C. Guerrero and Hall, 2; **30** R. Guerrero, Johnstone and Brayton, 1.
Championship positions and points totals provisional pending outcome of appeal by Penske following race at Portland.

EDS

CLEVELAND

1 – VILLENEUVE

2 – HERTA

3 – VASSER

The Medic Drug Grand Prix of Cleveland, presented by Dairy Mart, featured an extraordinary finish as Jacques Villeneuve contrived to score his fourth win of the season in Team Green's Player's Ltd. Reynard-Ford/Cosworth.

The real star of the show, however, was Gil de Ferran. The Brazilian belied his rookie status by qualifying on the pole and leading confidently until his advantage in the Pennzoil Reynard-Mercedes was negated by a full-course caution in the late stages.

A characteristic scramble for positions ensued on the wide-open Burke Lakefront Airport temporary circuit, during which de Ferran's superiority was challenged by Michael Andretti, Robby Gordon, Bryan Herta and Villeneuve. An ill-conceived attempt to take the lead by Gordon elevated Andretti to the front, only for the Toronto winner to be hobbled by an ignition problem. De Ferran then glimpsed an opportunity to regain first place with less than five laps remaining. At the same time, he attempted to pass the lapped car of Scott Pruett. The gambit ended in disaster as Pruett and de Ferran collided.

Andretti, Herta and Villeneuve each took a turn in front during the dramatic final four miles before Villeneuve emerged victorious. Herta finished close behind, a career-best second in Chip Ganassi's Target/Scotch Video Reynard-Ford, with teammate Jimmy Vasser snaring the final podium position after a strong charge in his similar Target/STP car.

Photos: Michael C. Brown

Main picture: Pole-sitter Gil de Ferran leads the field into the first corner while Jacques Villeneuve explores the wide expanses of the Cleveland circuit. An extraordinary race ended in cruel disappointment for the Brazilian and veteran team owner Jim Hall *(below).* A momentary lapse cost Bryan Herta *(left)* his maiden Indy Car victory but the ever-consistent Bobby Rahal *(below left)* picked up fourth place.

Michael C. Brown

QUALIFYING

The PPG Cup competitors served another reminder of the close-fought nature of the 1995 title-chase as each of the four timed sessions produced a different driver atop the scoring monitors. Paul Tracy was the first to show his hand, dipping underneath the existing track record of 59.168s in the first practice session on Friday morning with his Kmart/Budweiser Lola-Ford. Later in the day, New-man-Haas teammate Michael Andretti claimed the provisional pole at 58.328s, followed by fellow Lola drivers Tracy and Raul Boesel (Duracell Lola-Mercedes).

Saturday provided an altogether different scenario, with Reynard drivers this time to the fore. First, Vasser vaulted to the top in morning practice, then de Ferran posted a sensational improvement on the very last lap of qualifying to jump all the way from ninth to first!

'I believe this pole has been maturing,' said de Ferran after

securing his first pole and the first of the season for the Mercedes-Benz/Ilmor engine. 'I felt a little disappointed after Elkhart [where he was beaten on the last lap by Villeneuve], but finally it's happened. It was definitely a go-for-broke lap. You brake a little bit later than the lap before, you brake a little bit less than the lap before and you get on the power a little bit earlier. You take a couple of extra chances.'

Villeneuve maintained his competitive streak by holding onto the outside front row position ahead of Herta, who ended a disappointing sequence of races by bouncing right back into contention. Indeed, unofficial timing in Turn Eight tallied with his Reynard's on-board computer system, which revealed Herta's best lap would have been good enough for the pole had his engine not begun to starve for fuel as he negotiated the final chicane prior to the start/finish line.

'I'm not too concerned,' said Herta. 'I know what might have been – and

what's better is that the team knows what might have been. The important thing is that we are competitive again. The car feels good. I'm looking forward to the race.'

Teo Fabi posted another fine effort, fourth in his Combustion Engineering/Indeck Reynard-Ford after some drastic changes to the shock absorber settings which vastly improved the car's handling on the bumpy airfield track. Andre Ribeiro ensured five Reynards filled the front of the grid – powered by three different engines – following another strong drive in his LCI International Reynard-Honda.

Tracy headed the Lola contingent, a disappointed sixth, while Pruett (Firestone Lola-Ford) and Robby Gordon (Valvoline/Cummins Reynard-Ford) also were within 0.3 seconds of the pole-winner. Vasser, who set the pace in the morning, didn't find the expected improvement on fresh tires and wound up a lowly 15th on the tightly packed grid. In all, 20 cars qualified beneath the existing track record.

RACE

The hot and humid conditions so typical of summer in the Great Lakes region prevailed throughout the weekend. On race day the baking sun offered no respite from the steamy weather, especially with a stiff breeze blowing in across Lake Erie. The drivers knew they would be in for a tough race.

The action began even before the green flag was waved, with third row qualifiers Tracy and Ribeiro colliding as they exited the chicane in front of the pits. A close-following Pruett and the equally innocent Boesel also were involved.

Ribeiro was the biggest loser, retiring at the end of the first lap with a holed radiator. Tracy rejoined at the back of the pack, soon to retire with damaged suspension, while Pruett lost more than a lap before he was able to resume. Boesel also continued after forfeiting a handful of places.

De Ferran, untroubled by the chaos behind, took off into the lead, pursued by Villeneuve and Fabi,

Left: **As the city of Cleveland languishes in the intense humidity of the Great Lakes, Michael Andretti continues to charge. Ignition trouble hampered his bid for victory in the closing stages.**

Jimmy Vasser *(below)* climbed from 15th on the grid to a place on the rostrum with Chip Ganassi's Target/STP Reynard-Ford.

who usurped Herta at the first corner. Andretti profited most from the midfield melee, emerging in fifth after starting 10th. Gordon was next, while Al Unser Jr. mounted a strong early challenge, climbing from 13th on the grid to seventh inside just four laps. Unfortunately, the defending series champion descended the order with equal rapidity due to the manifestation of an electrical problem. A lengthy pit stop at least allowed Unser to run at a competitive pace before his day was ended by a transmission failure.

Villeneuve shadowed de Ferran closely during the early laps, but soon the yellow Pennzoil car began to pull clear. By lap 20, de Ferran had extended his lead to more than eight seconds. Fabi remained on Villeneuve's tail as Herta ran all alone in fourth after edging clear of the battling Andretti and Gordon.

Frustrated by being unable to find a way past Andretti, Gordon was the first of the leaders to make a pit stop on lap 25. He was followed four laps later by de Ferran. Fabi stayed out the longest, waiting until lap 33 before taking on fresh tires and a full load of methanol. The differing strategies saw de Ferran retain his comfortable advantage. Fabi, meanwhile, was able to oust Villeneuve from second. Excellent service by Walker Racing also elevated Gordon to fourth ahead of both Herta and Andretti.

De Ferran's margin decreased by three seconds on lap 40 as he attempted to put a stubborn Pruett two laps down. Even so, the Brazilian seemed secure at the front of the field. The gap to Fabi stabilized at around eight seconds.

Villeneuve, meanwhile, came under increasing pressure from Gordon. On lap 46, Gordon managed to outbrake his rival on the wide approach into Turn One. Villeneuve battled back on the exit, only to be squeezed almost to the edge of the grass as Gordon fought to maintain his advantage. Plumes of dust emanated from the rear of both cars as they roared through uncharted territory on the inside edge of the wide runway, and with neither willing to give an inch, it came as no surprise to see both men brake way too late for the ensuing right-hander. As their cars skated off onto the grass, Herta and Andretti nipped through gratefully on a more conventional line.

Gordon finally found a way past Villeneuve. He then charged back onto the tail of a battling Herta and Andretti before once again commencing the next round of pit stops (along with Herta) on lap 58.

As before, Fabi was the last of the leaders to stop. This time, after Phil LePan and the crew performed an incredibly fast service, Fabi resumed ahead of de Ferran. The team's strat-

egy had worked perfectly. Cruelly, however, Fabi's engine fell off-song on the very next lap. A wastegate exhaust pipe had fractured.

'That was a heart-breaker,' sighed Forsythe Racing team manager Tony Brunetti. 'Everything had gone as we planned. It was over, talk to you later.'

Fabi's bitter disappointment brought a sigh of relief from de Ferran, who now held a commanding lead over Andretti. Gordon followed a further seven seconds in arrears on lap 68, with Herta a similar distance back in fourth after losing time on his second pit stop. Villeneuve was a lonely fifth ahead of Adrian Fernandez (Tecate/Quaker State Lola-Mercedes), who was fighting to hold off Vasser. Their battle served to enliven what had otherwise threatened to degenerate into a high-speed procession.

But then came the one and only full-course caution of the afternoon, when Eric Bachelart lost control of Dale Coyne's ill-handling Agfa Lola T94/00-Ford in Turn Nine.

The restart came with 14 laps remaining. Gordon, his interest rekindled, attempted an impossible move into Turn One as he dived past not only the lapped car of Pruett but also Andretti and de Ferran! The Valvoline/Cummins Reynard led the race for a few moments before promptly skating far past the apex. Gordon resumed in third.

Michael C. Brown

There are two sides to every story . . .

Photos: Michael C. Brown

Not unexpectedly, Gil de Ferran and Scott Pruett *(right)* viewed the accident which terminated de Ferran's hopes of a well-earned maiden Indy Car victory from entirely different perspectives.

'I simply cannot conceive what was going on in his mind,' argued an angry de Ferran *(above)*. 'What was he thinking? He was two laps down. If I was fighting for the lead with him and it was the last corner of the last lap, then I'd say fair enough, that's racing, but . . .'

Pruett, however, vehemently defended his actions: 'Michael [Andretti] and I got hung up by a backmarker coming off the previous turn,' he explained, 'and Michael looked like he was having problems because I was closing up quickly on him. I pulled up alongside to pass him, and then, going into the chicane, Michael pulled to the inside of the backmarker, so we were three-wide. I just got a glimpse of de Ferran as we went into the corner.

'I feel it was just poor judgment on [de Ferran's] part. He put me in a situation where there was literally nowhere for me to go. If he had just

waited to get through the turn, he would have been able to go by me on the straight.'

Interestingly, neutral observers offered similarly diverse opinions as to the cause of the crash. Michael Andretti, for example, who had the best view of all, sided with Pruett: 'If de Ferran was smart, he would've seen that I was way off-line with Pruett passing me, so he should have waited until they came off the corner and then made the pass [on Pruett]. You can't go three-wide into that corner. But that's just inexperience.'

Nevertheless, several experienced drivers condemned Pruett for remaining in the thick of the action in spite of the fact he was two laps behind and out of contention for a top finish.

'I consider Scott a good friend and a very good driver, but he was out of line there,' stated former Indy Car driver Dominic Dobson, now a part-owner of the PacWest team. 'There were only a few laps to go and he shouldn't have been mixing it with the leaders.'

Andretti then took the challenge to de Ferran, whose tires had picked up some debris after running at reduced pace behind the pace car. Next time around, Andretti made a bid for the inside line in Turn One.

'I had him passed,' related Andretti. 'All of a sudden I look in my mirrors and, oh man, here comes Robby!'

Gordon once again came steaming through on an even tighter line, with little hope of making the corner. Andretti saw him coming and sagely backed off. De Ferran also was forced to take evasive action. The consequence of the drama was that Andretti emerged in front. Pruett avoided the melee and ran next ahead of de Ferran, Herta and Villeneuve as Gordon headed for the pits with a punctured left-rear tire.

Pruett defied convention by remaining in the thick of what was developing into a fantastic fight to the finish among the four leaders. His presence acted as a buffer for

Andretti, and as the laps ticked away it became clear he might need the assistance. Indeed, Andretti's engine fell sick inside the final five laps.

The drama intensified on lap 86, when Andretti was unintentionally held up in Turn Eight by Parker Johnstone, who was intent upon limping to the finish despite a broken suspension sustained in an impact with Carlos Guerrero. Pruett duly pulled alongside the stricken Andretti, followed closely by de Ferran as the leading pack accelerated toward the Turn Nine chicane.

Suddenly, Andretti realized his hopes were still alive: 'You can't go three abreast into that corner,' he noted. 'When I saw [de Ferran go alongside Pruett], I braked hard because I knew they were done.'

Sure enough, de Ferran and Pruett collided and slid into the tires, out of the race. Andretti had been reprieved. Briefly.

The focus then switched to Herta

and Villeneuve, who raced side by side for much of the 87th lap before Herta reasserted himself in second place. He then set his sights on Andretti. With a little more than one lap to go, Herta was caught slightly off-guard as Andretti's engine failed to pick up cleanly on the run toward Turn Nine. Herta, unable to believe his luck, ducked to the inside line as they approached the braking area . . . then realized to his horror that the yellow flags were still waving as a result of the Pruett/de Ferran incident.

'I wasn't planning on passing him but something was wrong and I didn't know what to do,' said Herta. 'My momentum carried me past him. Then I remembered a drivers' meeting a few races ago when [chief steward] Wally [Dallenbach] had said if you inadvertently pass someone under yellow, you won't get a penalty if you let them go back past.'

Accordingly, Herta slowed on the exit of the corner and Andretti duly

repassed him. But so too did Villeneuve, who had been tucked close behind in their draft.

Even then the drama wasn't over. Andretti, despite his badly misfiring engine, lunged to the inside of Villeneuve as the leaders braked hard for the final time into Turn One. It was a desperate maneuver that succeeded only in damaging Andretti's suspension. Villeneuve, fortunately, emerged unscathed from the assault and held off a last-ditch effort from Herta to take the victory.

'That was tough,' said an exhausted but elated Villeneuve. 'We didn't have enough downforce for the race. After a few laps, the car was really hard to drive. We were hanging in there. The yellow allowed us to cool down the tires and then I could push hard the last 10 laps.'

'The car wasn't working perfectly but this was a great day for the Player's team,' agreed his delighted car owner Barry Green. 'We'll take 'em any way we can.'

SNIPPETS

Photos: Michael C. Brown

• Among those who deserved more from their day were Raul Boesel and Adrian Fernandez *(above)*, both of whom moved up strongly into the top five before being halted by engine problems.

• Saturday was not a good day for Paul Tracy. First of all he arrived late for the morning practice session, then promptly slid off the track and made heavy contact with a landing light.

'Billy' Simmonds and the crew effected repairs, which took around 40 minutes, whereupon Tracy crashed again in Turn Eight, causing damage to his Lola's nose.

• Gil de Ferran provided the first pole for Jim Hall since the Texan re-formed his Indy Car team in 1991 following an absence of almost 10 years. Sadly, de Ferran wasn't quite able to provide Hall with the ultimate 60th birthday present on Sunday.

• The [...] accused action continued even after the checkered flag, when a frustrated Robby Gordon gesticulated angrily at Michael Andretti and initiated contact between their cars on the cool-down lap. Gordon alleged that Andretti had deliberately driven into him during the race, puncturing a tire and ending his hopes of a win. Andretti fervently rejected the claim and

Gordon of driving 'like a wild man.' The IndyCar stewards assessed Gordon *(below)* a $10,000 fine and placed both drivers on probation until the end of the season. 'It's a culmination of things that have happened this season and we've got to put a stop to it,' said assistant chief steward Dennis Swan in explaining Andretti's penalty.

• Gordon also came in for criticism from Villeneuve, who was embroiled in several close battles during the 90-lap contest: 'You can't run wheel to wheel with Robby and enjoy your racing,' said the race winner. 'This is Indy Car racing, not off-road racing. When you're going 170 mph there's no point in trying to hit the other car or push him onto the grass.' Contrastingly, Villeneuve praised Herta *(pictured with him above)* after their tussle in the later stages: 'When you race against someone like Bryan, it's a lot of fun. Even if you're close to each other, you have enough room and it's fun. That's the way racing should be.'

MEDIC DRUG GRAND PRIX OF CLEVELAND PRESENTED BY DAIRY MART

BURKE LAKEFRONT AIRPORT CIRCUIT, CLEVELAND, OHIO

JULY 23, 90 LAPS – 213.210 MILES

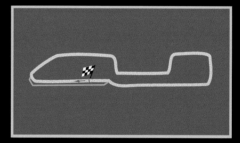

Place	Driver (Nat.)	No.	Team Sponsors Car-Engine	Tires	Q Speed	Q Time	Q Pos.	Laps	Time/Status	Ave.	Pts.
1	Jacques Villeneuve (CDN)	27	Team Green *Player's Ltd.* Reynard 95I-Ford	GY	147.484	57.826s	2	90	1h 38m 19.151s	130.113	20
2	Bryan Herta (USA)	4	Ganassi *Target/Scotch Video* Reynard 95I-Ford	GY	147.412	57.854s	3	90	1h 38m 20.308s	130.087	16
3	Jimmy Vasser (USA)	12	Ganassi *Target/STP* Reynard 95I-Ford	GY	145.476	58.624s	15	90	1h 38m 22.723s	130.034	14
4	Bobby Rahal (USA)	9	Rahal/Hogan *Miller Genuine Draft* Lola T95/00-Mercedes	GY	146.247	58.315s	11	90	1h 38m 23.028s	130.028	12
5	Danny Sullivan (USA)	17	PacWest Racing Group *VISA* Reynard 95I-Ford	GY	145.653	58.553s	14	90	1h 38m 28.475s	129.908	10
6	Robby Gordon (USA)	5	Walker *Valvoline/Cummins Special* Reynard 95I-Ford	GY	146.819	58.088s	8	90	1h 38m 38.050s	129.697	8
7	Michael Andretti (USA)	6	Newman-Haas *Kmart/Texaco Havoline* Lola T95/00-Ford	GY	146.463	58.229s	10	90	1h 38m 39.705s	129.661	6
8	Stefan Johansson (S)	16	Bettenhausen *Alumax Aluminum* Penske PC23-Mercedes	GY	144.146	59.165s	20	89	Running		5
9	Alessandro Zampedri (I)	34	Payton-Coyne *The Mi-Jack Car* Lola T94/00-Ford	FS	142.806	59.720s	24	89	Running		4
10	*Eliseo Salazar (RCH)	7	Dick Simon *Cristal/Mobil 1/Copec* Lola T95/00-Ford	GY	140.247	1m 00.810s	27	88	Running		3
11	Parker Johnstone (USA)	49	Comptech *Motorola Cellular* Reynard 95I-Honda	FS	144.297	59.103s	19	88	Running		2
12	Adrian Fernandez (MEX)	10	Galles *Tecate/Quaker State* Lola T95/00-Mercedes	GY	144.819	58.890s	18	87	Running		1
13	Hiro Matsushita (J)	25	Arciero-Wells *Panasonic/Duskin/YKK* Reynard 95I-Ford	FS	142.852	59.701s	23	86	Running		
14	*Gil de Ferran (BR)	8	Hall Racing *Pennzoil Special* Reynard 95I-Mercedes	GY	147.512	57.815s	1	85	Accident		2
15	Marco Greco (BR)	55	Galles *Brastemp/Int. Sports* Lola T95/00-Mercedes	GY	140.351	1m 00.765s	26	84	Running		
16	Scott Pruett (USA)	20	Patrick Racing *Firestone* Lola T95/00-Ford	FS	146.839	58.080s	7	83	Accident		
17	*Carlos Guerrero (MEX)	22	Simon *Herdez/Viva Mexico!* Lola T95/00-Ford	GY	141.325	1m 00.346s	25	82	Running		
18	Al Unser Jr. (USA)	1	Marlboro Team Penske Penske PC24-Mercedes	GY	145.683	58.541s	13	70	Transmission		
19	Teo Fabi (I)	33	Forsythe *Combustion Engineering/Indeck* Reynard 95I-Ford	GY	147.013	58.011s	4	67	Exhaust header		
20	Raul Boesel (BR)	11	Rahal/Hogan *Duracell Charger* Lola T95/00-Mercedes	GY	146.483	58.221s	9	65	Electrical		
21	Eric Bachelart (B)	19	Payton-Coyne *The Agfa Car* Lola T94/00-Ford	FS	142.986	59.645s	22	63	Accident		
22	Eddie Cheever (USA)	14	A.J. Foyt *Copenhagen Racing* Lola T95/00-Ford	GY	143.832	59.294s	21	48	Engine		
23	Mauricio Gugelmin (BR)	18	PacWest Racing Group *Hollywood* Reynard 95I-Ford	GY	146.240	58.318s	12	35	Fuel pressure		
24	*Christian Fittipaldi (BR)	15	Walker *Marlboro/Chapeco Special* Reynard 95I-Ford	GY	145.355	58.673s	16	22	Engine		
25	Emerson Fittipaldi (BR)	2	Marlboro Team Penske Penske PC24-Mercedes	GY	144.903	58.856s	17	22	Water line		
26	Paul Tracy (CDN)	3	Newman-Haas *Kmart/Budweiser* Lola T95/00-Ford	GY	146.920	58.048s	6	17	Suspension		
27	*Andre Ribeiro (BR)	31	Tasman Motorsports *LCI International* Reynard 95I-Honda	FS	146.996	58.018s	5	1	Holed radiator		

* denotes Rookie driver

Caution flags: Laps 70–75, accident/Bachelart. **Total:** one for six laps.

Lap leaders: Gil de Ferran, 1–28 (28 laps); Jacques Villeneuve, 29–31 (3 laps); Teo Fabi, 32 (1 lap); de Ferran, 33–60 (28 laps); Fabi, 61–66 (6 laps); de Ferran, 67–77 (11 laps); Andretti, 78–88 (11 laps); Villeneuve, 89–90 (2 laps). **Totals:** De Ferran, 67 laps; Andretti, 11 laps; Fabi, 7 laps; Villeneuve, 5 laps.

Fastest race lap: not given.

Championship positions: 1 Villeneuve, 138; **2** Rahal, 106; **3** Gordon, 99; **4** Andretti, 96; **5** Tracy, 78; **6** Vasser and Pruett, 73; **8** Fabi, 66; **9** Unser, 61; **10** Gugelmin, 56; **11** C. Fittipaldi and Boesel, 46; **13** Johansson, 42; **14** E. Fittipaldi, 41; **15** Fernandez, 38; **16** Sullivan, 32; **17** Cheever, 30; **18** Herta, 20; **19** Salazar, 19; **20** Ribeiro, 15; **21** de Ferran, 13; **22** Zampedri, 11; **23** Bachelart, 8; **24** Danner and Luyendyk, 6; **26** Matsushita, 5; **27** Greco and Johnstone, 3; **29** C. Guerrero and Hall, 2; **31** R. Guerrero and Brayton, 1.
Championship positions and points totals provisional pending outcome of appeal by Penske following race at Portland.

EDS

MICHIGAN

The outcome of an exciting Marlboro 500 seemed to have been settled when Al Unser Jr. rocketed past Scott Pruett on the outside line into Turn One as the top two protagonists sped onto their 250th and final lap. But not so fast. Pruett, in search of his maiden Indy Car triumph, wasn't beaten yet.

'I just concentrated on making a good run off Turn Two, so I could get a run on him down the back straight,' said Pruett, who proceeded to draft alongside Unser's Marlboro Penske-Mercedes. The huge crowd was on its feet, cheering wildly as Pruett drove brilliantly around the outside line in Turns Three and Four to claim victory in the second-closest finish in Indy Car history.

'Actually, I didn't think I was going to make it,' admitted Pruett, 'but I just had to go for it. When you have victory that close you just have to try a little bit harder.'

Pruett's last-lap maneuver secured not only his first win, by a scant 0.056 seconds, but also the first for Firestone and team owner Pat Patrick following their respective returns to the Indy Car scene this year.

Unser was full of praise for Pruett's audacious last-lap pass, while Adrian Fernandez delighted both team owner Rick Galles and an enthusiastic band of Mexican supporters by claiming a career-best third in his Tecate/Quaker State Lola-Mercedes.

After a thrilling duel that had the record crowd roaring with excitement, Scott Pruett bravely drafted past Al Unser Jr. on the last lap to give Firestone its first Indy Car win since 1974.
Photo: Michael C. Brown

QUALIFYING

A variety of talking-points had arisen prior to the end of the first day of official practice at Michigan International Speedway. Among them was the impressive resurfacing work undertaken over the winter and the decision by IndyCar to restrict engines to 40 inches of manifold boost pressure (down from the regular 45 inches) in order to minimize the escalation in speeds on Roger Penske's dauntingly fast, high-banked, two-mile superspeedway oval. Both issues earned unanimous praise from the drivers.

The omnipresent concern about safety also reared its head when

Robby Gordon crashed heavily on Friday afternoon. Once the cause of the accident had been pin-pointed to a rear suspension failure, the Reynard design engineers first of all advised their teams to replace any used wishbones with new components, then set to work on drawing a modified version. A fresh supply was manufactured overnight by Pratt & Miller in nearby Wixom, Mich.

The other main topic of conversation was the effectiveness of the Honda engines, especially after rookie Andre Ribeiro set the fastest speed in the opening session at 230.834 mph with Tasman's LCI Reynard-Honda. Paul Tracy's Kmart/Budweiser Lola-

Ford/Cosworth was 'best of the rest' at 229.757 mph.

Jacques Villeneuve jumped to the top of the charts the following morning, taking advantage of a monumental draft to achieve 233.985 mph in his familiar Player's Ltd. Reynard-Ford, but Parker Johnstone wasn't too far behind with a 231.708 mph in Comptech Racing's Motorola Cellular Reynard-Honda.

No one expected those speeds to be approached in the one-at-a-time qualifying session, held amid warmer conditions later on Saturday morning. Indeed, Michael Andretti, who was first out onto the track in Newman-Haas Racing's Kmart/Texaco Havoline Lola-Ford, expressed

his satisfaction after recording a lap at 228.413 mph: 'The car was good. As good as it gets. That's all we could get out of it.'

Teo Fabi, second to go, surprised Andretti by proving fractionally faster at 228.526 mph in Forsythe Racing's Combustion Engineering/Indeck Reynard-Ford.

'I think everyone is flat out all the way around, so if the temperature continues to rise, maybe we'll be lucky [and keep the pole],' said Fabi. 'It's all about speed on the straights and we're all running virtually no wing, so there's not much more we can do about that.'

Fabi's speed remained fastest for more than 45 minutes. Even Ribeiro

Parker Johnstone made a clean start from pole position to take control of the race with the Comptech team's Honda-powered Reynard. Michael Andretti, Teo Fabi, Jimmy Vasser, Jacques Villeneuve and Mauricio Gugelmin give chase.

Below: Al Unser Jr. recovered from an unscheduled pit stop in the closing stages to regain the lead on the last lap, only to have victory snatched from his grasp.

RACE

Perfect weather conditions and high speeds combined to attract a large crowd to the majestic MIS oval on race day. The bright blue sky and pastoral setting of the Irish Hills region of central Michigan provided a gentle contrast to the vivid colors which dominated the huge grandstands.

Expectations were high as the 26-car field (minus Gordon as the result of his crash on Friday) assembled in pit lane, especially among the Honda and Firestone contingents, whose hopes were raised still further during the race morning warmup when Ribeiro and Johnstone posted the fastest speeds.

After two false starts, Johnstone maintained his composure and made full use of the advice given to him earlier in the day by acknowledged oval track experts Rick Mears and Al Unser. Johnstone withstood a challenge from Fabi in Turn One and, for the first time in his career, confidently led the field around to complete the first green-flag lap.

Fabi, Andretti, Villeneuve and Jimmy Vasser (Target/STP Reynard-Ford) followed in grid order. Tracy charged from eighth to sixth ahead of Mauricio Gugelmin (Hollywood Reynard-Ford) and Bryan Herta (Target/Scotch Video Reynard-Ford). Ribeiro and Pruett completed the top 10.

The hot early pace was slowed on lap seven when Carlos Guerrero crashed in Turn Three, happily without serious injury.

Andretti passed Fabi almost immediately after the restart, while teammate Tracy continued his charge toward the front by relieving Villeneuve of fourth on lap 22. Tracy moved up one more position when Andretti slowed abruptly just three laps later.

'We started to develop a mis[fire] in the engine and it just got worse and worse,' said a frustrated Andretti, out of the race almost before it had started.

Tracy's Series II Cosworth XB didn't last much longer, eliminating the Canadian after he had run strongly in second place: 'I was cruising. It's a big disappointment,' he said.

The Honda brigade was also to be disillusioned. Johnstone led handsomely for most of the first 57 laps before slowing suddenly following a huge sideways slide in Turn Four. The Oregonian did well to maintain control of his Reynard and avoid contact with Eddie Cheever's Copenhagen Lola-Ford which he was lapping at the instant his right-rear wheel-bearing failed. Incidentally, several other drivers experienced a similar problem as the afternoon progressed.

Johnstone returned to the fray, albeit many laps down after repairs had been effected. He set the fastest lap of the race at 231.659 mph before being hobbled for keeps by a brake problem.

Ribeiro, meanwhile, inherited the lead after a magnificent drive through the pack in the early stages. The Brazilian remained in control until more electrical woes sidelined his Tasman car just after half-distance.

Johnstone and Ribeiro deserved more than merely one PPG Cup point apiece, for claiming the pole and leading the most laps respectively. Nevertheless, they had made their point. So had Honda. And Firestone.

The demise of the Honda cars elevated Pruett and Unser into the top two positions. Initially, Unser held a commanding advantage, but that was erased when the yellow flags flew on lap 150 after a tire problem caused Hiro Matsushita to spin his Panasonic/Duskin Reynard-Ford in Turn Four. The two leaders then commenced a protracted duel to the finish.

It was an intriguing contest: Lola vs. Penske, Ford vs. Mercedes and Firestone vs. Goodyear. There was much at stake, especially for the drivers, with Unser seeking to resuscitate his championship aspirations after a disappointing summer and Pruett anxious to score his very first Indy Car victory.

A high rate of attrition ensured that the two leaders were bereft of any serious challengers throughout the second half of the race. Gugelmin, for example, lost time due to a wheel-bearing failure, as did title contenders Villeneuve and Bobby Rahal (Miller Genuine Draft Lola-Mercedes). Cheever moved up steadily to a strong third before succumbing to a gearbox dog-ring failure after 163 laps. Herta also climbed to third before being involved in a nasty crash in Turn Two.

The incident began when Lyn St. James' Giant/Strum/Whitlock Lola-Ford suffered a major engine failure. A close-following Danny Sullivan (VISA Reynard-Ford) had nowhere to go and, unfortunately, suffered a broken pelvis when his car's right-front wheel penetrated the monocoque after making heavy contact with the retaining wall.

Buddy Lazier also posted an excellent performance in Payton-Coyne's Agfa Lola T94/00-Ford. The underrated Colorado driver was assessed a

couldn't come close, restricted to a disappointing 225.722 mph by a mysterious electrical gremlin. Then came Johnstone. His first warmup lap was a stunning 228.534 mph – faster than Fabi's best – and the speed continued to rise as he gathered momentum. Johnstone's final lap was an incredible 230.458 mph. No one else came close.

'I've been working with Honda for 11 years,' said Johnstone after securing the first Indy Car pole not only for himself but also Honda and Comptech – and the first for Firestone tires since March 1974. 'This year we started midseason in the toughest series in racing, so this is just fantastic.'

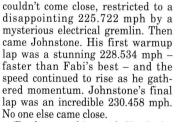

Photos: Michael C. Brown

Adrian Fernandez *(below)* survived a race of attrition to score his best result yet in the Tecate/Quaker State Lola-Mercedes.

stop-and-go penalty in the early stages for running over an air hose in the pits, despite which he rose inside the top 10 and passed Emerson Fittipaldi's eventual fifth-placed Marlboro Penske-Mercedes before losing many laps due to a c.v. joint failure.

Fernandez drove a sensible race to claim a personal best third at the finish, while Fabi was restricted to fourth by a chassis imbalance which caused several tires to blister.

Meanwhile, the battle between Unser and Pruett continued unabated. The pair exchanged the lead eight times during the 100 laps after Ribeiro's retirement, although the issue appeared to be settled when a blistered right-rear tire forced Unser to make an unscheduled pit stop just 20 laps from the finish.

'I thought it was all over,' said Unser, who lost almost a lap as Richard Buck and his crew changed all four Goodyear tires. But then came one final full-course caution when a punctured Firestone caused Alessandro Zampedri to crash his Mi-Jack Lola T94/00-Ford in Turn Four.

The incident prompted a five-lap dash to the finish. Pruett still appeared to have the upper hand, with several slower cars between them at the restart, but Unser took advantage of his fresher tires and was able to close onto Pruett's tail as the two leaders took the white flag signifying one lap to go. The record-sized crowd was on its feet as Unser made his move to the outside toward Turn One. The sound of the engines was literally drowned out as Unser's Penske sped past and took over the lead. Victory seemed almost assured.

But Pruett knew it wasn't over. Prior experience both in the Indy cars and the IROC stock cars had taught him that he still had a good opportunity – as long as he could stay in Unser's draft down the long back straightaway.

'He was weaving around on the straight, trying to break the draft, and I was trying to stay with him,' recounted Pruett. 'We were both using every trick in the book to try and win. I knew I had to run high in [Turns] Three and Four, and that's where my Firestone tires gave me the advantage. I could run high all day long and I was able to pass a lot of cars up there.

'We both went in deep and hard and high, and I managed to get up alongside him. We were virtually side by side all the way through Three and Four.'

Unser edged Pruett as high as he dared, but Pruett kept on coming. The momentum was on his side. Sure enough, he drew level with Unser's car in the middle of the corner, and then, with the crowd cheering wildly, he inched ahead as the two cars sped absolutely side by side out of Turn Four for the final time.

'I did that same move to Dale Earnhardt once in an IROC race,' said Unser, who was the first to congratulate Pruett on his courageous pass to ensure the victory. 'It was a great move. It was a fun race. What can I say? Both of us drove our hearts out today and the best man won.'

Unser, of course, was disappointed to finish second, especially after coming so close to the win, but he took solace from the fact his Penske had been a competitive force – and that it had taken a world-class maneuver to pry the spoils of victory from his grasp. Indeed, Unser garnered a huge ovation when he smiled broadly and proclaimed: 'Was that a show, or what?'

Johnstone steps into the spotlight

Parker Johnstone came of age as an Indy Car driver during the Marlboro 500. There's no question his Comptech Reynard-Honda was a major force at the daunting Michigan oval, yet the 34-year-old from Redmond, Ore., stepped up to the plate with a magnificent effort in qualifying, then withstood the pressure of starting from the pole and remained in control of the race until slowed by a mechanical failure.

Johnstone had waited a long time for his opportunity to establish himself as a top-flight Indy Car driver. He'd also taken a somewhat circuitous route in order to achieve his aims.

A gifted trumpet player in his youth, Johnstone sacrificed his musical ambitions in favor of a career in auto racing. Indianapolis always had been his ultimate goal, yet since making his first tentative step into the sport as a teenager, Johnstone competed almost exclusively in sedan or sports cars. Nevertheless, he carved quite a reputation for himself, especially after linking up with former SCCA National Champions Don Erb and Doug Peterson at Comptech Racing in 1987. Johnstone won the IMSA LuK Clutch Challenge for Comptech and Acura at his first attempt, then repeated as champion in 1988.

He also claimed a hat-trick of IMSA Camel Lights titles for the team.

When Honda made the move up into the Indy Car ranks in 1994, Comptech – and Johnstone – followed suit. Most of the time since then had been spent conducting engine tests, and despite the fact he had never before raced on an oval track, Johnstone quickly developed an affinity for the left-turn-only speedways.

It showed at MIS. Even so, after winning the pole, Johnstone wasn't above seeking advice: 'I was very fortunate today,' he said while relaxing in the Honda motorhome after the race, 'because I had an audience with Rick Mears and Al Unser this morning. They were fantastic.

'Rick Mears has always been a big hero of mine. I've studied his style on video, and today he talked me through all aspects of the race from green flag to checkered flag. He really helped me an awful lot.

'You know,' he continued, 'it's been quite a transformation in the course of only two days. Yesterday, in the press conference [after taking the pole], people were asking, "Parker Who?" And today I think we showed people that we really do belong at this level of the sport. It's been quite a thrill.'

SNIPPETS

• Robby Gordon's title hopes were virtually eliminated following his high-speed crash on Friday. Gordon, who was knocked unconscious by the impact *(below)* and spent one night in the hospital, returned to the track Saturday morning, brandishing a note from a neurologist who had apparently cleared him to drive. 'No chance,' replied the IndyCar medical team, invoking a rule prevalent throughout professional sports which precludes an athlete from participating in any activity for one week after sustaining a head injury.

• The broken left-rear lower A-arm which caused Gordon's crash was subjected to a thorough analysis by the Metallurgical Engineering department at Cummins, one of Walker Racing's primary sponsors. It was determined that the failure occurred as the result of improper chromium plating treatment. Reynard subsequently reclaimed and replaced all suspension components that had been so treated.

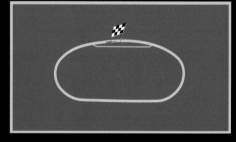

Photos: Michael C. Brown

• 'I got a bit anxious there on the last lap,' admitted Al Unser Jr. after his narrow defeat by Scott Pruett. 'I knew I needed to wait until Turn Three, but as soon as I caught up to him I thought, "What the heck, I have to go for it!" So I got him into [Turn] One and I should've waited until Turn Three. I kind of blew it. I tried to make my car as wide as I could coming off [Turn] Four but you gotta be safe out there and he had me up on the outside and there wasn't anything I could do. Still, it was a great race. I just hope everybody enjoyed the show.' No question about that, Al.

• Unser Jr. *(above)* was involved in another close finish Saturday afternoon, beating Trans-Am star Tom Kendall by a scant 0.112 seconds in the True Value Dodge International Race of Champions event.

• The drivers were unanimous in their praise for the new track surface – and grateful for the one-race-only boost limitation: 'No question it was the right thing to do,' declared Michael Andretti, who was fastest in the second practice session at 229.144 mph. 'We're flat out now, but believe me, we would have been anyway with the new surface, and I'll bet we would have been doing 240-plus, and I think that's crazy.'

PPG INDY CAR WORLD SERIES • ROUND 13

MARLBORO 500

MICHIGAN INTERNATIONAL SPEEDWAY, BROOKLYN, MICHIGAN

JULY 30, 250 LAPS – 500.000 MILES

Place	Driver (Nat.)	No.	Team Sponsors Car-Engine	Tires	Q Speed	Q Time	Q Pos.	Laps	Time/Status	Ave.	Pts.
1	Scott Pruett (USA)	20	Patrick Racing *Firestone* Lola T95/00-Ford	FS	224.841	32.023s	12	250	3h 07m 52.826s	159.676	20
2	Al Unser Jr. (USA)	1	Marlboro Team Penske Penske PC24-Mercedes	GY	224.296	32.100s	13	250	3h 07m 52.882s	159.675	16
3	Adrian Fernandez (MEX)	10	Galles *Tecate/Quaker State* Lola T95/00-Mercedes	GY	225.579	31.918s	11	249	Running		14
4	Teo Fabi (I)	33	Forsythe *Combustion Engineering/Indeck* Reynard 95I-Ford	GY	228.526	31.506s	2	247	Running		12
5	Emerson Fittipaldi (BR)	2	Marlboro Team Penske Penske PC24-Mercedes	GY	223.618	32.198s	17	245	Running		10
6	Stefan Johansson (S)	16	Bettenhausen *Alumax Aluminum* Penske PC23-Mercedes	GY	220.238	32.692s	21	244	Running		8
7	Jimmy Vasser (USA)	12	Ganassi *Target/STP* Reynard 95I-Ford	GY	227.982	31.582s	5	241	Running		6
8	Bobby Rahal (USA)	9	Rahal/Hogan *Miller Genuine Draft* Lola T95/00-Mercedes	GY	223.734	32.181s	16	240	Running		5
9	*Christian Fittipaldi (BR)	15	Walker *Marlboro/Chapeco Special* Reynard 95I-Ford	GY	224.649	32.050s	25	239	Running		4
10	Jacques Villeneuve (CDN)	27	Team Green *Player's Ltd.* Reynard 95I-Ford	GY	228.239	31.546s	4	235	Running		3
11	Mauricio Gugelmin (BR)	18	PacWest Racing Group *Hollywood* Reynard 95I-Ford	GY	227.839	31.601s	6	232	Running		2
12	*Gil de Ferran (BR)	8	Hall Racing *Pennzoil Special* Reynard 95I-Mercedes	GY	223.787	32.173s	15	226	Suspension		1
13	Alessandro Zampedri (I)	34	Payton-Coyne *The Mi-Jack Car* Lola T94/00-Ford	FS	218.197	32.998s	24	225	Accident		
14	Buddy Lazier (USA)	19	Payton-Coyne *Agfa/Raynor* Lola T94/00-Ford	FS	220.783	32.611s	20	223	Running		
15	Bryan Herta (USA)	4	Ganassi *Target/Scotch Video* Reynard 95I-Ford	GY	226.652	31.767s	7	193	Accident		
16	Danny Sullivan (USA)	17	PacWest Racing Group *VISA* Reynard 95I-Ford	GY	225.732	31.896s	9	189	Accident		
17	Lyn St. James (USA)	90	Dick Simon *Giant/Strum/Whitlock* Lola T95/00-Ford	GY	219.847	32.750s	22	188	Accident		
18	*Eliseo Salazar (RCH)	7	Dick Simon *Cristal/Mobil 1/Copec* Lola T95/00-Ford	GY	219.201	32.846s	23	175	Engine		
19	Eddie Cheever (USA)	14	A.J. Foyt *Copenhagen Racing* Lola T95/00-Ford	GY	223.546	32.208s	18	163	Transmission		
20	Hiro Matsushita (J)	25	Arciero-Wells *Panasonic/Duskin* Reynard 95I-Ford	FS	218.245	32.990s	26	139	Accident		
21	*Andre Ribeiro (BR)	31	Tasman Motorsports *LCI International* Reynard 95I-Honda	FS	225.722	31.898s	10	130	Electrical		1
22	Parker Johnstone (USA)	49	Comptech *Motorola Cellular* Reynard 95I-Honda	FS	230.458	31.242s	1	100	Brakes		1
23	Paul Tracy (CDN)	3	Newman-Haas *Kmart/Budweiser* Lola T95/00-Ford	GY	226.540	31.782s	8	91	Engine		
24	Raul Boesel (BR)	11	Rahal/Hogan *Duracell Charger* Lola T95/00-Mercedes	GY	224.266	32.105s	14	57	Engine		
25	Michael Andretti (USA)	6	Newman-Haas *Kmart/Texaco Havoline* Lola T95/00-Ford	GY	228.413	31.522s	3	40	Electrical		
26	*Carlos Guerrero (MEX)	22	Dick Simon *Herdez/Viva Mexico!* Lola T95/00-Ford	GY	223.480	32.218s	19	5	Accident		
NS	Robby Gordon (USA)	5	Walker *Valvoline/Cummins Special* Reynard 95I-Ford	GY	no speed	no time	–	–	Accident in practice		

* denotes Rookie driver

Caution flags: Laps 1–2, yellow start; laps 6–15, accident/Guerrero; laps 150–156, accident/Matsushita; laps 177–187, spin/Salazar; laps 194–207, accident/St. James and Sullivan; laps 237–244, accident/Zampedri. **Total:** six for 52 laps.

Lap leaders: Parker Johnstone, 1–45 (45 laps); Andre Ribeiro, 46 (1 lap); Paul Tracy, 47 (1 lap); Teo Fabi, 48 (1 lap); Eddie Cheever, 49–50 (2 laps); Johnstone, 51–57 (7 laps); Ribeiro, 58–88 (31 laps); Scott Pruett, 89–90 (2 laps); Mauricio Gugelmin, 91–92 (2 laps); Ribeiro, 93–128 (36 laps); Pruett, 129–131 (3 laps); Al Unser Jr., 132–152 (21 laps); Pruett, 153–154 (2 laps); Unser, 155–176 (22 laps); Pruett, 177–188 (12 laps); Unser, 189 (1 lap); Pruett, 190–207 (18 laps); Unser, 208–229 (22 laps); Pruett, 230–250 (21 laps). **Totals:** Ribeiro, 68 laps; Unser, 66 laps; Pruett, 58 laps; Johnstone, 52 laps; Cheever and Gugelmin, 2 laps; Tracy and Fabi, 1 lap.

Fastest race lap: Parker Johnstone, 31.080s, 231.659 mph, on lap 84.

Championship positions: 1 Villeneuve, 141; **2** Rahal, 111; **3** Gordon, 99; **4** Andretti, 96; **5** Pruett, 93; **6** Vasser, 79; **7** Tracy and Fabi, 78; **9** Unser, 77; **10** Gugelmin, 58; **11** Fernandez, 52; **12** E. Fittipaldi, 51; **13** C. Fittipaldi and Johansson, 50; **15** Boesel, 46; **16** Sullivan, 32; **17** Cheever, 30; **18** Herta, 20; **19** Salazar, 19; **20** Ribeiro, 16; **21** de Ferran, 14; **22** Zampedri, 11; **23** Bachelart, 8; **24** Danner and Luyendyk, 6; **26** Matsushita, 5; **27** Johnstone, 4; **28** Greco, 3; **29** C. Guerrero and Hall, 2; **31** R. Guerrero and Brayton, 1.
Championship positions and points totals provisional pending outcome of appeal by Penske following race at Portland.

EDS

MID-OHIO

1 – UNSER

2 – TRACY

3 – VILLENEUVE

There were three distinct phases to the Miller Genuine Draft 200. In the early stages of the 83-lap race, which took place amid sweltering 95-degree conditions on the challenging Mid-Ohio Sports Car Course, pole-winner Jacques Villeneuve held the advantage with Team Green's Player's Ltd. Reynard-Ford/Cosworth. Then Michael Andretti took up the running. But with just four laps to go and the #6 Kmart/Texaco Havoline Lola-Ford seemingly cruising toward its second victory of the season, Andretti slowed dramatically. His engine had let him down.

Andretti's misfortune played into the hands of Al Unser Jr., who took advantage of an inspired strategic call by Roger Penske and was perfectly positioned to guide his Marlboro Penske-Mercedes home to a superbly judged victory.

'It's awesome,' said a delighted Unser. 'It's great to be back. It was a long, hard-fought race. It's a shame Michael broke, because he had a great drive all day long, but what can you say?'

Paul Tracy gained some consolation for Paul Newman and Carl Haas by finishing second in his Kmart/Budweiser Lola-Ford, while fellow Canadian Villeneuve maintained his relentless charge toward the PPG Cup title with another sensible drive to third place for team owner Barry Green.

'It was a tough race,' admitted a thoroughly exhausted Villeneuve. 'The car was great in the first laps, then it picked up a lot of understeer and the brakes began to go away. It was really hot. I was dying!'

The shortcomings of the Marlboro Penske had not been entirely eliminated but a combination of astute tactics, slick pit work and Michael Andretti's perennial misfortune – not forgetting his own skill and indomitable spirit – enabled Al Unser Jr. *(below left)* to score a timely victory.

Bottom left: Adrian Fernandez enjoys plenty of encouragement from his Mexican sponsors.

Michael C. Brown

QUALIFYING

Villeneuve arrived at Mid-Ohio brimful with confidence following an impressive Formula 1 test in England. Despite that – or perhaps because of it – the 24-year-old made what he described as 'a stupid mistake' while shaking down his backup #27X machine during first practice on Friday. Villeneuve was fortunate that the car sustained only minor damage to its right-side suspension and undertray after sliding wide and hitting the wall at the exit of the final corner in front of the pits. Later in the afternoon, after switching to his primary car, Villeneuve made amends by claiming his fourth pole out of the last six races and his third in a row on permanent road courses.

'The car was really good,' he said after recording a stunning best of 1m 06.836s, shattering the existing track record of 1m 07.773s. 'Testing here earlier this year made all the difference in the second half of the season. We really have a good handle on the car.'

In fact, either of Villeneuve's three best laps would have been good enough for the pole, although one last attempt to find even more speed resulted in a lurid slide over the curbs in Turn One which saw the car momentarily teetering onto two wheels.

'I was being a little greedy,' he admitted. 'I tried to go in really, really fast. When I hit the curb, that launched me up in the air. It was nearly a big accident.'

Luckily, once again, the car escaped serious damage. Midway through the Friday qualifying session, during which most of the fastest times were set, Bryan Herta briefly looked set to challenge Villeneuve's best.

'I was pretty pleased when I got within one-tenth of Jacques,' said Herta, showing a good turn of pace in Chip Ganassi's Target/Scotch Video Reynard-Ford, 'but then he went and embarrassed us all.'

Herta was unable to respond to Villeneuve's improvement, although he did retain second place on the grid. Herta, incidentally, set the fastest time during qualifying on Saturday, albeit fractionally slower than his own Friday best.

Andretti, in the best-placed Lola, had to be content with a place on row two of the grid, followed by the Reynard-Fords of Mauricio Gugelmin (Hollywood/PacWest) and Robby Gordon (Valvoline/Cummins/Walker

Villeneuve confirms a future in Formula 1

On the day before the commencement of official practice at Mid-Ohio, Jacques Villeneuve came clean: He would not be racing in the PPG Cup series in 1996. Instead he would accept a lucrative and personally challenging offer to compete in the FIA Formula 1 World Championship. The move was not unexpected. Indeed, speculation had been rife for several months that the young French-Canadian would follow in the footsteps of his late, lamented father, Gilles, who carved a spectacular reputation with the charismatic Ferrari team before tragically losing his life in a crash during practice for the Belgian Grand Prix in 1982.

The rumors intensified during the two-week gap between the races at Michigan and Mid-Ohio, especially after Villeneuve completed an extremely impressive three-day test for the Williams-Renault team in England. In fact, despite having no prior experience of a Formula 1 car, nor of the Silverstone Grand Prix circuit, Villeneuve recorded lap times only slightly slower than the team's regular drivers Damon Hill and David Coulthard. His destiny seemed assured.

For a week or so after the test, Villeneuve remained tight-lipped on the subject of where he would compete in 1996. Formula 1 team owner Frank Williams also refused to

comment, other than to say he was excited by the 24-year-old's performance.

But Villeneuve's mind was made up. First of all, via his manager, Craig Pollock, he notified Indy Car team owner Barry Green of his intentions, then long-time sponsor Player's Ltd. issued a statement on his behalf which confirmed the switch to Formula 1 without specifically naming the team for which he would be driving.

'This was one of the toughest decisions I have ever had to make,' said Villeneuve. 'I am honored to have been associated with Player's Ltd., Barry Green and the entire crew. They are a first-class team and they gave me the opportunity to gain valuable experience.'

A couple of weeks later, Williams finally confirmed that Villeneuve would indeed drive alongside Hill, whose own father, Graham, numbered two Formula 1 World Championships and the 1966 Indianapolis 500 among his illustrious list of achievements.

Not surprisingly, Villeneuve's decision was greeted with mixed feelings by Barry Green: 'Obviously we are saddened to lose Jacques as part of our team but at the same time we are proud that we have made a significant contribution to his development.

'Jacques is one of the most talented drivers I have ever worked with and he will be a star in Formula 1,' he predicted.

Racing), who vaulted a couple of positions during Saturday's slightly slower session. Other notable improvements were posted by Gil de Ferran, who moved from 12th to sixth in his Pennzoil Reynard-Mercedes, Unser (13th to eighth), and Indy Car debutante Juan Fangio II, who found 1.5 seconds and moved from 22nd to 14th in the PacWest team's #17 VISA Reynard-Ford.

RACE

A vast crowd assembled on race day, with just about every vantage point taken on the picturesque parkland circuit. The sea of bright colors ensured a superb spectacle.

As usual at Mid-Ohio, the 28-car field was unleashed midway along the long, downhill back straightaway rather than at the finish line in front of the pits. Villeneuve took full advantage of his pole position to lead into the first corner. Andretti emerged as his nearest challenger, sweeping past on the inside of Herta, who confessed he simply braked too soon for the first turn. Gugelmin also took the opportunity to pass Herta.

The two leaders soon extended a comfortable advantage over Gugelmin, who in turn stretched away from Herta's already understeering Target/Scotch car. De Ferran ran strongly

in fifth, while Gordon rebounded from losing two positions at the start by repassing Tracy on lap three. This group also included local favorite Bobby Rahal, who was in desperate need of a strong result in his Miller Genuine Draft Lola-Mercedes to keep his championship aspirations alive, and Unser, who followed closely without ever looking especially menacing.

By lap 20, Andretti had clawed back from an early two-second deficit to the leader. Gugelmin was already 10 seconds in arrears, chased by Herta, who remained in fourth, albeit another six seconds farther behind. Unser, meanwhile, had begun to fall away slightly, and on lap 23, rather earlier than originally scheduled, he peeled off into the pit lane for service.

'I was using up my tires too much,' related Unser, who continued in ninth after the first round of pit stops had been completed. 'The car's still not working as well as we'd like it to – it just uses up the tires.'

The lap after Unser's pit stop, Andretti made a bid for the lead under braking at the end of the main straightaway. Villeneuve jealously guarded the inside line, whereupon Andretti instead tried to make a pass by going the long way around . . . only to be forced almost into the grass on the exit. Clearly, Villeneuve was in

an uncompromising mood. Andretti decided to bide his time.

Both men made their first pit stops on lap 28. They rejoined in the same order, but Andretti knew his best chance of making a pass would come before Villeneuve was properly back into his stride. Once again Villeneuve rebuffed the predictable challenge at the end of the main straightaway. A couple of corners later, however, with both cars still sliding around, their fresh tires not yet up to optimum working temperature, Andretti squeezed through by virtue of a typically brave and incisive maneuver in the Esses. This time Villeneuve was unable to respond.

Andretti quickly left Villeneuve far behind in his mirrors, pulling away by a second per lap. Villeneuve, meanwhile, soon came under threat from de Ferran and Rahal, both of whom had made up ground as a result of sensationally fast pit stops.

On lap 39, de Ferran executed a fine outside-line pass under braking at the end of the straight. Villeneuve lost valuable momentum as he tried in vain to rebuff the challenge, and moments later a determined Rahal sought to take advantage. Rahal drew level with Villeneuve as they accelerated toward the crest of the hill, where the road arcs sharply to the left, and at that point he was on the unfavored outside line. If Rahal had managed to maintain position, he would have assumed the inside line as the pair dived downhill into the next corner – but he didn't make it that far. Instead, a clash of wheels saw Rahal's Lola ricochet into the barriers (ironically clad with Miller Genuine Draft signage) and out of the race.

Rahal emerged uninjured but almost apoplectic with rage, convinced that Villeneuve had pushed him off the road on purpose. One lap later, with the field now circulating at reduced speed behind the pace car, Rahal stepped onto the track and, encouraged by cheers from the partisan crowd, gestured angrily toward Villeneuve, who had continued in third place.

'I was racing with de Ferran and he outbraked Jacques at the end of the back straight,' explained Rahal. 'I think Jacques was getting tired or running out of brakes. I moved on the outside where two cars have plenty of room. I think he got sideways and then he nailed me.'

Villeneuve, who dismissed the clash of wheels as 'a racing incident,'

Bobby Rahal fights to correct a slide as Al Unser Jr. closes in. Rahal's hopes of regaining the PPG Cup were dealt a mortal blow when the Miller Genuine Draft Lola crashed out of the race after a clash with Jacques Villeneuve.
Photo: Michael C. Brown

Left: Scott Goodyear, who had come so close to winning the Indianapolis 500 for Tasman, scored a PPG Cup point on his return to the series with one of the team's Reynard-Hondas.

Paul Tracy *(bottom)* enjoyed better luck than his Newman-Haas teammate, bringing the Kmart/Budweiser Lola home in second place.

was indeed experiencing some difficulty under braking. Nevertheless, after the race, he did claim to sympathize, at least to some degree, with three-time PPG Cup champion Rahal's point of view: 'He was fighting for the championship,' noted Villeneuve. 'I'm leading the championship and I'm the one who banged wheels with him, so it doesn't look too good. But it was just a mistake. It happens in racing. If it had been a guy that wasn't in the championship hunt it wouldn't have looked as bad. When you're side by side and you're going for it, sometimes [the car] slides and you just barely touch wheels.'

The hiatus caused by the first and only full-course caution of the day allowed Unser's team owner, Roger Penske, a chance to roll the dice.

'Al was running strong but he couldn't pass,' reasoned Penske, who calls the shots on Unser's car. 'We put some front wing in the car at the first stop and the thing really picked up. It was a good move. We figured let's unhook him and take a shot.'

So Penske called for Unser to make a pit stop under the yellow. Typically expert work by Richard

Buck and the crew had Unser on his way inside 10 seconds, since he needed only a partial load of fuel. In doing so he lost only two positions.

'We were on full tanks and on fresh tires,' continued Penske, 'and we knew we'd be in good shape if we could stay within 20 seconds of the leader.'

Of course, Unser, who resumed 11th, still needed the cards to fall his way. And for a change, they did. De Ferran's Mercedes engine began to lose power immediately after the restart. On lap 50 he coasted to a halt on the back straight, engine blown. Yet another potential podium finish had slipped away.

The status quo was maintained until around two-thirds distance, when one by one the remaining frontrunners peeled off into pit lane for regularly scheduled service. Unser, meanwhile, spurred on by the scent of a challenge, maintained a fast pace which enabled him to inherit the lead on lap 63 when Tracy became the last of the leaders to stop. Unser, of course, still required one more pit stop, which came on lap 70, but exceptional work by the Marlboro Penske

team and the need for only enough fuel for the final 13 laps ensured he was stationary for less than 11 seconds. Unser rejoined with the loss of only one position.

Andretti duly regained control of the race. A well-deserved victory was virtually assured. But then, incredibly, just as in Cleveland a mere three weeks earlier, his Ford/Cosworth engine suddenly gave up the ghost.

'I was just in shock, disbelief, especially when I drove so hard to get that far,' said Andretti, his frustration compounded by the fact his team had opted to err on the side of caution by selecting an older Series I XB engine for the race instead of the more potent but not fully reliable Series II. 'I worked my butt off. It was really disappointing.'

Andretti's cruel misadventure allowed Unser, his long-time nemesis, to regain the lead on lap 80. Unser encountered some delay in the closing stages, mired behind the lapped car of Eliseo Salazar, but finally acknowledged the checkered flag 2.037 seconds clear of Tracy.

'I owe this win to my crew,' praised Unser. 'Roger made a great

call and my guys did a fabulous job in the pits. We were using up the tires a little bit and so we needed to get out of sequence [on the pit stops]. Everything worked out just great.'

Tracy secured the runner-up placing – for the third time in four years at Mid-Ohio – thereby gaining some relief for Newman-Haas Racing after overhauling Villeneuve during the second pit stop sequence, while countryman Villeneuve padded his already considerable championship lead by taking third.

'It was hard work,' said Villeneuve in between taking gasps of air. 'Even if we didn't run as strong as we wanted, it's great for the points.'

Adrian Fernandez finished close behind, among the PPG Cup points for the eighth successive race in his Tecate/Quaker State Lola-Mercedes after moving up steadily as the afternoon progressed. Herta ran next, driving hard and overcoming a couple of mediocre pit stops as well as excessive understeer to fend off the vastly more experienced Gugelmin, who killed his hopes of a podium finish by stalling the engine during his first pit stop.

SNIPPETS

Photos: Michael C. Brown

• Raul Boesel *(above)* experienced yet another disappointing weekend. An oil leak obliged him to switch to his backup Duracell Lola-Mercedes on Friday morning, while his progress in qualifying was restricted by an electrical problem. After starting 13th, stifled by a lack of grip, Boesel fell back to 20th when he made contact with Christian Fittipaldi, then was

assessed a stop-and-go penalty for inadvertently overtaking another car under yellow flags. Undaunted, the Brazilian charged from 24th to eighth – setting third fastest lap of the race – before being halted by an engine failure 10 laps from the finish.

• Adrian Fernandez was not at all happy with the balance

of his Lola-Mercedes on Friday. Saturday, however, brought a substantial improvement after a lengthy debrief with engineer Ed Nathman and crew chief Owen Snyder. 'It's much better now,' said Fernandez. 'Yesterday we were completely lost. We didn't have a good test here so we didn't learn as much as we wanted about the car.'

• Andre Ribeiro's hopes of a solid result quite literally went up in smoke when his LCI Reynard-Honda caught fire following a minor fuel spillage during his first scheduled pit stop. Tasman crew member Randy Lampard selflessly dived into the cockpit to assist Ribeiro's escape from the invisible

methanol flames, which were quickly doused by other equally quick-thinking team members. No injuries were reported.

• Patrick Racing crew chief Tony Van Dongen suffered torn leg ligaments when he was inadvertently bowled over in the pit lane by Scott Pruett's Firestone Lola-Ford during the final warmup session.

• Mauricio Gugelmin was a factor all weekend in the PacWest team's Hollywood Reynard, although a problem within the cockpit hindered his progress in the race. 'A long piece of cable, maybe a radio cable, dropped by my feet,' revealed Gugelmin.

'So besides driving I was playing football with the bloody thing inside the car. I was really mad about that. Then, on the first pit stop, I made a mistake. I let the engine die. But that thing on my foot really screwed me up all day.'

• Another notable performance was posted by

Gugelmin's new teammate, Juan Fangio II *(below)*, who substituted for the injured Danny Sullivan and enjoyed a fine run to seventh on his Indy Car debut. 'He did a brilliant job,' praised chief engineer Alan Mertens. 'Very impressive. He was a pleasure to work with. He had a great demeanor and he drove the hell out of the car.'

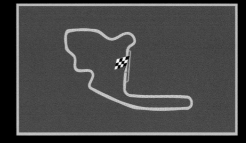

PPG INDY CAR WORLD SERIES • ROUND 14

MILLER GENUINE DRAFT 200

MID-OHIO SPORTS CAR COURSE, LEXINGTON, OHIO

AUGUST 13, 83 LAPS – 185.800 MILES

Place	Driver (Nat.)	No.	Team Sponsors Car-Engine	Tires	Q Speed	Q Time	Q Pos.	Laps	Time/Status	Ave.	Pts.
1	Al Unser Jr. (USA)	1	Marlboro Team Penske Penske PC24-Mercedes	GY	118.859	1m 08.148s	8	83	1h 44m 04.774s	107.110	20
2	Paul Tracy (CDN)	3	Newman-Haas *Kmart/Budweiser* Lola T95/00-Ford	GY	118.978	1m 08.080s	7	83	1h 44m 46.811s	107.075	16
3	Jacques Villeneuve (CDN)	27	Team Green *Player's Ltd.* Reynard 95I-Ford	GY	121.192	1m 06.836s	1	83	1h 44m 54.299s	106.947	15
4	Adrian Fernandez (MEX)	10	Galles *Tecate/Quaker State* Lola T95/00-Mercedes	GY	118.501	1m 08.354s	11	83	1h 44m 55.552s	106.926	12
5	Bryan Herta (USA)	4	Ganassi *Target/Scotch Video* Reynard 95I-Ford	GY	120.150	1m 07.416s	2	83	1h 44m 58.655s	106.873	10
6	Mauricio Gugelmin (BR)	18	PacWest Racing Group *Hollywood* Reynard 95I-Ford	GY	119.326	1m 07.881s	4	83	1h 44m 59.528s	106.858	8
7	*Juan Fangio II (RA)	17	PacWest Racing Group *VISA* Reynard 95I-Ford	GY	118.196	1m 08.530s	14	83	1h 45m 10.949s	106.663	6
8	Robby Gordon (USA)	5	Walker *Valvoline/Cummins* Special Reynard 95I-Ford	GY	119.104	1m 08.008s	5	83	1h 45m 12.492s	106.637	5
9	Jimmy Vasser (USA)	12	Ganassi *Target/STP* Reynard 95I-Ford	GY	118.744	1m 08.214s	10	83	1h 45m 26.074s	106.407	4
10	Eddie Cheever (USA)	14	A.J. Foyt *Copenhagen Racing* Lola T95/00-Ford	GY	116.269	1m 09.666s	23	83	1h 45m 46.327s	106.065	3
11	Scott Pruett (USA)	20	Patrick Racing *Firestone* Lola T95/00-Ford	FS	117.327	1m 09.038s	21	82	Running		2
12	Scott Goodyear (CDN)	24	Tasman Motorsports *LCI/CNN/Motorola* Reynard 95I-Honda	FS	117.547	1m 08.908s	19	82	Running		1
13	*Eliseo Salazar (RCH)	7	Dick Simon *Cristal/Mobil 1/Copec* Lola T95/00-Ford	GY	115.715	1m 10.000s	24	82	Running		
14	Alessandro Zampedri (I)	34	Payton-Coyne *The Mi-Jack Car* Lola T94/00-Ford	FS	114.385	1m 10.813s	28	81	Running		
15	Hiro Matsushita (J)	25	Arciero-Wells *Panasonic/Duskin* Reynard 95I-Ford	FS	114.993	1m 10.439s	26	81	Running		
16	Eric Bachelart (B)	19	Payton-Coyne *The Agfa Car* Lola T94/00-Ford	FS	114.802	1m 10.556s	27	81	Running		
17	Teo Fabi (I)	33	Forsythe *Combustion Engineering/Indeck* Reynard 95I-Ford	GY	118.027	1m 08.629s	16	80	Running		
18	*Carlos Guerrero (MEX)	22	Dick Simon *Herdez/Viva Mexico!* Lola T95/00-Ford	GY	115.710	1m 10.002s	25	80	Running		
19	Michael Andretti (USA)	6	Newman-Haas *Kmart/Texaco Havoline* Lola T95/00-Ford	GY	120.065	1m 07.463s	3	79	Engine		1
20	Raul Boesel (BR)	11	Rahal/Hogan *Duracell Charger* Lola T95/00-Mercedes	GY	118.220	1m 08.516s	13	74	Engine		
21	Emerson Fittipaldi (BR)	2	Marlboro Team Penske Penske PC24-Mercedes	GY	117.586	1m 08.886s	18	65	Engine		
22	Marco Greco (BR)	55	Galles *Brastemp/Int. Sports* Lola T95/00-Mercedes	GY	116.450	1m 09.558s	22	62	Out of fuel		
23	Stefan Johansson (S)	16	Bettenhausen *Alumax Aluminum* Penske PC23-Mercedes	GY	117.847	1m 08.733s	17	61	Engine		
24	*Gil de Ferran (BR)	8	Hall Racing *Pennzoil Special* Reynard 95I-Mercedes	GY	119.039	1m 08.045s	6	49	Engine		
25	*Christian Fittipaldi (BR)	15	Walker *Marlboro/Chapeco Special* Reynard 95I-Ford	GY	118.091	1m 08.591s	15	46	Fire		
26	Bobby Rahal (USA)	9	Rahal/Hogan *Miller Genuine Draft* Lola T95/00-Mercedes	GY	118.805	1m 08.179s	9	38	Accident		
27	*Andre Ribeiro (BR)	31	Tasman Motorsports *LCI International* Reynard 95I-Honda	FS	118.344	1m 08.445s	12	32	Fire		
28	Parker Johnstone (USA)	49	Comptech *Motorola Cellular* Reynard 95I-Honda	FS	117.446	1m 08.968s	20	0	Accident		
NQ	*Hubert Stromberger (A)	64	Project Indy *No-Touch/Van Dyne/Marcelo* Reynard 94I-Ford	GY	112.891	1m 11.751s	28	–	Did not qualify		

* denotes Rookie driver

Caution flags: Laps 39–44, accident/Rahal. **Total:** one for six laps.

Lap leaders: Jacques Villeneuve, 1–29 (29 laps); Gil de Ferran, 30–31 (2 laps); Michael Andretti, 32–59 (28 laps); Villeneuve, 60 (1 lap); Paul Tracy, 61–62 (2 laps); Al Unser Jr., 63–69 (7 laps); Andretti, 70–79 (10 laps); Unser, 80–83 (4 laps). **Totals:** Andretti, 38 laps; Villeneuve, 30 laps; Unser, 11 laps; de Ferran and Tracy, 2 laps.

Fastest race lap: Al Unser Jr., 1m 09.947s, 115.802 mph, on lap 73.

Championship positions: 1 Villeneuve, 156; **2** Rahal, 111; **3** Gordon, 104; **4** Unser and Andretti, 97; **6** Pruett, 95; **7** Tracy, 94; **8** Vasser, 83; **9** Fabi, 78; **10** Gugelmin, 66; **11** Fernandez, 64; **12** E. Fittipaldi, 51; **13** C. Fittipaldi and Johansson, 50; **15** Boesel, 46; **16** Cheever, 33; **17** Sullivan, 32; **18** Herta, 30; **19** Salazar, 19; **20** Ribeiro, 16; **21** de Ferran, 14; **22** Zampedri, 11; **23** Bachelart, 8; **24** Danner, Luyendyk and Fangio, 6; **27** Matsushita, 5; **28** Johnstone, 4; **29** Greco, 3; **30** C. Guerrero and Hall, 2; **32** R. Guerrero, Goodyear and Brayton, 1.

Championship positions and points totals provisional pending outcome of appeal by Penske following race at Portland.

EDS

NEW HAMPSHIRE

Making good use of the advantage offered by the combination of Honda power and Firestone tires, Andre Ribeiro dives inside the Kmart/Texaco Havoline Lola of Michael Andretti to take the lead.
Photo: Michael C. Brown

Andre Ribeiro joined an elite group of first-time winners when he guided the Tasman Motorsports Group's LCI International Reynard-Honda to a stunning victory in the New England 200. In doing so he joined Nigel Mansell and Jacques Villeneuve as the only drivers within the past 10 years to have won a round of the PPG Indy Car World Series during their rookie campaign.

'I can't believe it,' said an emotional Ribeiro after dominating the second half of the race and beating Michael Andretti to the finish line by 14.482 seconds – the third largest margin of victory this season. 'This is the greatest moment in my life. It's incredible. Incredible.'

Ribeiro, who started from the pole and led most laps, also secured a well-deserved maiden victory for Honda.

'It's a tribute to all the hard work, the long hours that went into this program,' said Robert Clarke, general manager of Honda Performance Development. 'The new engine, the HRH, has been strong from the first time we raced it at Indy. We could see a win was coming; we could feel it.'

Ribeiro displayed his maturity by being content to bide his time during the early stages of the race. Teo Fabi, who started on the outside of the front row, led confidently from the start, only to fade to 12th by the finish. Andretti took up the running, although ultimately neither he nor third-place finisher Al Unser Jr. was able to halt Ribeiro's charge.

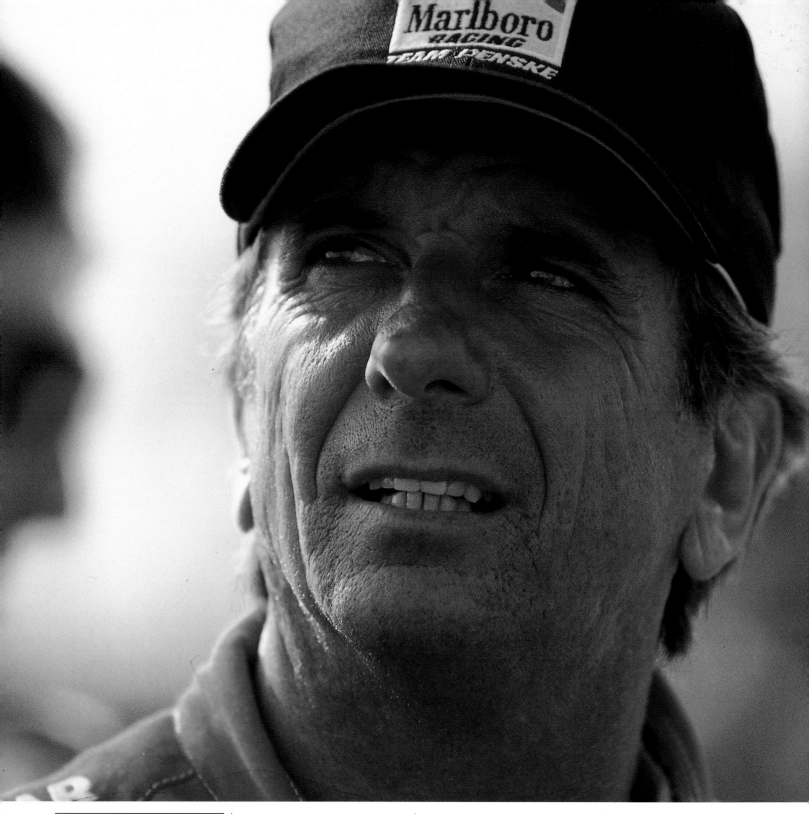

QUALIFYING

Ribeiro was among the fastest drivers from the outset of practice on Friday, although it wasn't until qualifying that he showed his true colors. Running sixth in the lineup, Ribeiro unleashed a stunning first lap at 21.477 seconds – more than a half-second quicker than anyone else to that point and three-tenths quicker than his previous best. Ribeiro's second lap was even faster at 21.466. The 29-year-old then had to sit back and wait to see if anyone would topple him from the coveted pole position.

'It was much harder to watch the others than drive myself,' declared Ribeiro. 'It was almost too exciting at the end. It was very, very close.'

Indeed, the final stages of the single-car qualifying session were enlivened first of all by Walker Racing teammates Christian Fittipaldi

(Marlboro/Chapeco Reynard-Ford) and Robby Gordon (Valvoline/Cummins Reynard-Ford), both of whom dipped below the 22-second barrier. They were promptly eclipsed by Scott Pruett (21.506), whose Firestone/Patrick Racing Lola-Ford had been fastest on the first day of practice. Then Fabi caused Ribeiro's heart to skip a few beats when he stopped the clocks at 21.498 on his first flying lap with Jerry Forsythe's Combustion Engineering/Indeck Reynard-Ford.

Fabi's second lap looked like being even faster . . . until he attempted to carry just a little too much speed into Turn Three. The resultant understeer scrubbed off valuable momentum. Ribeiro's pole was assured.

'It's a great feeling to be on the pole for the first time,' said Ribeiro. 'I think we have a very good combination. Tasman has put together a very good package with the Honda

engine and Firestone tires, and it's all coming together. We've definitely proved we can run up front.'

Fabi and Pruett also bettered Emerson Fittipaldi's existing track record, the top three all averaging more than 177 mph. Fittipaldi himself languished way back in 16th, one place ahead of Marlboro Penske-Mercedes teammate Al Unser Jr.

'Both cars picked up a humongous understeer in qualifying,' reported Fittipaldi's race engineer, Tom Brown. 'It cost us half a second. Other than that the cars are running well. If we can get rid of that push, we'll be looking good for the race.'

Series leader Jacques Villeneuve's Player's Ltd. Reynard-Ford also was afflicted by inconsistent handling, which restricted him to 15th on the grid, equaling the worst qualifying position of his Indy Car career. Adrian Fernandez suffered the opposite problem, a sudden snap-oversteer

causing him to crash heavily on Friday afternoon after setting the second fastest time in Rick Galles' Tecate/Quaker State Lola-Mercedes. The Mexican did well to salvage 10th on the tightly packed grid.

In all, 20 cars were within one second of the pole-time, and it was rather poignant to note that the last among that group was Bobby Rahal, who turned his back on the Honda program at the end of last season and instead opted for Mercedes-Benz power for his Miller Genuine Draft Lola.

RACE

Perfect weather conditions persisted into race day, with clear blue skies and comfortable temperatures in the 80s helping to attract a healthy crowd of 47,000 to the Bahre family's state-of-the-art 1.058-mile New Hampshire International Speedway.

Seemingly now more at home on ovals than on the road courses where he started his career, Emerson Fittipaldi *(left)* enjoyed one of the more rewarding races of a largely disappointing season, climbing from 16th in the starting order to fifth place at the finish. By contrast, the veteran's young nephew, Christian *(below)*, qualified superbly in fifth place but had faded to eighth by the flag.

The start was clean, although Ribeiro did not make best use of his pole position: 'I was a bit loose coming off Turn Four,' he admitted, 'so I lost two positions. Then I decided to just wait, be patient. That was the main word that was in my head, especially at the beginning of the race.'

Fabi edged ahead of Ribeiro at the green flag, while Gordon drove deep and high into Turn One to move into second place. Ribeiro tucked in behind, followed by Pruett, Jimmy Vasser (Target/STP Reynard-Ford) and Christian Fittipaldi. Farther back, Fernandez abruptly lost control on the exit of Turn Two and slammed backward into the wall.

'I really feel bad for my team because they've worked so hard this weekend,' said Fernandez, who emerged unscathed from his second major impact in just three days. Miraculously, everyone else was able to avoid the errant Mexican, although a lengthy caution period ensued while the wreckage was cleared.

The leading positions remained unchanged when the race was restarted, with Fabi continuing to run strongly out in front. Ribeiro finally found a way past Gordon on lap 24, and soon afterward Gordon began to plunge down the order as his Valvoline/Cummins Reynard started to oversteer dramatically.

'It was the same as at Nazareth,' noted Gordon, who slipped to a disappointed ninth at the finish. 'We were quick all weekend and as soon as we go racing we get loose about 15 to 20 laps in and I just have to

hang on for 30 more laps until I can make a pit stop. That makes for a real long day.'

Ribeiro took over the pursuit of Fabi, while Pruett also displayed the competitiveness of the Firestone tires by running comfortably in third until losing control amid traffic on lap 41 while under intense pressure from Andretti.

'We were dicing real hard,' said Pruett, who hit the wall backward with considerable force. 'Michael and I went down into Turn Three and it got away from me. I don't know if we may have touched. I don't know if it was the turbulence or what. The car just got away from me real quick.'

There was no evidence of any contact, although Andretti certainly was fortunate to avoid the spinning Patrick machine as it revolved directly in front of him.

'I think he might have got down on the apron [the flat area on the inside of the turn] and he lost it,' reported Andretti. 'It got my heart going a bit, but we missed him.'

The second full-course caution of the day triggered the first round of pit stops, which resulted in several significant changes in the order. First of all, an air-wrench failure cost Fabi valuable time, dropping him from first to eighth. Worse, a decision to switch to the harder Goodyear option compound backfired as his car began to oversteer drastically soon after the restart. Another air-gun failure cost more time for the diminutive Italian, who slipped to 12th after making an extra pit stop

to change back to the primary tires in the later stages.

Ribeiro also lost a little ground, due to a minor mix-up over which set of tires were supposed to be fitted. The Brazilian rejoined in fourth behind Andretti, Newman-Haas teammate Paul Tracy (Kmart/Budweiser Lola-Ford), who took advantage of an exceptionally fast pit stop, and Vasser.

Unser also had made tremendous progress. The defending series champion moved up quickly from 17th to 10th in the early stages, then leapt to sixth following a very efficient pit stop.

Ribeiro, though, was the man to watch. He made short work of Tracy and Vasser once the race was resumed. Soon he was setting his sights on Andretti in the lead.

'In the middle of the race, when I was behind Michael, I had a very good balance on the car and I felt that was the moment to go,' said Ribeiro.

And go he did. Ribeiro remained tucked into Andretti's draft for several laps, heeding the advice of team owner Steve Horne on the radio and waiting for the opportunity to make a legitimate move for the lead. Finally, on lap 100, Ribeiro saw his chance and dived for the inside under braking. The pass was incisive and perfectly executed. Andretti was unable to respond.

'I was bogged down a bit in traffic and that's when he was able to make a run at me,' said Andretti. 'He took advantage of that. He braked real late into Turn One and

Photos: Michael C. Brown

Michael C. Brown

Underrated Italian Teo Fabi *(bottom)* put in another strong qualifying performance with the Combustion Engineering/Indeck Reynard but, once again, misfortune on race day cost him all chance of victory.

it was a real good move. I tried to come back at him but he managed to put a couple of [slower] cars between us and that was it.'

Ribeiro never looked back. He relinquished the lead for a few laps after making his second pit stop on lap 122, then regained his advantage when Andretti stopped a handful of laps later. By then the two leaders had pulled a full lap clear of Unser, who had moved up to third place after Tracy was forced out by an oil leak. The Tasman team expressed some minor concern about fuel consumption immediately after Ribeiro had stopped for the second time, but judicious use of the throttle and gearing soon allayed any fears.

'With the gap that we had, we were able to conserve the fuel and the tires,' said Ribeiro. 'It really wasn't a problem. The car was perfect. The tires were perfect. The engine was perfect. Today we had the best combination.'

Andretti concurred with the Brazilian's assessment, especially with regard to the tires.

'I think our car was quite good,' declared Andretti. 'It seemed like the longer we ran on the tires, the better off Andre was. That's what got us, I think. Firestone did a pretty good job this weekend. We definitely had the best Goodyear car out there. On the second [pit] stop, the guys asked me what adjustments I wanted to make and I didn't know what to say. I didn't know what else to do. It was very well balanced. I could run with Andre the first half of the fuel stint, but then the last half is where he was able to gain a bit on us and that was the difference.'

Unser continued his sequence of podium finishes, claiming third, one lap off the ultimate pace, while Villeneuve moved steadily up the order to finish fourth for Team Green. The result was good enough to virtually clinch the PPG Cup title with two races remaining. Indeed, only Unser retained a theoretical chance of beating the French-Canadian – and only then if the Penske team managed to overcome the odds and win its appeal against Unser's disqualification at Portland.

'We're very happy,' said Villeneuve, smiling broadly. 'It was a great effort from everybody on Team Green. We knew we just had to go out and be aggressive. We made some changes to the car and it was very strong at the end of the race. We were just trying to get up through the pack. We weren't really

Maiden victory for Tasman

New Zealander Steve Horne *(above)* has made an enormous impression on the North American scene over the past 15 years or so. After guiding Australian Geoff Brabham to the SCCA Can-Am Championship, he was hired in 1982 by Jim Trueman to establish the Truesports Indy Car team. Bobby Rahal was to be the driver. The combination was successful almost right away. Horne, Rahal and Truesports won a pair of PPG Indy Car World Series championships in the middle 1980s and added a victory in the Indianapolis 500.

Ultimately, however, after Trueman had succumbed to a lengthy battle with cancer, the relationship soured. Rahal left to pursue other options. Horne quit the foundering team in 1992. Instead he established his own Tasman Motorsports Group in partnership with a pair of Columbus, Ohio businessmen, Ben Dillon and Stan Ross.

Horne wisely set his sights on the burgeoning PPG-Firestone Indy Lights Championship as a means of proving his team's worth, and with a strong nucleus of people from the old Truesports operation, including

team manager/Tasman part-owner Jeff Eischen and race engineer Don Halliday, they swept to the championship in both 1993 (Bryan Herta) and 1994 (Steve Robertson).

Graduation to the PPG Cup series represented the next logical step. Once again, Tasman was competitive almost from the start, with Scott Goodyear narrowly missing out on victory in the Indianapolis 500 and Ribeiro leading strongly at Michigan until being halted by an electrical problem.

The victory in New Hampshire was richly deserved. 'I know some people say I'm unemotional,' said Horne. 'But today I got emotional. We have a lot of young guys on the team and some of them have never won an Indy Car race, so it was a great experience for me just to see their faces.

'Personally, too, it was very satisfying – the last win for me in the Indy cars was in 1988 at Pocono with Bobby Rahal. Perhaps this was kind of a payback after Indy and Michigan. We had the best package today; we had the best tires, the best engine and the best driver.'

worried about the championship at that point.'

Emerson Fittipaldi also overcame a poor qualifying run, rising to fifth in

the second Marlboro Penske-Mercedes, while Vasser, who had run strongly in third for a large portion of the race, survived excessive oversteer

– and a near-miss while lapping the year-old Mi-Jack Lola-Ford of Alessandro Zampedri – to finish sixth.

De Ferran lost time on his pit stops due to an inoperative clutch (again), but was rewarded with his best result to date, seventh, while the Walker Racing pair, Christian Fittipaldi and Gordon, overcame handling problems to take the next two positions. Rahal, like Gordon, finished three laps down, and 10th place wasn't enough to keep him in contention for the PPG Cup championship, which seemed set to make its first trip north of the border, thanks to the efforts of young Mr. Villeneuve.

'Mathematically, Junior still has a chance if they give him back his points from Portland,' said Villeneuve. 'So, until we know for sure, I won't tell myself that it's won because it's still possible to lose it.'

The champagne therefore remained on ice in the Team Green enclave. Not so in the Honda motorhome, where Steve Horne and the Tasman contingent prepared to celebrate in style. Their victory was overdue and thoroughly deserved.

Michael C. Brown

SNIPPETS

• Rookie driver Gil de Ferran *(below)* overcame inconsistent handling (a common complaint after the race) to reach the finish line for the first time since Portland in June. 'I saw this funny little black-and-white flag,' quipped the Brazilian. 'I almost forgot what it looked like.'

• Hiro Matsushita set a respectable best lap of 22.393s on his qualifying run, which should have been good enough for 20th on the grid despite suffering an engine failure as he exited Turn Four on the final lap. According to veteran race engineer Gordon Coppuck, the car's telemetry showed the lap should have resulted in a time of around 22.27s – good for 15th – if the engine hadn't expired. The conjecture was irrelevant, however, for the Japanese driver's time was disallowed after his Panasonic/Duskin Reynard-Ford failed the mandatory post-qualifying minimum-weight check – by one pound!

• The IndyCar officials lost no time in displaying the black flag after noticing a fine trail of oil smoke emanating from Paul Tracy's Lola almost halfway through the race. The signal required Tracy to make a pit stop, so that the cause of the apparent leak could be detected. Tracy, however, having just moved up to third place, chose to ignore the flag for several laps. Then, after finally relenting and pulling into the Newman-Haas pit, he vented his spleen on IndyCar Director of Logistics Billy Kamphausen, who was merely attempting to explain the reason for the black flag. Tracy's actions earned him a record total of $12,000 in fines. The leak, incidentally, was traced to a cracked oil tank, which effectively ended Tracy's day.

• Michael Andretti's second-place finish was sufficient to clinch the inaugural Indy Car Manufacturers Championship for Ford/Cosworth. Andretti also secured the Nations Cup award for the United States.

• Several drivers reported that their cars went severely loose as the race progressed. Among them was Bryan Herta *(above)*, who qualified a solid 11th in Chip Ganassi's Target/Scotch Video Reynard-Ford but slipped back to a disappointed 19th at the finish. 'We took 13 turns of front wing out of the car and it was still loose,' he lamented. A broken engine mount subsequently was discovered to have exacerbated the problem.

• The quote of the weekend came from Scott Pruett after he had narrowly avoided collecting the spinning Adrian Fernandez on Friday afternoon. 'We got lucky,' confessed Pruett. 'Maybe I should go out tonight and buy a lottery ticket or something.'

Photos: Michael C. Brown

PPG INDY CAR WORLD SERIES • ROUND 15

NEW ENGLAND 200

NEW HAMPSHIRE INTERNATIONAL SPEEDWAY, LOUDON, NEW HAMPSHIRE

AUGUST 20, 200 LAPS – 211.600 MILES

Place	Driver (Nat.)	No.	Team Sponsors Car-Engine	Tires	Q Speed	Q Time	Q Pos.	Laps	Time/Status	Ave.	Pts.
1	*Andre Ribeiro (BR)	31	Tasman Motorsports *LCI International* Reynard 95I-Honda	FS	177.436	21.466s	1	200	1h 34m 36.192s	134.203	22
2	Michael Andretti (USA)	6	Newman-Haas *Kmart/Texaco Havoline* Lola T95/00-Ford	GY	172.398	22.093s	9	200	1h 34m 50.674s	133.861	16
3	Al Unser Jr. (USA)	1	Marlboro Team Penske Penske PC24-Mercedes	GY	170.347	22.359s	17	199	Running		14
4	Jacques Villeneuve (CDN)	27	Team Green *Player's Ltd.* Reynard 95I-Ford	GY	170.784	22.302s	15	199	Running		12
5	Emerson Fittipaldi (BR)	2	Marlboro Team Penske Penske PC24-Mercedes	GY	170.446	22.346s	16	199	Running		10
6	Jimmy Vasser (USA)	12	Ganassi *Target/STP* Reynard 95I-Ford	GY	173.049	22.010s	6	198	Running		8
7	*Gil de Ferran (BR)	8	Hall Racing *Pennzoil Special* Reynard 95I-Mercedes	GY	172.747	22.048s	8	198	Running		6
8	*Christian Fittipaldi (BR)	15	Walker *Marlboro/Chapeco Special* Reynard 95I-Ford	GY	174.479	21.830s	5	198	Running		5
9	Robby Gordon (USA)	5	Walker *Valvoline/Cummins Special* Reynard 95I-Ford	GY	174.758	21.795s	4	197	Running		4
10	Bobby Rahal (USA)	9	Rahal/Hogan *Miller Genuine Draft* Lola T95/00-Mercedes	GY	169.844	22.425s	20	197	Running		3
11	Mauricio Gugelmin (BR)	18	PacWest Racing Group *Hollywood* Reynard 95I-Ford	GY	172.950	22.022s	7	196	Running		2
12	Teo Fabi (I)	33	Forsythe *Combustion Engineering/Indeck* Reynard 95I-Ford	GY	177.167	21.498s	2	196	Running		1
13	*Eliseo Salazar (RCH)	7	Dick Simon *Cristal/Mobil 1/Copec* Lola T95/00-Ford	GY	165.307	23.041s	25	196	Running		
14	Alessandro Zampedri (I)	34	Payton-Coyne *The Mi-Jack Car* Lola T94/00-Ford	FS	170.224	22.375s	19	195	Running		
15	*Juan Fangio II (RA)	17	PacWest Racing Group *VISA* Reynard 95I-Ford	GY	171.740	22.178s	12	194	Running		
16	*Carlos Guerrero (MEX)	22	Dick Simon *Herdez/Viva Mexico!* Lola T95/00-Ford	GY	167.791	22.700s	22	193	Running		
17	Eddie Cheever (USA)	14	A.J. Foyt *Copenhagen Racing* Lola T95/00-Ford	GY	170.253	22.371s	18	191	Running		
18	Raul Boesel (BR)	11	Rahal/Hogan *Duracell Charger* Lola T95/00-Mercedes	GY	171.163	22.252s	13	191	Running		
19	Bryan Herta (USA)	4	Ganassi *Target/Scotch Video* Reynard 95I-Ford	GY	171.931	22.153s	11	189	Running		
20	Marco Greco (BR)	55	Galles *Brastemp/Int. Sports* Lola T95/00-Mercedes	GY	168.816	22.562s	21	184	Accident		
21	Buddy Lazier (USA)	19	Payton-Coyne *The Agfa Car* Lola T94/00-Ford	FS	166.916	22.819s	23	184	Accident		
22	Hiro Matsushita (J)	25	Arciero-Wells *Panasonic/Duskin* Reynard 95I-Ford	FS	no speed	no time	26	184	Running		
23	Paul Tracy (CDN)	3	Newman-Haas *Kmart/Budweiser* Lola T95/00-Ford	GY	171.138	22.256s	14	101	Oil leak		
24	Scott Pruett (USA)	20	Patrick Racing *Firestone* Lola T95/00-Ford	FS	177.101	21.506s	3	40	Accident		
25	Stefan Johansson (S)	16	Bettenhausen *Alumax Aluminum* Penske PC23-Mercedes	GY	166.856	22.827s	24	17	Oil leak		
26	Adrian Fernandez (MEX)	10	Galles *Tecate/Quaker State* Lola T95/00-Mercedes	GY	172.367	22.097s	10	0	Accident		

* denotes Rookie driver

Caution flags: Laps 1–10, accident/Fernandez; laps 41–51, accident/Pruett; laps 198–200, accident/Greco and Lazier. **Total:** three for 24 laps.

Lap leaders: Teo Fabi, 1–42 (42 laps); Michael Andretti, 43–99 (57 laps); Andre Ribeiro, 100–122 (23 laps); Andretti, 123–127 (5 laps); Ribeiro, 128–200 (73 laps). **Totals:** Ribeiro, 96 laps; Andretti, 62 laps; Fabi, 42 laps.

Fastest race lap: Teo Fabi, 22.968s, 165.833 mph, on lap 15.

Championship positions: 1 Villeneuve, 168; **2** Rahal, 114; **3** Andretti, 113; **4** Unser, 111; **5** Gordon, 108; **6** Pruett, 95; **7** Tracy, 94; **8** Vasser, 91; **9** Fabi, 79; **10** Gugelmin, 68; **11** Fernandez, 64; **12** E. Fittipaldi, 61; **13** C. Fittipaldi, 55; **14** Johansson, 50; **15** Boesel, 46; **16** Ribeiro, 38; **17** Cheever, 33; **18** Sullivan, 32; **19** Herta, 30; **20** de Ferran, 20; **21** Salazar, 19; **22** Zampedri, 11; **23** Bachelart, 8; **24** Danner, Luyendyk and Fangio, 6; **27** Matsushita, 5; **28** Johnstone, 4; **29** Greco, 3; **30** C. Guerrero and Hall, 2; **32** R. Guerrero, Goodyear and Brayton, 1.

Championship positions and points totals provisional pending outcome of appeal by Penske following race at Portland.

EDS

VANCOUVER

Al Unser Jr. seems to relish the West Coast street circuit races in Long Beach and Vancouver. Since 1988, he has won 10 out of the 14 events run on the two temporary venues, including three straight in the Molson Indy Vancouver.

The seeds of Unser's latest victory, achieved in perfect weather conditions before another record crowd, were planted during qualifying, when he opted to concentrate on Goodyear's more durable 'option' tire instead of the 'recommended' compound preferred by the majority of his rivals.

'We had to choose between a soft one and a hard one,' explained Unser, who qualified only ninth in his Marlboro Penske-Mercedes but soon began to work his way toward the front. 'I ran the soft ones and they were quicker but they went off faster. I really felt we made a good decision going with the backup tires. We gave up a little bit in qualifying because of that, but it paid off in the race.'

Michael Andretti also chose the harder compound tires for his Kmart/Texaco Havoline Lola-Ford/Cosworth, although his hopes of victory were dashed by a broken transmission.

Second place fell to a deserving Gil de Ferran, who finally profited from a slice of good fortune and posted a fine drive for Jim Hall's team following a hectic last-minute switch to his backup Pennzoil Reynard-Mercedes.

Benefiting from an astute tire choice, Al Unser Jr. carved his way through from ninth place on the grid to score a commanding victory for Marlboro Team Penske.
Photo: Michael C. Brown

Michael C. Brown

Alessandro Zampedri *(left)* did well to finish ninth in the Payton-Coyne team's year-old Mi-Jack Lola despite being black-flagged when one of his nose wings became detached.

Right: Robby Gordon runs ahead of Gil de Ferran and Al Unser Jr. in the early stages of the race. The trio filled the rostrum positions at the flag, but by then the order had been reversed.

Stefan Johansson took fourth place with the Alumax Penske, the best result for the hard-working Bettenhausen team since the Nazareth race in April.

QUALIFYING

In marked contrast to his rookie campaign, Jacques Villeneuve has developed a real affinity for the Canadian street circuits this year. As in Toronto, Team Green's familiar #27 Player's Ltd. Reynard-Ford was to the fore throughout practice and qualifying. Villeneuve ultimately posted a substantial improvement in the warmth of Saturday's final session to secure his fifth pole of the season.

'I am happy we got the pole here because, like Toronto last year, Vancouver was a horrible weekend,' noted Villeneuve. 'We weren't expecting to be fast.'

Villeneuve, like the majority of Goodyear runners, chose the 'primary' tires. The Canadian was happy with the level of grip they produced, although, significantly, he did notice some drop-off in performance as the tires wore down: 'My Player's Ltd. Reynard was great on new tires. It's been fairly good on old tires but the tires go down [in performance] and we need to do some work tonight for the race.'

Jimmy Vasser produced another superb display in Chip Ganassi's Target/STP Reynard-Ford. The Californian annexed second on the grid despite being forced into the team's backup car, the original '94 prototype chassis, after a broken fuel line caused his primary machine to catch fire on Friday morning. It was the third time this season Vasser had started from the outside of the front row.

'The car's working pretty good,' he said, 'but I'm getting pretty tired of being second all the time – and it always seems to be second to Jacques.'

Bobby Rahal was next, taking advantage of some development pieces in Ilmor Engineering's Mercedes-Benz engine to secure his highest starting position of the season in the Miller Genuine Draft Lola. Rahal was pleased with the progress, although he hardly looked it, for he had been suffering all week from a nasty case of strep throat.

'The doctors told me not to run today,' admitted Rahal. 'Dr. Olvey said I should skip at least the morning practice because I have the effects of tonsillitis. So I didn't run many laps this morning. This afternoon I had a good car. In fact, good enough for the front row. But Jimmy just got by me. I just wish I didn't feel this bad because I think we have a car to win this race.'

Scott Goodyear made an impressive return to the Tasman team's #24 LCI/CNN/Motorola Reynard-Honda, setting the fourth fastest time, best of the Firestone contingent, while Andretti proved fastest of those who preferred to concentrate on the Goodyear 'option' tires.

RACE

Villeneuve brought the full 28-car field up toward the starter's stand at a slow pace and then jumped on the gas so that he was able to maintain his advantage through the flat-out Turn One kink and onto the fastest part of the race course. Vasser, Rahal and Goodyear tucked in dutifully behind, although a little farther down the field things weren't quite so orderly.

'The start got a little messed up,' said Unser. 'Jacques brought us up kind of slow and it caused havoc in the fourth, fifth and sixth rows [of the grid]. I passed Gil [de Ferran] at the start and then we were all protecting our position at the hairpin. But Gil went past me and a couple other cars on the outside. I thought that was a pretty good move, so the next corner I tried the outside of Gil. We went into the chicane together and he climbed over my left-front [wheel] and that put him into the fence.'

'There just wasn't enough room when we both came to turn right,' concurred de Ferran, whose car tipped up onto two wheels and caromed into the tire barrier.

The track was all but blocked as several cars came to a halt in order to avoid the fracas. Chief steward Wally Dallenbach had little option but to display the red flag and bring the race to an immediate halt. The stoppage ensured the race would be restarted over its entire 100-lap distance – which spelled excellent news for de Ferran, whose day once again seemed to have been brought to a premature conclusion.

'When I saw myself facing the tires, I thought, "Oh no, another weekend wasted," ' said the Brazilian. But suddenly he had been granted a second chance. His primary car was too badly damaged to continue, so Alex Hering and the crew quickly fetched the backup from the transporter and began transferring as much of the setup from the other car as possible. New brakes, tires, shock absorbers, rear wing and gear ratios were all fitted in record time, and de Ferran duly took up his position on the grid.

'The guys did a fantastic job,' praised de Ferran. 'The only thing they didn't have time to fit was the drink bottle!'

The first attempt at a restart was waved off when Villeneuve jumped clear of Vasser before the green flag, but the second time worked a charm. The leading contenders quickly settled down into their grid order, and once again it was the midfield that provided the fireworks. This time the two Fittipaldis, Emerson and Christian, were involved in some wheel-banging.

'I am very disappointed with my nephew, Christian, because he squeezed me out on both of the starts,' said a furious Emerson, who rejoined at the back of the pack. 'It is unbelievable. In my 11 years of Indy Car racing I have never had this situation on a start.'

Villeneuve soon began to pull away at the front, and almost as quickly it became apparent why: Vasser's engine was misfiring. A broken spark plug was discovered to be the reason for his demise after only nine laps.

'This was a real disappointment,' said Vasser. 'This is the sixth race this year when a mechanical problem took us out and cost us a race that we had a good shot at winning.'

Rahal took up the chase of Villeneuve, feeling rather better on race day than he had earlier in the weekend, and Goodyear chased along in third until momentarily locking his brakes and spinning in Turn 10.

'I just went too hot into the turn,' admitted the Canadian, who fell to the back of the pack. Goodyear clambered back to 11th in the late stages, only to be inadvertently punted from behind by Villeneuve. The resultant spin cost him any chance of finishing among the points.

Rahal was the next to run into difficulty as his tires began to lose their effectiveness. Indeed, after losing places on successive laps to Andretti and Unser, he opted to make a pit stop on lap 25.

Villeneuve began to experience a similar lack of grip, and on lap 27 Andretti executed a perfectly judged pass under braking for the Turn 10 hairpin. Unser attempted to follow suit but met with sterner resistance from the Canadian, such that by the time Unser found a way past, on lap 33, Andretti was already 12 seconds up the road.

Villeneuve then peeled off into the pits, to be followed on the next lap by Robby Gordon, who had been running strongly in fourth with Derrick Walker's Valvoline/Cummins Reynard-Ford. Andretti and Unser continued to press home their tire advantage, and by the time the first round of pit stops had been completed it was clear the race would be decided between them.

Marlboro Team Penske managed to halve Andretti's advantage during the pit stops, and before long Unser had taken care of the rest of the deficit. By lap 48, just before half-distance, the two leaders were together on the road. Unser was on a charge. Nevertheless, catching Andretti and passing him represented two altogether different challenges.

A change of luck at last for de Ferran

Gil de Ferran served notice of his capabilities almost from the moment he first drove an Indy car in anger. The 27-year-old Brazilian caused a major shock – at least among the Indy Car establishment – when he claimed the provisional pole for his very first race in Miami, and ever since then he had been knocking on the door of success. Indeed, the only real surprise was that it took until the 16th race for him to record his first podium finish.

Among hard-core auto racing fans, de Ferran has long been touted as a star in the making. He cut his racing teeth in Brazil, then moved to Europe in 1988 and progressed rapidly through the ranks. He won the prestigious British Formula 3 Championship in 1992 for Paul Stewart Racing, owned and managed by the son of three-time Formula 1 World Champion Jackie Stewart, and narrowly missed out on the Formula 3000 Championship in 1994. It seemed only a matter of time before he would graduate into Formula 1.

But then came an opportunity for a fresh start. De Ferran was intro-

duced to veteran Indy Car team owner Jim Hall midway through the 1994 season and the pair immediately struck up a rapport. He was instantly impressive, too, when Hall invited him to test-drive his Pennzoil Reynard.

'When I was offered the opportunity, basically, I jumped,' said de Ferran. 'I spoke to Jackie [Stewart] and he was very, very supportive. No question, it was too good an opportunity to let go, because this is one of the top teams in Indy Car racing and Pennzoil is one of the best and most traditional sponsors. When Jim asked me to drive for him, I said "yes" right away.'

Born in France and raised in Brazil, it should come as no surprise to learn that the cosmopolitan de Ferran has settled easily in North America with his English wife, Angela, and their baby daughter, Anna Elizabeth. His rookie season has been punctuated by a host of mechanical problems and a few accidents, yet through it all the team never lost faith in de Ferran, nor he in them. The second-place finish in Vancouver was long overdue and, without question, a portent of things to come.

Michael C. Brown

Below right: Out of the shadows at last. Gil de Ferran heads for the first podium finish of his short Indy Car career with Bryan Herta's Target/Scotch Video Reynard in pursuit.

Paul Tracy lost a possible top-three finish when a desperate attempt to pass Bryan Herta ended in an embarrassing spin. Teo Fabi, Scott Pruett and Scott Goodyear thread their way past the Canadian's stranded Kmart/Budweiser Lola.

'To pass Michael Andretti is one of the toughest things in this world. He and Jacques [Villeneuve] definitely know how to block – or drive defensively, how's that?' Unser added with a wry smile. 'Mikey blocked me one time real good and I almost drilled him going into the hairpin.'

A couple of brief cautions served to tighten up the pack. They also offered an opportunity for everyone to make their second scheduled pit stops. Andretti and Unser resumed at the front, but Unser pounced almost immediately after the restart, gaining a jump on his rival on the drag race along Pacific Boulevard and roaring past into the lead as they passed by the Plaza of Nations complex for the 61st time.

One lap later, Andretti slowed abruptly at the hairpin. Second gear had broken. His day was done.

'Well, I guess I gave Junior another one,' groaned Andretti. 'I just couldn't pick up any of the gears. I tried to hold it in third and fourth but it would just jump right out.'

Rahal instead looked set to challenge Unser, but having stopped early, out of sequence, he was obliged to make an extra pit stop on lap 84. Unser was left with a clear run to the finish. His only concern was with regard to fuel consumption, although judicious application of the throttle and short-shifting through the gears allowed him to make up any shortfall well before the finish.

'We started saving fuel right after the second pit stop because we knew it was going to be close,' declared Unser, who maintained his advantage despite cutting his pace by as much as two seconds per lap. 'My car was perfect. The Goodyear tires were great, the Mercedes engine was super and we had plenty of fuel left in the car at the end.'

Bryan Herta drove well in Chip Ganassi's Target/Scotch Video Reynard-Ford, despite damaging a nose wing in an earlier incident with Teo Fabi, although his hopes of a good finish were thwarted on lap 66 when Tracy dived down the inside into the hairpin, locked up his brakes and slid sideways into Herta's path. Mauricio Gugelmin also became involved in the melee, ending his day after a solid run in the Hollywood Reynard-Ford. De Ferran gratefully picked his way through to emerge in third place, which became second when Rahal pulled off into the pits.

'I just kept driving hard the whole

us,' said de Ferran, who, like Unser, was required to adopt a fuel-saving strategy in the closing stages.

The various dramas enabled Gordon to emerge in third place, despite struggling throughout most of the race with an ill-handling car: 'We were just trying to hold on,' said Gordon, who earned his first podium finish since winning at Detroit in June. 'It seemed like our tires would last about 10 laps and then they were virtually octagon-shaped. It was so bad, I could hard-

ly see going down the straights. My tires were just junk.'

Scott Pruett, who ran consistently well in Pat Patrick's Firestone Lola-Ford, looked set to challenge Gordon until being forced to back off and save fuel. Stefan Johansson therefore moved up into a close fourth, despite having started a lowly 17th in his Alumax Penske-Mercedes. Rahal also was right there at the finish line, the third of three drivers separated by just a half-second. Pruett also was in contention, with Emerson Fittipaldi's

Marlboro Penske-Mercedes the final unlapped finisher.

Villeneuve, who had moved into fourth place at two-thirds distance, was hobbled soon afterward by a failing transmission. He fell back to a disappointed 12th at the finish. Thus, provisionally at least (pending the outcome of the appeal against Unser's disqualification at Portland), the championship was still up for grabs as the contenders began to pack up and move south for the season finale at Laguna Seca Raceway, Calif.

Michael C. Brown

SNIPPETS

Photos: Michael C. Brown

• Brian Till was invited to drive A.J. Foyt's Copenhagen Lola-Ford following the decision to part company with Eddie Cheever one week earlier. Till *(above)*, a veteran of 19 previous Indy Car starts with a best finish of ninth at Cleveland in 1993, found it difficult to adapt from the Trans-Am sedan he had been driving regularly this season, especially when a broken transmission precluded him from completing a lap on Saturday morning, but he qualified handily.

• Team Green scooped many of the top honors during the Championship Association of Mechanics' annual awards presentation. Chief mechanic Kyle Moyer was named the Snap-On 'Top Wrench,' while Mike LaFontain was voted as the transmission specialist of the year. In addition, Team Green's Tony Cotman, Eric Haverson, Dave Popielarz and tire specialist Jim Wilson were voted onto the Raybestos 'All-Star' team of mechanics. Hall Racing chief mechanic Alex Hering was presented the George Bignotti Preparation Award, sponsored by Earl's Performance Products, in recognition of the most consistently well-prepared car in the series. Her-ing was [...] selected by a panel comprising IndyCar officials Billy Kamphausen, Dick Perry and Dennis Swan, as well as USAC technical chief Mike Devin.

• Domenico 'Mimmo' Schiattarella *(below)*, who contested a few Toyota Atlantic races in 1994 and then drove for Andreas Leberle's Project Indy team in the PPG Cup races at Toronto and

Mid-Ohio, also returned to the Indy Car ranks in Vancouver. Schiattarella, who began the season with the ill-fated Simtek Formula 1 team, survived several dramas to finish 18th.

• Tony Bettenhausen was absent from the race due to the fact his wife's mother, Shirley, the wife of former Indy Car racer Jim McElreath, had been hospitalized in Arlington, Texas, after suf-fering a heart attack. Shirley was reportedly making a good recovery on Sunday, hopefully buoyed by the news of Stefan Johansson's fourth-place finish.

• Ross Bentley, from nearby Port Coquitlam, B.C., narrowly failed to qualify Payton-Coyne Racing's #19 Agfa Lola T94/00-Ford. The affable Bentley had not driven an Indy car all year, and despite the handicap of no prior testing he looked set to make the show until being bumped in the closing minutes.

• Scott Goodyear *(above right)* lost a potential podium finish when he spun his LCI Reynard-Honda in the early stages. Tasman teammate Andre Ribeiro later crashed in Turn One while trying to pass de Ferran for fifth. Laconic New Zealander Steve Horne, owner of the Tasman team, classified the mistakes as 'DDBF – Double Driver Brain Fade.'

• Did the red-flag interruption cause any problems for Al Unser Jr.? 'No,' he replied with a grin. 'It gave me a chance to go have a cigarette, actually.'

PPG INDY CAR WORLD SERIES • ROUND 16

MOLSON INDY VANCOUVER

CONCORD PACIFIC PLACE STREET CIRCUIT, VANCOUVER, BRITISH COLUMBIA, CANADA

SEPTEMBER 3, 100 LAPS – 170.300 MILES

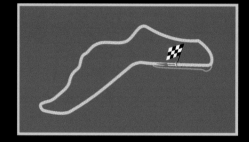

Place	Driver (Nat.)	No.	Team Sponsors Car-Engine	Tires	Q Speed	Q Time	Q Pos.	Laps	Time/Status	Ave.	Pts.
1	Al Unser Jr. (USA)	1	Marlboro Team Penske Penske PC24-Mercedes	GY	109.400	56.040s	9	100	1h 46m 54.900s	95.571	21
2	*Gil de Ferran (BR)	8	Hall Racing *Pennzoil Special* Reynard 95I-Mercedes	GY	109.612	55.932s	8	100	1h 47m 09.913s	95.348	16
3	Robby Gordon (USA)	5	Walker *Valvoline/Cummins Special* Reynard 95I-Ford	GY	109.732	55.870s	7	100	1h 47m 21.007s	95.184	14
4	Stefan Johansson (S)	16	Bettenhausen *Alumax Aluminum* Penske PC23-Mercedes	GY	108.397	56.559s	17	100	1h 47m 21.423s	95.178	12
5	Bobby Rahal (USA)	9	Rahal/Hogan *Miller Genuine Draft* Lola T95/00-Mercedes	GY	110.420	55.523s	3	100	1h 47m 21.524s	95.176	10
6	Scott Pruett (USA)	20	Patrick Racing *Firestone* Lola T95/00-Ford	FS	109.387	56.047s	10	100	1h 47m 24.373s	95.134	8
7	Emerson Fittipaldi (BR)	2	Marlboro Team Penske Penske PC24-Mercedes	GY	108.658	56.423s	14	100	1h 47m 46.686s	94.806	6
8	Paul Tracy (CDN)	3	Newman-Haas *Kmart/Budweiser* Lola T95/00-Ford	GY	108.809	56.344s	12	99	Running		5
9	Alessandro Zampedri (I)	34	Payton-Coyne *The Mi-Jack Car* Lola T94/00-Ford	FS	108.256	56.632s	18	99	Running		4
10	Raul Boesel (BR)	11	Rahal/Hogan *Duracell Charger* Lola T95/00-Mercedes	GY	107.901	56.819s	20	99	Running		3
11	Parker Johnstone (USA)	49	Comptech *Motorola Cellular* Reynard 95I-Honda	FS	107.544	57.007s	22	99	Running		2
12	Jacques Villeneuve (CDN)	27	Team Green *Player's Ltd.* Reynard 95I-Ford	GY	111.013	55.226s	1	98	Running		2
13	*Eliseo Salazar (RCH)	7	Dick Simon *Cristal/Mobil 1/Copec* Lola T95/00-Ford	GY	107.761	56.893s	21	98	Running		
14	Scott Goodyear (CDN)	24	Tasman Motorsports *LCI/CNN/Motorola* Reynard 95I-Honda	FS	110.193	55.637s	4	98	Running		
15	*Carlos Guerrero (MEX)	22	Dick Simon *Herdez/Viva Mexico!* Lola T95/00-Ford	GY	106.948	57.325s	23	97	Running		
16	Bryan Herta (USA)	4	Ganassi *Target/Scotch Video* Reynard 95I-Ford	GY	108.581	56.463s	15	96	Running		
17	Hiro Matsushita (J)	25	Arciero-Wells *Panasonic/Duskin* Reynard 95I-Ford	FS	105.813	57.940s	26	95	Running		
18	*Mimmo Schiattarella (I)	64	Project Indy *No-Touch/Van Dyne/Marcelo* Reynard 94I-Ford	GY	105.556	58.081s	28	93	Running		
19	Teo Fabi (I)	33	Forsythe *Combustion Engineering/Indeck* Reynard 95I-Ford	GY	110.135	55.666s	6	73	Cooling system		
20	Mauricio Gugelmin (BR)	18	PacWest Racing Group *Hollywood* Reynard 95I-Ford	GY	108.976	56.258s	11	65	Accident		
21	Michael Andretti (USA)	6	Newman-Haas *Kmart/Texaco Havoline* Lola T95/00-Ford	GY	110.143	55.662s	5	63	Transmission		
22	Adrian Fernandez (MEX)	10	Galles *Tecate/Quaker State* Lola T95/00-Mercedes	GY	108.085	56.722s	19	61	Handling		
23	*Andre Ribeiro (BR)	31	Tasman Motorsports *LCI International* Reynard 95I-Honda	FS	108.419	56.547s	16	55	Accident		
24	*Christian Fittipaldi (BR)	15	Walker *Marlboro/Chapeco Special* Reynard 95I-Ford	GY	108.674	56.415s	13	49	Exhaust		
25	Marco Greco (BR)	55	Galles *Brastemp/Int. Sports* Lola T95/00-Mercedes	GY	105.685	58.010s	27	46	Transmission		
26	Brian Till (USA)	14	A.J. Foyt *Copenhagen Racing* Lola T95/00-Ford	GY	106.494	57.570s	25	26	Accident		
27	Jimmy Vasser (USA)	12	Ganassi *Target/STP* Reynard 95I-Ford	GY	110.459	55.503s	2	8	Engine		
28	*Juan Fangio II (RA)	17	PacWest Racing Group *VISA* Reynard 95I-Ford	GY	106.579	57.523s	24	8	Accident		
NQ	Ross Bentley (CDN)	19	Payton-Coyne *The Agfa Car* Lola T94/00-Ford	FS	104.931	58.427s	29	–	Did not qualify		

* denotes Rookie driver

Caution flags: Lap 1, yellow start; laps 7–9, tow start/Schiattarella; laps 49–51, tow/Greco; laps 56–59, accident/Ribeiro. **Total:** four for 11 laps.

Lap leaders: Jacques Villeneuve, 1–26 (26 laps); Michael Andretti, 27–60 (34 laps); Al Unser Jr., 61–100 (40 laps). **Totals:** Unser Jr., 40 laps; Andretti, 34 laps; Villeneuve, 26 laps.

Fastest race lap: Bobby Rahal, 56.906s, 107.735 mph, on lap 86.

Championship positions: 1 Villeneuve, 170; **2** Unser, 132; **3** Rahal, 124; **4** Gordon, 122; **5** Andretti, 113; **6** Pruett, 103; **7** Tracy, 99; **8** Vasser, 91; **9** Fabi, 79; **10** Gugelmin, 68; **11** E. Fittipaldi, 67; **12** Fernandez, 64; **13** Johansson, 62; **14** C. Fittipaldi, 55; **15** Boesel, 49; **16** Ribeiro, 38; **17** de Ferran, 36; **18** Cheever, 33; **19** Sullivan, 32; **20** Herta, 30; **21** Salazar, 19; **22** Zampedri, 15; **23** Bachelart, 8; **24** Danner, Luyendyk, Fangio and Johnstone, 6; **28** Matsushita, 5; **29** Greco, 3; **30** C. Guerrero and Hall, 2; **32** R. Guerrero, Goodyear and Brayton, 1.
Championship positions and points totals provisional pending outcome of appeal by Penske following race at Portland.

EDS

LAGUNA SECA

1 – DE FERRAN

2 – TRACY

3 – GUGELMIN

Laguna Seca Raceway lived up to its reputation for providing a fitting finale to the PPG Indy Car World Series. Indeed, the Toyota Grand Prix of Monterey, featuring the Bank of America 300, produced two deserving victors.

Brazilian rookie Gil de Ferran took the checkered flag in Hall Racing's Pennzoil Reynard-Mercedes, becoming the ninth different winner during this extraordinarily competitive season, while sophomore driver Jacques Villeneuve overcame several time-consuming delays before securing the PPG Cup championship title with an 11th-place finish in Team Green's Player's Ltd. Reynard-Ford/Cosworth.

'It was a long race,' said Villeneuve's car owner, Barry Green. 'We were going backward for a while – we had two flat tires and we knocked the front wing off after Jacques hit some debris – but I'm just so proud of my guys. They stayed focused, Jacques stayed focused and we pulled it off. It's fantastic.'

'It means a lot,' added Villeneuve. 'It's my first championship in any series so it is very special.'

De Ferran was equally elated, having followed up his second-place finish in Vancouver with his maiden victory. Along the way, he earned enough points to win the prestigious Jim Trueman Rookie of the Year Award.

'My first win in an Indy car is very, very significant for me,' he said, 'especially against such strong competition.'

Flying the flag. Gil de Ferran *(left)* ended his first season in Indy Car racing with a richly deserved maiden victory. The Brazilian's win also enabled him to snatch the coveted Rookie of the Year award from fellow countryman Christian Fittipaldi, whose patriotically liveried Marlboro/Chapeco Reynard *(below)* failed to finish.

Right: Al Unser Jr.'s hopes of retaining the PPG Cup were ended when he could finish no higher than sixth. Although his Portland win was subsequently restored on appeal, Villeneuve's points total remained beyond reach.

Michael C. Brown

PPG Cup championship settled on the track

So far as the PPG Cup title was concerned, with the appeal against the disqualification of Al Unser Jr. at Portland still pending, there were two potential scenarios as the combatants gathered for the final race of the season at scenic Laguna Seca Raceway. First, if the appeal was subsequently denied, Jacques Villeneuve was effectively the new champion already, since his points tally was unassailable. But if Unser's victory in Portland was restored, he would gain an additional 21 points, bringing his total to within 16 markers of Villeneuve.

The odds, of course, remained in favor of Villeneuve, and, thankfully, his 11th-place finish was enough to put the issue beyond doubt.

'It's great to have won the championship, so we don't have to wait until the appeal,' said a relieved and delighted Villeneuve. 'If they'd told us in a week or two, "Hey, by the way, you've won the championship," it wouldn't mean nearly as much. We'd take it but it wouldn't be the same.'

One week after the dust had settled in California, Marlboro Team Penske was back in action – this time in Michigan, where lawyers presented their case to an Appeals Court panel composed of Chief Judge Philip C. Elliott and court members Steven R. Hearn,

an experienced Michigan lawyer, and former NASCAR technical director Richard Leon 'Dick' Beaty.

The judges considered a wealth of exhibits as well as testimony from 18 witnesses during three days of depositions, then deliberated for two days before announcing their verdict in favor of the appellant. Unser was therefore reinstated as the winner at Portland.

The actual means of measuring Unser's Penske proved to be the crux of the matter. At Portland, three volunteer technical inspectors had been responsible for scrutinizing all the cars, including Unser's, and they apparently employed a slightly different method of measurement than the IndyCar officials who supervised the proceedings and directly participated in the inspection of the winning car. The two different techniques produced dissimilar results – and continued to do so when the #1 Penske, which had been voluntarily impounded since the race meeting in Oregon, was reinspected during the hearing. The panel decided in Penske's favor after noting that the volunteer inspectors successfully cleared the car while utilizing the same method of measurement employed on all other competing cars during the Portland race weekend.

QUALIFYING

There are no prizes for guessing who started from the pole. Yep, Jacques Villeneuve. Once again, though, the massively impressive young French-Canadian had to produce something special to eclipse Bryan Herta, who, less than 10 seconds earlier, had leapt to the top of the timing charts with a new record 1m 09.992s, an average speed of 113.877 mph around the supremely challenging 2.214-mile road course.

'It was a great 10 seconds,' smiled Herta after claiming his third front row grid position in Chip Ganassi's Target/Scotch Video Reynard-Ford. 'I really can't complain. I got a really good lap out of the car. I'm just pleased to be on the front row and have a good starting position.'

Villeneuve steadily improved his car as the weekend progressed. He traded positions with Herta a couple of times during an exciting final half-hour session, then vaulted to the top with less than one minute remaining.

'The last lap is when you have to give it everything you have,' said Villeneuve, who would start from the pole for the sixth time in the last nine races.

De Ferran displayed the value of a productive test session at Laguna Seca earlier in the season by setting the fastest time in the opening practice session on Friday. In qualifying, however, the team lost its way on the setup and it was only during the final session Saturday that de Ferran and race engineer Bill Pappas were able to rediscover the car's poise.

'It was difficult to get a balance,' said de Ferran, who opted to switch to the backup Goodyear tires on Saturday. 'We made a change to the car before we went out on our final set of tires. I knew it was my last chance. I just went for it and it worked out.'

Teo Fabi earned the provisional pole on Friday with Forsythe Racing's Combustion Engineering/Indeck Reynard-Ford, but was unable to find any improvement on the second day. He therefore slipped to fourth on the grid ahead of the fastest Lola of Scott Pruett (Firestone Lola-Ford) and Mauricio Gugelmin (Hollywood Reynard-Ford).

Al Unser Jr., Villeneuve's only potential rival for the PPG Cup title, languished a disappointing 14th on the grid in Roger Penske's Marlboro Penske-Mercedes. In common with de Ferran and the Newman-Haas pair, Paul Tracy (8th) and Michael Andret-

ti (12th), he chose to run the Goodyear 'option' tire but found his efforts restricted by excessive understeer.

'We can't get the car to turn,' lamented Unser. 'Starting back like this isn't fun at all, but we'll give it our best shot tomorrow and go from there.'

RACE

Unser, as usual, had concentrated more on preparation for the race than for qualifying, and it came as no surprise to see the #1 Penske up toward the top of the time sheets during the final warmup session on

Sunday morning. Indeed, Unser's time of 1m 11.777s was beaten only by the Target/STP Reynard of Jimmy Vasser.

The parched, dusty hillsides overlooking the picturesque Laguna Seca Raceway, with spectacular views also extending across the Salinas Valley and Monterey Bay, were transformed on race day as a huge and colorful crowd basked in glorious California sunshine. An exciting 84-lap race was in prospect.

The initial start was clean, with the front two rows, comprising four cars, accelerating absolutely in uni-

son across the start/finish line, over the brow of the hill in Turn One and then downhill again toward the tight, left-handed hairpin in Turn Three. Villeneuve's pole position enabled him to grasp the lead under braking, while Herta, after initially considering a move around the outside of the champion elect, wisely decided to tuck in behind at the exit. De Ferran and Fabi were similarly engaged in a tussle for third. Behind, though, Robby Gordon, who qualified a distant 16th in his Valvoline/Cummins Reynard-Ford, spun off at the hairpin, after being hit from behind by Adrian Fernandez, and stalled the engine.

After a brief full-course caution, Villeneuve once again took off into the lead. Almost right away, though, Herta's hopes took a nose-dive when his engine began to misfire badly. A faulty coil was found to be the cause. Herta lost several laps while a replacement was fitted. He continued, although his disappointing afternoon ended prematurely when, after making a routine pit stop, he rejoined the track immediately in front of the race leader, de Ferran. Unfortunately, as he glanced in his mirrors, Herta failed to see Andre Ribeiro's LCI Reynard-Honda, which drew alongside Herta on the outside line and was accidentally punted off the road as Herta concentrated on making room for de Ferran.

Herta's early problem elevated de Ferran to second place, and it wasn't long before he began to close on Villeneuve. The two leaders established their fastest laps, in the high 1m 13s range, very early in the proceedings, but then, as had been the case during practice and qualifying, their tires began to lose adhesion. By lap 25, Villeneuve was struggling to circulate in the 1m 16s. Nevertheless, he managed to maintain station ahead of de Ferran. Fabi, Gugelmin, Pruett and Tracy also followed in line astern.

Villeneuve and Gugelmin chose to make their first scheduled pit stops on lap 29, while de Ferran, Fabi, Tracy and Pruett waited one more lap before taking on service. The Hall team, shrewdly, sent de Ferran on his way without completely filling the fuel tank. The strategy was devised in the belief that de Ferran would save perhaps a couple of seconds and yet still have enough fuel to complete the race with only one more stop. It worked like a charm. De Ferran accelerated out of the pits ahead of Villeneuve and soon began to stretch out a commanding lead.

Michael C. Brown

183

Michael C. Brown

Mauricio Gugelmin maintained his late-season return to form with a polished drive to third place in the PacWest team's Hollywood Reynard.

Bottom: **With the title theirs at last, team owner Barry Green *(left)* celebrates with newly crowned PPG Cup champion Jacques Villeneuve.**

Unser also gained an advantage during the pit stops, moving ahead of Ribeiro, Andretti and Bobby Rahal (MGD Lola-Mercedes) into seventh place. He then began to close on Pruett as the race neared its halfway mark. Villeneuve, meanwhile, encountered his first problem on lap 34, when he slowed abruptly and dived into the pits after he felt the handling on his car go suddenly awry.

Team Green changed all four tires and sent Villeneuve back into the race, discovering afterward that the left-front tire had been losing air. Eleven laps later, Villeneuve darted onto pit road again. Same problem. It was later surmised that the damage was caused by Villeneuve consistently bouncing off the curb at the notorious Corkscrew turn.

Villeneuve resumed in 13th, and suddenly the chase for the PPG Cup came alive, since Unser by now had moved up inexorably to fourth after passing both Pruett and Fabi, who lost time in a scary moment while endeavoring to lap Carlos Guerrero's Team Herdez/Viva Mexico! Lola-Ford. If Unser could make it to second, Villeneuve would need to finish at least 12th to clinch the title. Given his tire problems, that seemed far from a certainty.

'I knew we had a strong car, but after the second blow-up I thought that was the end of my race,' said Villeneuve.

Fabi's problems, which included collecting a plastic cone in his front wing as he drove off-course to pass the errant Guerrero, enabled Tracy to move into second place, albeit some 11 seconds adrift of de Ferran, who motored serenely on his way. Gugelmin, in turn, was happily ensconced in third as Unser, having pressed too hard and taken the competitive edge off his tires, began to drift back in fourth. Before long, Unser came under attack not only from Pruett but also Andretti.

De Ferran surrendered his lead briefly to Gugelmin when he made his second pit stop, slightly earlier

than some of the other leading contenders, on lap 54. After the pit stops, he enjoyed an even healthier advantage of more than 15 seconds. Even a full-course caution caused him no undue concern. De Ferran remained fully in command and rewarded Jim Hall's faith in his ability by romping home to Victory Lane.

'The Pennzoil team gave me a beautiful car,' declared de Ferran. 'It was a great day. You know, when we got by Jacques on the pit stops – which, by the way, was fantastic strategy from the team – and we started to pull away from him, I thought, hmm, we might have a good day. It was a beautiful way to finish the season.'

De Ferran's victory catapulted him past Christian Fittipaldi and

Ribeiro in the Rookie of the Year title-chase. Fittipaldi, who had led the standings ever since Miami, was hindered by inconsistent handling on his Marlboro/Chapeco Reynard-Ford and, finally, a stuck throttle which caused him to run off the road and damage the suspension while running a distant 13th.

'To come out as Rookie of the Year is an extra bonus,' said de Ferran, who trailed Fittipaldi by 17 points at the start of the weekend. 'I kind of gave up on that because we were so far behind. It's a nice bonus, a big surprise.'

Tracy was content to finish his season on a high note, having proven faster than Andretti, his Newman-Haas teammate, all weekend. The Canadian, though, was hanging on

for dear life in the closing stages as his rear tires were well past their best. Gugelmin and Andretti both closed up dramatically in the run to the flag, the trio covered by a fraction over one second.

Pruett held on for fifth, despite the loss of fifth gear, while Unser, who mysteriously lost ground during the second round of pit stops, just held off Rahal for sixth.

'My car was pretty loose after the second pit stop,' related Unser. 'I hustled the car to make up some time and because of that I ended up being a little too hard on my tires.'

Villeneuve had one final scare when a large piece of debris damaged his Reynard's nose, causing yet another unscheduled pit stop. Even so, his 11th-place finish was enough to put the PPG Cup beyond the reach of Unser.

'It was a fun race because we fought all the way,' said a delighted – and relieved – Villeneuve. 'We had to drive aggressively, we had to pass some cars, so the driving side of it was fun.

'It feels great to win the championship. To come down to the last race was tough but we fought hard to win it. I couldn't be happier.'

Michael C. Brown

SNIPPETS

Photos: Michael C. Brown

• Carl Haas (above) and Paul Newman hosted a press conference on Friday at which they announced that Christian Fittipaldi would replace Paul Tracy in the Kmart/Budweiser car for next season. Haas also confirmed his team would continue to use Ford/Cosworth engines in 1996, although he admitted to having held

lengthy discussions with Honda. 'It came down to a very hard choice,' said Haas. 'Ford and Cosworth very much wanted to keep this team, so we made a commitment to them and we stayed the course.'

• Retired San Francisco 49ers NFL quarterback star Joe Montana, who is now a partner in Chip Ganassi's Target-backed team, served as Grand Marshal for the season finale, while Danny Sullivan, injured in a crash at MIS in July, made a welcome reappearance to issue the time-honored 'Gentlemen, start your engines' command.

• Mauricio Gugelmin was obliged to miss the final qualifying session after a right-rear suspension failure

caused  him to run off the road in Turn Five on Saturday morning. The Brazilian, who set the second-fastest time on Friday, was fortunate not to fall any lower than sixth on the final grid.

• Parker Johnstone (below) posted his best qualifying performance to date on a road course, thanks to the addition of experienced race

• Robby Gordon endured a frustrating weekend, starting

engineers John Bright, who joined the Comptech team in Vancouver, and Tim Wardrop. Unfortunately, Johnstone's efforts on race day were hindered by an elusive boost-control problem which robbed him of vital horsepower and resisted all attempts at a cure.

a disappointing 16th and finishing only one place higher after being involved in several incidents with Derrick Walker's Valvoline/Cummins Reynard-Ford. 'We had understeer, oversteer and probably side-steer,' said a disgruntled Gordon after qualifying.

• Fredrik Ekblom (above) thoroughly impressed A.J.

Foyt's Copenhagen team, despite having driven an Indy car only once before. (He finished 15th at Detroit in 1994 with a year-old car.) The likable and talented 24-year-old Swede showed a good turn of speed, a willingness to learn and admirable maturity as he was content to pick up experience rather than attempt any heroics.

PPG INDY CAR WORLD SERIES • ROUND 17

TOYOTA GRAND PRIX OF MONTEREY
FEATURING THE BANK OF AMERICA 300

LAGUNA SECA RACEWAY, MONTEREY, CALIFORNIA

SEPTEMBER 10, 84 LAPS – 185.986 MILES

Place	Driver (Nat.)	No.	Team Sponsors Car-Engine	Tires	Q Speed	Q Time	Q Pos.	Laps	Time/Status	Ave.	Pts.
1	*Gil de Ferran (BR)	8	Hall Racing Pennzoil Special Reynard 95I-Mercedes	GY	113.526	1m 10.208s	3	84	1h 53m 17.579s	98.493	21
2	Paul Tracy (CDN)	3	Newman-Haas Kmart/Budweiser Lola T95/00-Ford	GY	112.637	1m 10.762s	8	84	1h 53m 25.538s	98.378	16
3	Mauricio Gugelmin (BR)	18	PacWest Racing Group Hollywood Reynard 95I-Ford	GY	112.920	1m 10.585s	6	84	1h 53m 25.910s	98.372	14
4	Michael Andretti (USA)	6	Newman-Haas Kmart/Texaco Havoline Lola T95/00-Ford	GY	112.250	1m 11.006s	12	84	1h 53m 26.613s	98.362	12
5	Scott Pruett (USA)	20	Patrick Racing Firestone Lola T95/00-Ford	FS	112.989	1m 10.541s	5	84	1h 53m 40.241s	98.166	10
6	Al Unser Jr. (USA)	1	Marlboro Team Penske Penske PC24-Mercedes	GY	112.232	1m 11.017s	14	84	1h 53m 41.518s	98.147	8
7	Bobby Rahal (USA)	9	Rahal/Hogan Miller Genuine Draft Lola T95/00-Mercedes	GY	112.305	1m 10.971s	11	84	1h 53m 42.025s	98.140	6
8	Jimmy Vasser (USA)	12	Ganassi Target/STP Reynard 95I-Ford	GY	112.816	1m 10.650s	7	84	1h 53m 43.697s	98.116	5
9	Teo Fabi (I)	33	Forsythe Combustion Engineering/Indeck Reynard 95I-Ford	GY	113.012	1m 10.527s	4	84	1h 53m 44.358s	98.106	4
10	Adrian Fernandez (MEX)	10	Galles Tecate/Quaker State Lola T95/00-Mercedes	GY	111.896	1m 11.231s	15	84	1h 54m 23.725s	97.544	3
11	Jacques Villeneuve (CDN)	27	Team Green Player's Ltd. Reynard 95I-Ford	GY	114.476	1m 09.625s	1	83	Running		3
12	Raul Boesel (BR)	11	Rahal/Hogan Duracell Charger Lola T95/00-Mercedes	GY	112.247	1m 11.008s	13	83	Running		1
13	*Juan Fangio II (RA)	17	PacWest Racing Group VISA Reynard 95I-Ford	GY	110.953	1m 11.836s	19	83	Running		
14	Stefan Johansson (S)	16	Bettenhausen Alumax Aluminum Penske PC23-Mercedes	GY	111.054	1m 11.771s	18	83	Running		
15	Robby Gordon (USA)	5	Walker Valvoline/Cummins Special Reynard 95I-Ford	GY	111.782	1m 11.303s	16	83	Running		
16	Emerson Fittipaldi (BR)	2	Marlboro Team Penske Penske PC24-Mercedes	GY	110.586	1m 12.074s	20	83	Running		
17	Parker Johnstone (USA)	49	Comptech Motorola Cellular Reynard 95I-Honda	FS	112.349	1m 10.943s	10	83	Running		
18	*Carlos Guerrero (MEX)	22	Dick Simon Herdez/Viva Mexico! Lola T95/00-Ford	GY	109.851	1m 12.556s	22	83	Running		
19	*Fredrik Ekblom (S)	14	A.J. Foyt Copenhagen Racing Lola T95/00-Ford	GY	109.923	1m 12.509s	21	82	Running		
20	Alessandro Zampedri (I)	34	Payton-Coyne The Mi-Jack Car Lola T94/00-Ford	FS	109.241	1m 12.962s	24	82	Running		
21	*Mimmo Schiattarella (I)	64	Project Indy No-Touch/Van Dyne/Marcelo Reynard 94I-Ford	GY	109.162	1m 13.015s	25	81	Running		
22	Hiro Matsushita (J)	25	Arciero-Wells Panasonic/Duskin Reynard 95I-Ford	FS	108.862	1m 13.216s	26	81	Running		
23	Marco Greco (BR)	55	Galles Brastemp/Int. Sports Lola T95/00-Mercedes	GY	109.418	1m 12.843s	23	80	Running		
24	*Christian Fittipaldi (BR)	15	Walker Marlboro/Chapeco Special Reynard 95I-Ford	GY	111.738	1m 11.331s	17	70	Suspension		
25	Bryan Herta (USA)	4	Ganassi Target/Scotch Video Reynard 95I-Ford	GY	113.877	1m 09.992s	2	66	Suspension		
26	*Andre Ribeiro (BR)	31	Tasman Motorsports LCI International Reynard 95I-Honda	FS	112.489	1m 10.855s	9	63	Accident		
NQ	*Eliseo Salazar (RCH)	7	Dick Simon Cristal/Mobil 1/Copec Lola T95/00-Ford	GY	108.461	1m 13.487s	27	–	Did not qualify		
NQ	*Franck Freon (F)	19	Payton-Coyne The Agfa Car Lola T94/00-Ford	FS	107.185	1m 14.361s	28	–	Did not qualify		

* denotes Rookie driver

Caution flags: Lap 1, tow start/Gordon; laps 8–10, tow start/Gordon; laps 64–68, accident/Ribeiro. **Total:** three for nine laps.

Lap leaders: Jacques Villeneuve, 1–28 (28 laps); Gil de Ferran, 29–54 (26 laps); Mauricio Gugelmin, 55–56 (2 laps); de Ferran, 57–84 (28 laps). **Totals:** de Ferran, 54 laps; Villeneuve, 28 laps; Gugelmin, 2 laps.

Fastest race lap: Gil de Ferran, 1m 13.705s, 108.139 mph, on lap 7.

Final championship positions: 1 Villeneuve, 173; **2** Unser, 140; **3** Rahal, 130; **4** Andretti, 125; **5** Gordon, 122; **6** Tracy, 115; **7** Pruett, 113; **8** Vasser, 96; **9** Fabi, 83; **10** Gugelmin, 82; **11** E. Fittipaldi and Fernandez, 67; **13** Johansson, 62; **14** de Ferran, 57; **15** C. Fittipaldi, 55; **16** Boesel, 50; **17** Ribeiro, 38; **18** Cheever, 33; **19** Sullivan, 32; **20** Herta, 30; **21** Salazar, 19; **22** Zampedri, 15; **23** Bachelart, 8; **24** Danner, Luyendyk, Fangio and Johnstone, 6; **28** Matsushita, 5; **29** Greco, 3; **30** C. Guerrero and Hall, 2; **32** R. Guerrero, Goodyear and Brayton, 1.

Championship positions and points totals provisional pending outcome of appeal by Penske following race at Portland. Amended standings given on page 79.

EDS

HEARN TURNS THE TABI

Photos: Michael C. Brown

Once again the championship was fought out between Richie Hearn *(far left)* and David Empringham *(left)*. Hearn claimed only three wins in the Food 4 Less Ralt *(main picture)* to his rival's six, but took the title by four points.

Canadian Patrick Carpentier *(right)* scored two early-season wins but had to settle for third place in the final standings.

The 1995 edition of the Player's Ltd./Toyota Atlantic Championship served almost as a replay of the 1994 title-chase – with one notable exception. This time Californian Richie Hearn turned around a two-point deficit to Canada's David Empringham from one year ago and rebounded to claim the championship honors by a similarly scant four-point margin. Hearn, 24, clinched the crown by guiding John Della Penna's Food 4 Less Ralt RT41 to a second-place finish in the season finale at Laguna Seca Raceway.

'I wanted this so bad for myself, my team and especially [team owner] John [Della Penna], because he's been so close to the championship a couple of times,' said Hearn. 'I thought there was no way I could go to the [awards] banquet and finish second again, especially after finishing so close last year.'

Hearn and Empringham, who narrowly failed in his bid to win three successive titles in Brian Robertson's Motomaster/Slick 50/BDJS Motorsport Ralt, fought tooth and nail for the championship. Both displayed exceptional consistency, with Hearn earning three wins, six seconds, one third-place finish and two fourths from the 12-race season to Empringham's tally of six wins, one second, two thirds and two fourths.

'David pushed me to my absolute limit,' praised Hearn, 'not only on the track, physically, but mentally too. I'm relieved it's all come to an end.'

Ultimately, the difference came down to a single, costly mistake by Empringham during the second of two races on Quebec's challenging Trois Rivieres street circuit in August. 'I was too impatient,' he said, referring to an incident early in the race while he was trying to pass Case Montgomery's similar Ralt. 'I should have waited.'

Empringham, who had won the first race the previous day, was relegated to a distant 13th, and with all 12 races counting toward the championship, that one poor finish proved decisive. Nevertheless, the 29-year-old from Willowdale, Ontario, was satis-

'I'm disappointed but life goes on,' he said with a wry smile. 'I'm really happy with the season. It's a hell of a lot tougher to defend a championship than it is to win it.'

Indeed, Empringham has much to look forward to, having signed a long-term contract with Forsythe Racing and Player's Ltd. that likely will see him graduate into the PPG-Firestone Indy Lights Championship in 1996 and then, with luck, to the premier PPG Indy Car World Series the following season.

Fellow Canadian Patrick Carpentier finished third in the standings for Lynx Racing. The amiable young man from Joliette, Quebec, began the season with a fine victory in Miami and added another triumph on the oval at Nazareth, but strangely seemed to go off the boil in the second half of the season. Next year, however, he will start as a firm favorite for honors along with Californian Case Montgomery, who overcame a meager budget with veteran driver-turned-team owner Sandy Dells and rewarded his new sponsors, Microsoft, with a magnificent pole-to-checkered flag victory in the final round at Laguna Seca.

Toyota Atlantic veteran Colin Trueman endured a disappointing

season with his Hogan Motor Leasing Ralt, highlighted by third-place finishes at Long Beach and his home track, Mid-Ohio.

On the other end of the experience scale, Brazilian brothers Felipe and Zequinha ('Zeca') Giaffone waged a season-long battle for the coveted Rookie of the Year title. The pair signed on with veteran team owner Pierre Phillips and both enjoyed some strong races, albeit punctuated by several mechanical problems. Ultimately, three straight non-finishes at the end of the season cost Zeca dearly and allowed older brother Felipe to scoop the honors. Canadian rookie Lee Bentham was perhaps even more impressive, finishing just one point adrift of Zeca despite taking part in only seven races with Bill Fickling's excellent P-1 team. Bentham, too, will be a man to watch in 1996.

Six different drivers shared the spoils of victory in the sometimes well-supported C2 category, for older cars. Bernie Schuchmann successfully defended his title, by virtue more of consistency than outright speed, although Michael David made good progress after missing several races and then winning the class four times in his similar Swift DB-4.

1995 SCCA PLAYER'S LTD./TOYOTA ATLANTIC CHAMPIONSHIP
Final point standings after 12 races:

1	Richie Hearn (USA), Food 4 Less Ralt RT41	201
2	David Empringham (CDN), Motomaster/Slick 50 Ralt RT41	197
3	Patrick Carpentier (CDN), Player's/Cari-All Ralt RT41	129
4	Case Montgomery (USA), Microsoft Ralt RT40	114
5	Colin Trueman (USA), Hogan Motor Leasing Ralt RT41	83
6	Felipe Giaffone (BR), Phillips Motorsports Ralt RT41	80
7	Zeca Giaffone (BR), Phillips Motorsports Ralt RT41	73
8	Lee Bentham (CDN), NTN Bearings/TMI Racing Ralt RT41	72
9	Clint Mears (USA), Food 4 Less Ralt RT41	67
10	Eric Lang (USA), Lang Communications/Pizza-Pizza Ralt RT41	62

Performance chart

Driver	Wins	Poles
Empringham	6	1
Hearn	3	5
Carpentier	2	3
Montgomery	1	1

Note: Qualifying was canceled at two races due to inclement weather

Jeremy Shaw

Photos: Michael C. Brown

MOORE

Brilliant young Canadian Greg Moore swept aside all opposition, winning no fewer than 10 of the season's 12 races for Jerry Forsythe's Player's-backed team. Next year he graduates to the PPG Indy Car World Series with the same entrant.

THE MASTER

Jerry Forsythe's Player's Ltd. Racing team – and lead driver Greg Moore – succeeded in their aim of taking over the mantle of Steve Horne's Tasman Motorsports Group, which this year graduated into the PPG Indy Car World Series after dominating the PPG-Firestone Indy Lights Championship in 1993 and 1994. Indeed, Moore came within a nudge and a few ticks of the watch of the perfect season, beaten only twice in 12 starts – once, narrowly, by Robbie Buhl in Detroit and then when he was punted out of the lead by Pedro Chaves in Vancouver.

The fact that Moore emerged as the champion should come as no surprise. In 1993, as a raw rookie, not yet 18 years old when the season began, he served notice of his capabilities by earning four top-five finishes with a close-knit team run by his father, Ric, a veteran sedan racer, in concert with chief mechanic/engineer/general guru Steve Challis and number one mechanic Kent Holden. One year on, the same combination earned three victories to break the Tasman stranglehold, with Moore finishing a strong third in the point standings. The young man from Vancouver, Canada, therefore began 1995 as a firm favorite for honors. He did not disappoint.

By the end of the season, Moore had virtually rewritten the record book. He started out with five straight victories and ended with 10 wins to his name. Both are records. His career tally of 13 triumphs also constitutes a new standard of excellence.

'The records are just a reflection on the relationship I have with my sponsors, Player's, and my team, Forsythe Racing,' said Moore, who mirrored Steve Robertson's achievement in winning the 1994 Indy Lights series by completing every lap of every event during the 12-race campaign. 'They took a gamble on a 19-year-old kid and it kind of paid off for them. It makes me very proud. It's really been a dream season.'

Moore led a total of 375 laps, or 64 percent, of the 583 that made up the season. His racecraft was exemplary, especially on the ovals, where he always contrived to come through strongly despite a tendency to qualify only on the second, third or even fourth row of the grid.

Moore tied up the title at Cleveland, with three races still to run, and completed the year with a massive 102-point margin over his nearest challenger. No wonder he has become a hot property. Wisely

Forsythe and Player's have a long-term contract with this enthusiastic and ambitious young man, and in 1996 he will doubtless be a strong challenger for Rookie of the Year honors in the premier Indy Car category.

The 1995 season saw a continued growth of the Indy Lights category which, under its original guise as the American Racing Series, was conceived in 1986 by veteran Indy Car team owner U.E. 'Pat' Patrick. Sure, Moore was the class of the field, but there was no shortage of worthy challengers. In fact, with an average of better than 23 cars turning up at every race – four more than one year ago, thanks to the unstinting efforts of series general manager Roger Bailey – the championship could boast better support than ever.

The only driver to beat Moore in a 'straight' fight was Robbie Buhl, who took something of a gamble by returning to the series he had won in 1992 as a means of trying to bump-start his stalled career. Buhl realigned himself with veteran crew chief Burke Harrison, who guided Buhl to the title in '92 in the culmination of an unprecedented hat-trick, having also won the championship the previous two years with Paul Tracy and Eric Bachelart. Now with Dorricott Racing, Harrison and Buhl picked up virtually where they had left off. If not for Moore they would likely have won the crown again.

The highlight of Buhl's year was his pole-to-checkered flag victory in his hometown, Detroit. Buhl knew the importance of starting out in front on the tortuous parkland circuit and posted a sensational lap in qualifying to make sure he would do just that. He then withstood intense pressure from Moore, finally winning by just 0.170 seconds.

'I'm happy,' concluded Buhl after a campaign which also included three poles and another half-dozen podium finishes. 'I think I proved to people that I am competitive. The Player's guys, they just dominated, unfortunately, but we were the best after that.'

Brazilian Affonso Giaffone and Californian Doug Boyer also enjoyed good seasons. Giaffone chose to align himself with Brian Stewart Racing and engineer Steve Erickson for his rookie season, and with even a modicum of good fortune he deserved to emerge with at least one victory. At Phoenix, indeed, in his very first start on an oval, Giaffone had everyone covered, including Moore, only to be penalized for jumping ahead too

quickly on a restart following a full-course caution with just a few laps to go. The team was incensed at the imposition of a one-lap penalty, although a few weeks later Giaffone learned there could have been more at stake when he watched Scott Goodyear lose almost certain victory in the Indianapolis 500 following an identical infraction.

Giaffone also led at Nazareth until missing a shift on a restart. In all, four runner-up finishes ensured he was a deserving recipient of the Turbo-Mac Rookie of the Year Award.

Boyer began the year with a solid fifth-place finish at Miami and ended with a flourish, taking four podium finishes from the last five races. Under the tutelage of Bob Lesnett's Summit Motorsports team, Boyer made strides toward overcoming a lack of confidence on the ovals and came on strong in the final oval race of the year at New Hampshire, rising from a distant 15th to a promising ninth with absolutely no attrition to aid his progress.

The lack of a budget for testing hindered Pedro Chaves in his switch from Brian Stewart's team to Mark Weida's Leading Edge Motorsport operation, although the amiable Portuguese did claim a long-overdue maiden victory after three years in the series. The win came in controversial circumstances in Vancouver, however, when he inadvertently punted home-town favorite Moore into a spin soon after a full-course caution.

Buzz Calkins displayed steady improvement in his third season of Indy Lights. The addition of experienced race engineer Ken Anderson proved a major boon to the family-run team, and Calkins responded by claiming podium finishes on the ovals at Phoenix and Milwaukee.

Rookie Mark Hotchkis posted some very promising drives in a second Leading Edge Lola-Buick, albeit punctuated by several accidents. His drive from 17th on the grid to fourth at Cleveland served to show he could develop into a title contender in 1996.

Sinden Racing Services kept faith in former motocross star Jeff Ward, who posted especially strong performances at Miami (where he finished second) and Detroit (third). Ward learned above all that consistency comes with experience, and he did well to finish among the top 10 in the point standings despite the restriction of a minimal budget.

Nick Firestone and David DeSilva

by Jeremy Shaw

The only real threat to Moore's supremacy was posed by 1992 champion Robbie Buhl *(left)*, who beat the youngster by the narrowest of margins in Detroit.

Experienced Portuguese driver Pedro Chaves *(below)* finally scored his first Indy Lights win, although the circumstances of his victory inevitably detracted from his achievement somewhat.

Brazilian Affonso Giaffone *(bottom left)* did not enjoy the best of luck but still salvaged third place in the final points standings.

were afflicted by a dire loss of confidence, yet they, too, showed flashes of what might have been as they claimed one podium finish apiece.

Among those finishing outside the top 10 in points, Alex Padilla might have achieved more had he not split the eight races he contested among four different teams, while Claude Bourbonnais' hopes of being able to apply pressure to Player's teammate Greg Moore were dashed by a massive accident during practice at Nazareth. Bourbonnais suffered a broken neck and was forced to sit out five races. He promptly crashed again on his return at New Hampshire, although his crew managed to repair the damage and the French-Canadian responded with an excellent drive to second place.

Countryman Bertrand Godin, fresh out of Formula Ford 1600, was very impressive in a couple of races when invited to substitute for the injured Bourbonnais. Mike Borkowski, the 1994 SCCA American Continental (Formula Ford 2000) Champion, also displayed great promise in an abbreviated campaign with Steve Medlin's new team. Bob Dorricott Jr. starred briefly on a couple of the ovals, winning the pole at Nazareth for the second year running and qualifying

second fastest at New Hampshire before crashing heavily. Canada's Trevor Seibert (Canaska Racing), Argentina's Jose Luis di Palma, plus Brazil's Niko Palhares (both with QwikCars/PacWest) and Colombian Diego Guzman (Dick Simon Racing/QwikCars) were among others to show not only their talent but also the ever-increasing worldwide interest in Indy Lights as a viable and attractive stepping-stone toward the PPG Indy Car World Series.

1995 PPG-FIRESTONE INDY LIGHTS CHAMPIONSHIP

Final point standings after 12 races:

	Driver	Points
1	Greg Moore (CDN), Player's Ltd./Indeck	242
2	Robbie Buhl (USA), Patrick Media/Copper & Brass Sales	140
3	Affonso Giaffone (BR), STP	122
4	Doug Boyer (USA), Red Line Oil	108
5	Pedro Chaves (P), Castrol of Portugal/Trench	99
6	Buzz Calkins (USA), Bradley Food Marts	77
7	Mark Hotchkis (USA), Fountainhead Water/Top Dawg	57
8	Jeff Ward (USA), Primm Investment/Arizona Executive Air	56
9	Nick Firestone (USA), STP/Firestone Vineyards	52
10	David DeSilva (USA), DeSilva Gates/Cruttenden Roth	33
11	Alex Padilla (USA), SP Aviation	32
12	Mike Borkowski (USA), Spirit of Connecticut	31
13	Claude Bourbonnais (CDN), Player's Ltd./Indeck	29
14	Diego Guzman (COL), Colombiana/Comcel/Marlboro	29
15	Jose Luis di Palma (RA), YPF/Marlboro	24
16	Bertrand Godin (CDN), Player's Ltd./Indeck	16
17	Trevor Seibert (CDN), Microsoft Canada	16
18	Bob Reid (USA), Ingersoll Rand/Grainger	15
19	Jeff Andretti (USA), Procter & Gamble Motorsports	12
20	Niko Palhares (BR), PacWest/QwikCars	9

Note: All drivers run identical Lola T93/20-Buick cars

Performance chart

Driver	Wins	Poles
Moore	10	7
Buhl	1	3
Chaves	1	–
Bourbonnais	–	1
Dorricott	–	1